L·I·S·T·E·N·S·P·E·A·K

Ease in Communication for Second Language Speakers of English

Irene Alterbaum · Joyce Buck

New York City Technical College
City University of New York

KENDALL/HUNT PUBLISHING COMPANY
4050 Westmark Drive   Dubuque, Iowa 52002

Book Team

Chairman and Chief Executive Officer Mark C. Falb
Vice President, Director of National Book Program Alfred C. Grisanti
Editorial Development Supervisor Georgia Botsford
Developmental Editor Liz Recker
Prepress Project Coordinator Sheri Hosek
Prepress Editor Jenifer Chapman
Permissions Editor Colleen Zelinsky
Design Manager Jodi Splinter
Designer Deb Howes
Senior Vice President, College Division Thomas W. Gantz
Vice President and National Field Manager Brian Johnson
Managing Editor, College Field Paul Gormley
Associate Editor, College Field Sue Ellen Saad

Previously titled *LISTENSPEAK: Pathways to Better Speech*

Contents

---

* / ʌ / is a central vowel.

Preface

The third edition of *Listenspeak* has been extensively revised and updated to reflect the increasingly diverse backgrounds of the large number of non-native students currently enrolled in our schools of higher education including community colleges, four-year colleges, and universities. They come from countries as geographically and linguistically disparate as Russia, India, Pakistan, China, Vietnam, Korea, Mexico, Brazil, Egypt, and Puerto Rico.

These students are aware of the many challenges they face, the most immediate of which is the need to communicate in English, their second language. Business and professional advancement is often affected by the ability to communicate effectively and intelligently. A major concern is intelligibility, the ability to use appropriate sound, stress, and intonation patterns in a way that ensures listener comprehension.

While speakers of English as a second language have the difficult problem of learning a new language, there are two other groups that have other needs.

1. *Speakers of English as a second dialect.** More than 400,000 of these student are currently enrolled in our colleges and universities and their numbers continue to swell. These include students who come from countries such as Nigeria, Kenya, and Guyana. Their first language is English, but their phonological patterns are at variance with American English.

2. *Native speakers with nonstandard dialects.* These students speak a dialect perceived as nonstandard because of phonological, grammatical, and lexical differences from mainstream English.

While all three groups have a common goal, their problems are different. Non-native students need to master a new sound and stress system. Second-dialect speakers must modify their patterns to fit the mold of American English. Native speakers of nonstandard English must discard poor speech models and learn acceptable ones, by sharpening their listening skills, acquire proficiency in self-monitoring techniques, and develop self-confidence in speaking standard American English.

There are several aspects to this book that we consider unique:

♦ We teach the intonation pattern of the language before the sound system. This is not done through the step system but through an understanding of stress—how duration, volume, and pitch affect the melody pattern of the language. Phrasing, pausing, and linking are also taught.

♦ We use the International Phonetic Alphabet, which provides the fastest access to correct sound production.

♦ We believe in extensive modeling, immediate feedback, and self-monitoring. The student hears, repeats, and is immediately corrected.

♦ We use humor in our dialogue to encourage the understanding of idiomatic English.

The book is divided into five parts: (1) an overview of the speech mechanism and the International Phonetic Alphabet (IPA), (2) stress patterns, (3) consonants, (4) vowels, and (5) diphthongs. While conso-

---

* We recommend this text for students on the intermediate ESL level and above.

nants and vowels are grouped together, with the consonants preceding vowels, they can be taught individually in any sequence desired by the instructor.

Each chapter follows the same highly structured sequence.

Listening/Speaking. Identifying and perceiving differences between target sounds.

Listening/Writing. Underlining, circling, and segmenting words into sounds and syllables to sharpen listening skills.

Homework/Review. Reenforcing class work with written exercises on removeable pages; reading dialogues at home in preparation for presentation in class.

Reading Aloud. Using dialogues to attune the student's ear to the casual patterns of interpersonal communication.

We trust that this guide and workbook will satisfy both students and teachers who are seeking mature and lively college-level exercises designed for the improvement of phonological skills.

Irene Alterbaum and Joyce Buck
New York City Technical College
City University of New York

syllable

vowels

Overview

consonants

lateral and glides

diphthongs

Proverbs from Around the World

◆

About Guests:

African saying:

Treat your guest as a guest for two days—then, on the third day give him a hoe.

Spanish saying:

Guests always have nice backs.

Turkish saying:

If your guest becomes a cook, your larder will be empty.

Indian saying:

Fish and guests smell when they are three days old.

Miscellaneous:

Africa:

If it's not here and now, who cares about what or when.

Arabia:

Blind eyes are better than blind hearts.

Spain:

At twenty, a man will be a peacock
At thirty, a lion
At forty, a camel
At fifty, a serpent
At sixty, a dog
At seventy, a monkey
At eighty—nothing.

To live in fear is a life half lived.

CHAPTER ONE

Basic Speech Concepts

How many sounds are there in the English language? How many sounds do you hear in the word **six?** How are these sounds made? Questions like these are rarely raised. Native American speakers never think about the sound patterns of their language. Yet, it is often helpful to second-language learners to understand the mechanics involved in the speech process as they begin their study of spoken English.

As college students pursuing your studies and planning for a career, you may want to improve your speech patterns in English. The introduction to this course focuses on the organs of speech to show how you can control them to form the sounds that convey your thoughts. You will find that the American English sound system may differ in many ways from your native language. Knowing the sounds of English will clear up confusions you may have in understanding and in pronouncing certain words.

The Speech Mechanism

The speech organs—the tongue, the lips, the lower jaw, and the soft palate—are capable of considerable movement. When these articulators work together, they shape various sounds: the consonants, the vowels, and the diphthongs. Contributing to this speech machinery are the hard palate and the upper and lower teeth. These organs are stationary and incapable of movement but they serve as points of contact for the active articulators. The vocal cords are also essential to the speech process. Figure 1 shows the components involved in the speech process.

Tongue

The most flexible articulator in the speech system is the tongue. Think of all the movements your tongue can make. You can point it, groove it, move it from side to side, extend it past the lips, raise or lower it, or let it lie flat in your mouth. Any of the four sections of the tongue may be involved in speaking: the tongue tip, the blade, the midsection, and the back.

When you raise the tongue tip and press it firmly against the hard palate just behind the upper teeth, you can produce any one of these frequently used sounds / t d l n / as in **tight, deed, lull,** and **noon.** These sounds are often known as lingua-alveolar sounds. *Lingua* refers to the tongue, *alveolar* to the upper gum

3

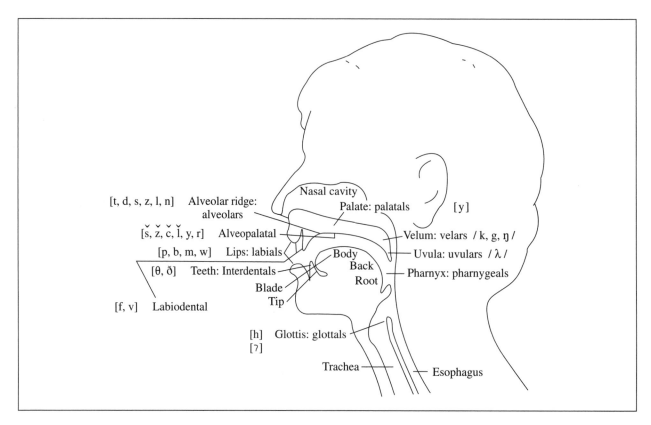

FIGURE I. The speech mechanism. From *Why Tesol? Theories and Issues in Teaching English as a Second Language for K-12 Teachers,* 2nd edition by Ariza et al. Copyright © 2002 by Kendall/Hunt Publishing Company.

ridge of the hard palate. You are also using the tongue tip when you produce the / s z tʃ dʒ / sounds in these words: **cease, zoos, church,** and **judge.**

As you make the sounds / k g ŋ /, as in **coke, gag,** and **singing,** can you tell what part of the tongue you are using? It is the back section, which is raised and pressed against the soft palate, known as the *velum.* These sounds are called lingua-velar because the velum is the point of contact for these two articulators.

The midsection of the tongue is active for the production of the / j / sound in **yellow, young,** and **cure.** The abiity to extend the tongue between the upper and lower front teeth enables us to produce the **th** sounds in **think, they,** and **everything.** These sounds do not exist in most languages.

The sides of the tongue can also assist in the production of the sounds / s z ʃ ʒ tʃ dʒ /.

Lips

The lips can function alone or they can be used in conjunction with other articulators. You can round your lips or unround them. You can close them firmly or very lightly. The shape of the lips and the degree of tension of the lips may vary so that different vowel sounds can be formed. To produce the vowel sounds / oʊ / and / u / as in **toe** and **two,** the lips are rounded. To produce the vowel sounds / i /, / ɪ /, and / eɪ / as in **fee, fit,** and **fate,** the lips are unrounded. They are stretched and tense for **feet** and relaxed for **fit.**

The lips also play a large part in the production of some consonants. The consonant sound / w / as in **war** and **queen** requires considerable lip rounding. The lips can close firmly for / m /, / p /, and / b / as in **man, put,** and **buy.** Sounds that are formed by the action of two lips are called *bilabial.* The contact between the lips and the teeth results in the labio-dental sounds / f / and / v / in **few** and **view.** The word *dental* refers to teeth.

Lower Jaw

Unlike the upper jaw, which is fixed, the lower jaw can open and close. The lower jaw opens widely for / ɑ / in **stop,** a little less widely for / ɔ / in **law** and / æ / in **add.** To produce / ʌ / in **cup,** / ɝ / in **first,** and / ɛ / in **end,** the jaw is slightly open.

Palate

The roof of the mouth is called the palate. It separates the nose or nasal cavity from the mouth, or oral cavity (see Figure 1). There are two major sections.

1. The hard palate which is bony, extends from the upper front teeth to the middle of the roof of the mouth,

2. The soft palate, which consists of muscles and tissue, extends from the middle to the back part of the roof of the mouth. The tip of the soft palate ends in a flap of tissue that hangs down called the uvula. This can be seen when you open your mouth very wide as you look in the mirror.

Hard Palate

If you touch the upper front teeth with your tongue and then move it slowly back along the hard palate, you can feel a bump or a ridge. This is called the upper gum ridge, or alveolar ridge. When you produce the sounds / t d n l /, this is where the tongue tip rests. The affricates / tʃ /, as in **cheap,** and / ʤ /, as in **jeep,** start at this point with the tongue tip resting lightly on the gum ridge before moving quickly away from the palate. The / ʃ / and / ʒ / sounds along with the / r / sounds are made with the tongue tip curled back toward, but *not touching* the hard palate. They are known as lingua-palatal sounds.

Soft Palate

Unlike the hard palate, the soft palate is capable of movement. It can be raised and lowered. When the soft palate is raised, it closes off the passageway to the nose. Nearly all English consonants and vowels are emitted through the mouth. Sounds that are made in this way are known as oral sounds. When the soft palate is lowered, sounds are directed through the nose. These sounds are called nasal sounds, and there are only three in the English language, / m n ŋ /, as in **my, know,** and **sang.**

When you raise the back of your tongue to produce / k g ŋ /, the point of contact for these lingua-velar sounds is the soft palate or the velum.

Teeth

The upper and lower (front and side) teeth are used with other articulators to produce sounds. The biting edges of the upper and lower teeth are close together for the production of / s z tʃ ʤ /. The sides of the tongue meet the upper side teeth to form the / s / and / z / sounds, and the voiced and voiceless **th** in **they** and **thumb.** Can you feel your upper front teeth pressing lightly on your lower lip when you produce / f / and / v / in **few** and **view**? When you observe your face in a mirror, you can easily see the point of contact for these labio-dental sounds.

Vocal Cords

If you place your fingers at your throat and swallow, you can feel a bump moving up and down. What you are feeling is the larynx, or voice box. It is situated on top of the trachea, the windpipe leading to the lungs, and contains two small powerful muscles known as the vocal cords or vocal bands.

As you breathe in, air is taken into the lungs. As you breathe out, the air passes through the vocal cords. The force of that exhaled breath stream causes the vocal cords to vibrate as they are pushed together and apart. When the vocal bands are apart, there is no vibration, and voiceless sounds such as / p / in **pipe,** / f / in **fish,** and / h / in **who** are produced. When the vocal bands come together and vibrate, you produce voiced sounds such as / m / in **my,** / b / in **boy,** and / i / in **eat.** The opening or space between the vocal cords is called the glottis. This opening is very wide in whispered speech. Figure 2 shows the location of the vocal cords, and vocal chords in the act of normal speaking and whispering.

The process of speaking, then, depends on two closely related systems. When we talk, we are using the following:

1. The articulatory system, which includes the tongue, the lips, the lower jaw, the teeth, and the hard and the soft palate. These organs shape the sounds we produce to form words.

2. The phonatory system, which includes the breathing apparatus and the vocal cords, responsible for producing voiced and voiceless sounds, an important feature in English speech. In addition, this system enables us to convey feeling and meaning through the vocal techniques of raising or lowering pitch, increasing or decreasing loudness, and lengthening or shortening vowel sounds.

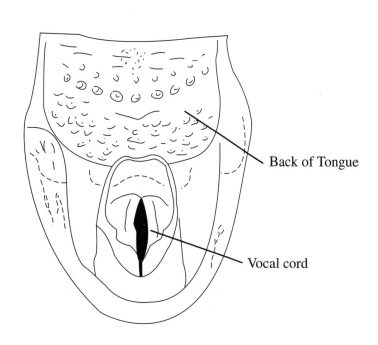

The Larynx: A Downward View

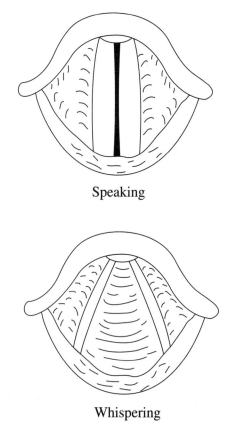

Speaking

Whispering

FIGURE 2. The vocal cords.

The Sound System of American English

A key to understanding and speaking a second language is knowing the sound system that is used to form words. An efficient tool for perceiving sounds quickly, the International Phonetic Alphabet (IPA) is used all over the world for the transcription of sounds (see Table 1); this table is also located on the front inside cover.

When you review the IPA aloud with your instructor, you will note that every sound is represented by a written symbol marked by a pair of slash lines. The letters *s* and *ce* are sounded as / s / in the words **see** and **race.** The letter *s* in the word **his** is pronounced / z /. Although there are twenty-six letters in the alphabet, there are approximately forty-six sounds, as shown on the IPA chart. We have all been taught in school that there are twenty-one consonants and five vowels (**a, e, i, o, u**). However, according to the IPA transcription of General American Dialect, there are twenty-five consonant sounds, fourteen vowel sounds, and six diphthong sounds.*

As you become more familiar with this phonological system, the difference between the sounds of your native language and those of American English will become more apparent. Spanish, French, and Italian speakers do not use the breathy / p / in **pie;** therefore, their pronunciation of this word will be similar to **buy.** Speakers of Asian languages often confuse / l / and / r /, so that there is no distinction between **glass** and **grass.** In numerous instances, you will find yourself using the lips, tongue, and jaw a little differently. Learning to identify the sounds of standard American English and knowing how to produce them will give you a better feeling about yourself when you speak.

At times you will find that there is no consistent relationship between English spelling and pronunciation patterns. The IPA will help you to note that a sound may be represented by different spelling patterns. The vowel sound / i / in **eat** is represented by different spelling patterns as in **meat, meet, ski,** and **receive.**

Let's look at the word **six.** How many letters do you see? Obviously, the answer is three. But how many sounds do you hear? Let's transcribe the word **six** into phonetics. Remember, one symbol represents one sound. The first sound is / s /, the second is the vowel sound / ɪ /, the third is the / k /, and the last sound is / s /. Therefore, there are four sounds in the three-letter word **six.** This system of recording the sounds of the spoken language will help you see as well as hear the actual pronunciation of the spoken word.

In addition to affecting pronunciation, the sounds you make affect the meaning of your words for the listener. How well you are understood by listeners determines your intelligibility and your effectiveness as a speaker. The substitution of / s / for **sh,** as in **sip** instead of **ship,** or the omission of the final / t /, producing the word **can** instead of **can't,** may change the word and consequently its meaning for the listener.

Sounds such as / s / and / t / that signal differences in meaning, as in the examples **sip** for **ship** and **can** for **can't,** are known as phonemes. Each phoneme possesses its own characteristics or distinctive features. These may be acoustic or articulatory. We may hear sounds that differ because they are voiced or voiceless, such as / b / or / p /. Most phonemes are orally produced and emitted through the mouth, but three, the / m n ŋ /, can be distinguished as nasal sounds emitted through the nose. Some sounds such as the plosives / d / and / g / may be perceived as "exploding" after a brief stoppage of air. The fricatives / s / and / z / are distinguished from other phonemes on the basis of their hissing and buzzing qualities. A phoneme may share articulatory features with other phonemes, such as / m / or / b /, which are produced with the two lips close togther; yet a distinctive feature of / m / is nasality. So in contrasting the words **me** and **bee,** the listener is alerted to the differences in these words and in their respective meanings by the phonemes or sounds at the beginning of the words.

A phoneme can be defined as a family of sounds. You may know a family where everyone looks a little different, but they all have the same last name. The / t / phoneme may be viewed in a similar way. If you

---

* The Kenyon symbol system is used phonemically in this text to record General American Dialect (GAD), the most commonly used speech pattern heard on television and radio.

TABLE I SOUND SYSTEM OF AMERICAN ENGLISH
CONSONANT SOUNDS

IPA Symbol	Examples					Dictionary Symbol
Plosives						
/ p /	pay	cup	supper	stopped		p
/ b /	buy	rub	rubber	robbed		b
/ t /	take	hit	letter	missed		t
/ d /	dime	hide	ladder	wanted		d
/ k /	keep	take	banker	ache		k
/ g /	go	egg	again			g
Fricatives						
/ s /	sit	bus	past	cats		s
/ z /	zero	does	easy	dogs		z
/ ʃ /	she	cash	issue	ocean	motion	sh
/ ʒ /		beige	leisure			zh
/ f /	fish	rough	laughing	physics		f
/ v /	very	have	ever			v
/ θ /	think	earth	nothing			th
/ ð /	these	breathe	brother			th
/ h /	house		ahead	who		h
Affricates						
/ tʃ /	church	each	capture	cello		ch
/ ʤ /	jump	judge	danger	page	giant	j
Nasals						
/ m /	me	come	summer			m
/ n /	no	run	money	hand	know	n
/ ŋ /		sing	singing			ŋ
Lateral and Glides						
/ l /	like	pool	allow	glass		l
/ w /	we		award	quart		w
/ hw /	when		nowhere	what		hw
/ r /	rain		sorry	grow		r
/ j /	you		onion	music	million	y

TABLE I (continued)

VOWEL SOUNDS

IPA Symbol	Examples					Dictionary Symbol
Front						
/ i /	eat	meet	ski	believe		ē
/ ɪ /	it	city	different			i
/ e /, / eɪ /[1]	ate	obey	rain	pay		ā
/ ɛ /	red	ready	sweater	guest	egg	ĕ
/ æ /	at	sad	hand	salmon		ă
Back						
/ u /	too	sue	chew	fruit	rude	ōō ü
/ ʊ /	wood	would	push	crook		ŏŏ u̇
/ oʊ /[1]	go	hello	stone	widow		ō
/ ɔ /	all	jaw	taught	boss	thought	ô ŏ
/ ɑ /	arm	calm	stop	clock	father	ä o
Central						
/ ʌ /[2]	under	cut	sun	son	flood	u ŭ
/ ə /[3]	among	banana	above	Russia		ə
/ ɜ˄ /[2]	murder	bird	world	search	purpose	ər ûr
/ ɚ /[3]	father	actor	scholar			ər
Diphthongs						
/ eɪ /	late	raid	rain	strange		ā
/ aɪ /	time	cry	lie	why	sigh	ī
/ ɔɪ /	boy	oil	noise			oi
/ aʊ /[4]	now	house	doubt	power		ou au
/ ɪɚ /[5]	peer	sheer	beer			ê
/ ɛɚ /[5]	pear	share	bear			â
/ ɔɚ /[5]	pour	shore	bore			
/ ʊɚ /[5]	poor	sure	boor			

[1] The diphthongs / eɪ / and / oʊ / are variations of the / e / and / o / phonemes. For teaching purposes, the / eɪ / and / oʊ / are indicated phonemically to signal differences in meaning in GAD.
[2] Stressed syllables
[3] The schwa is used in unstressed syllables.
[4] / aʊ / is also acceptable.
[5] In certain regions such as New York City, New England, and the South, where / r / is omitted, the variants / ɪə ɛə ɔə ʊə / are often heard. For teaching purposes, the variants listed in the table are indicated phonemically to signal differences in meaning in GAD. Phonemic representations are usually / ɪr ɛr ɔr ʊr /.

produce the following words—**time, attend, letter, hit**—you will discover that the / t / sounds in these words do not sound exactly the same nor are they produced in the same way. The initial / t / in **time** or the / t / followed by a vowel in the stressed syllable in **attend** is breathier and more aspirated than the short medial / t / in **letter.** The / t / in **hit** is even more weakly aspirated in final position. All three / t / variants are slightly different from each other and are known as allophones. But all the / t / allophones are voiceless and recognizable as members of the / t / family.

Speech Communication Barriers

It is equally frustrating and confusing for the speaker and the listener when speech patterns are unclear. One student told us that while taking this course, she learned why people had laughed at her when she said she liked "Chinese foot" instead of "Chinese food." Her pronunciation changed the meaning of the message, and therefore the student received a different reaction from her listener than she had expected.

There are several reasons why a speaker may have difficulty in getting a message across to a listener. One problem may be that the speaker fails to produce final consonants. When the final / p / in **pipe** is omitted, another word, **pie,** is heard. Failure to distinguish **row, road,** and **wrote** because of the omission of the final consonant imposes an unnecessary burden on the listener. Unless the tongue tip is raised to the upper gum ridge for the / d / in **cold,** this word is reduced to **coal.** Another problem may be that the voiced / z / in **knees** is replaced by the voiceless / s / in **niece,** thereby misleading the listener. Inaccurate placement of the articulators and incorrect voicing of sounds may result in indistinct or unintelligible speech. Failure to use the lower jaw actively may cause you to sound indistinct and muffled. Speaking with the jaw clenched or nearly tightly shut results in considerable listener discomfort.

The omission, substitution, addition, and distortion of sounds alter the words produced, obscure meaning, and interfere with listener comprehension.

Another problem in pronunciation is misplacing stress or accenting the wrong syllable, as in the words **pro mise, stu dent, eco no mics.** Often the native listener loses interest because this speech pattern is different from what he or she expects to hear.

These problems tend to increase when you are speaking for longer periods of time in more formal speech situations. In these more complex public communication events, you may be giving oral presentations or reports before a group, providing explanations and directions, or receiving and giving long telephone messages.

Applying Basic Phonological Concepts

Knowing the sound and stress patterns of standard American English is fundamental to the improvement of your listening, speaking, reading, and writing skills. The homework exercises at the end of this chapter will help you learn and practice basic phonological concepts. They can be done in class or at home and corrected in the class over a period of several lessons. The exercises will help you to do the following:

1. Pronounce the sound, not the letter.

     EXAMPLE: / g / not "gee,"   / b / not "bee"

2. Recognize if the sound is voiced or voiceless.*

     EXAMPLE: / t / is voiceless (VL),   / d / is voiced (V)

---

* If a sound is *voiceless,* you can feel considerable air emitted through your mouth and no vibration at your larynx. If a sound is *voiced,* you can feel the vibration at your larynx and no air emitted through your mouth. All vowels are voiced. Contrast / p / and / b / to feel the difference in vibration more easily.

3. Divide a word into its component sounds.

> **EXAMPLE:** The word **fix** has four sounds: / f ɪ k s /.

4. Recognize and produce the final consonant.

> **EXAMPLE:** have / v /   half / f /   come / m /

5. Recognize and produce consonant clusters.

> **EXAMPLE:**

/ st /	stop	meant	/ nt /
/str /	street	reached	/ tʃt /
/ ʃr /	shrink	helped	/ lpt /

Summary of Objectives

This program is designed to help you to develop basic skills in oral communication. Daily practice and frequent use of a tape recorder will improve your ability to

1. listen carefully and distinguish target sounds and stress patterns in American English.

2. use pitch, loudness, duration, and pause to create appropriate stress patterns.

3. use target sounds and stress patterns in the context of structured social discourse, namely reading passages and dialogues.

Chapter 1 Homework Review

A. An essential feature of each phoneme is its voiced or voiceless quality.

Pronounce each word in the list below and isolate the underlined sound. As you pronounce the sound indicated between slashes place your hand at your throat. Do you feel vibration for the production of the / m / sound? Yes, there is vibration. Do you feel any air emitted at your lips? No. Then the sound / m / is voiced.

Are the following sounds voiced or voiceless? Write V for voiced sounds and VL for voiceless sounds.

    EXAMPLE: / p / paid <u>VL</u>

1. / n /	know	_____	11. / l /	late	_____
2. / b /	bury	_____	12. / h /	have	_____
3. / v /	very	_____	13. / s /	same	_____
4. / g /	gate	_____	14. / i /	piece	_____
5. / w /	away	_____	15. / eɪ /	lake	_____
6. / ʃ /	sugar	_____	16. / u /	true	_____
7. / ʤ /	judge	_____	17. / ɑ /	orange	_____
8. / z /	easy	_____	18. / ɪ /	sick	_____
9. / m /	movie	_____	19. / f /	physical	_____
10. / k /	key	_____	20. / s /	rice	_____

B. The intellibility of speech is dependent on the perception and production of the final consonant sounds. In some instances, the final letter **e** is silent, as in **have;** in other words, the final sound does not resemble the final letter. For example, in the word **basic,** the **c** letter represents the / k / sound.

Write the final sound in each word using the symbols of the IPA.

    EXAMPLE: raise / z /

1. class / /	4. mate / /	7. son / /
2. come / /	5. does / /	8. race / /
3. mat / /	6. some / /	9. bomb / /

10. ache   /   /   12. mail   /   /   14. choose   /   /

11. arts   /   /   13. male   /   /   15. eggs   /   /

C. Most consonants in English appear in three positions. Sounds occuring in the beginning of the word are in the initial position. Sounds in the middle of the word are known as medial sounds, and those at the end of the word are final sounds.

All variants of the / p / phoneme are voiceless. They can occur in different positions and yet belong to the same family.

> **EXAMPLE:**   / p /   pie   apple   appear   wipe   jumped

Fill in the missing sounds in the following words. As you do, note the position in which the sound is located: initial, medial, or final.

1. / s /   ___oup   te___t   a___k   thi___   book___

2. / l /   ___ake   he___p   ho___d   meda___   whist___e

3. / m /   ___oon   hi___   sta___p   fa___ous   la___b

D. The final consonant sound distinguishes different words, both in pronunciation and in meaning. Therefore the production of their final consonant sound is crucial to intelligibility. Using the symbols of the IPA, fill in the missing final consonant sound and pronounce each word aloud.

> **EXAMPLE:**   bus / bʌ<u>s</u> /   buzz / bʌ<u>z</u> /   bud / bʌ<u>d</u> /   but / bʌ<u>t</u> /

1. have / hæ___ /   half   / hæ___ /   has   / hæ___ /

2. mine / maɪ___ /   mind   / maɪn___ /   mined   / maɪn___ /

3. raid / reɪ___ /   rate   / reɪ___ /   raids / reɪ___ ___ /   rates / reɪ___ ___ /

4. rope / roʊ___ /   robe   / roʊ___ /   road   / roʊ___ /   wrote / roʊ___ /

5. hide / haɪ___ /   height / haɪ___ /   hike   / haɪ___ /

E. In some words, the spelling and the pronunciation are quite different. Using the symbols of the IPA, fill in the missing sounds. Then write the number of sounds in the word.

> **EXAMPLE:**   laugh   / <u>l</u> æ <u>f</u> /   <u>3</u>

1. one   / ___ ʌ ___ /   _____   6. his   / hɪ___ /   _____

2. once   / ___ ʌ ___ ___ / _____   7. locked / lɑk___ /   _____

3. tack   / ___ æ ___ /   _____   8. sick   / ___ ɪ ___ /   _____

4. tax   / ___ æ ___ ___ / _____   9. six   / ___ ɪ ___ ___ / _____

5. exam   / ɪ___ ___ æm /   _____   10. expect / ɪ___ ___ pɛ ___ t /   _____

F. In other words, there are several consonants combined together (creating consonant clusters). All the consonants must be pronouced for intelligibility. Fill in the missing sounds using the IPA symbols. Then write the number of sounds in the word.

EXAMPLE: least / list / _____   helped / hɛlpt / _____   strive / straɪv / _____

1. stand   / __ __ æ __ __ / _____

6. went   / wɛ __ __ /   _____

2. tests   / tɛ __ __ __ /   _____

7. bill   / bɪ __ /   _____

3. friends / frɛ __ __ __ /   _____

8. build   / bɪ __ __ /   _____

4. clocks   / __ __ ɑ __ __ / _____

9. built   / bɪ __ __ /   _____

5. against / əgɛ __ __ __ /   _____

10. asks   / æ __ __ __ / _____

G. In many instances, the spelling and the pronunciation of a vowel sound do not match. Fill in the missing sounds using the symbols of the IPA. Then write the number of sounds in the word.

EXAMPLE: meat   / m _i_ t /   _3_

1. train   / tr __ n / _____

6. court   / k __ rt / _____

2. boat   / b __ t / _____

7. caught   / k __ t / _____

3. boot   / b __ t / _____

8. through / θr __ / _____

4. book   / b __ k / _____

9. said   / s __ d / _____

5. arm   / __ rm / _____

10. say   / s __ / _____

syllable

consonants

Patterns of Stress

vowels

lateral and glides

diphthongs

Proverbs from Around the World

Turkey:

A man is his own mirror.

Uruguay:

A woman's beauty cannot warm a winter's night.

India:

Not all the buds on a bush will blossom.

A doctor is only a doctor when he has killed one or two patients.

Jamaica:

Clothes cover up character.

Japan:

Eggs and promises are easily broken.

Russia:

One can get sick of cake, but never of bread.

A wife should be humble as a lamb, busy as a bee, beautiful as a bird of paradise, and faithful as a turtle dove.

A pessimist is a well informed optimist.

Botswana:

Life is but memories unborn.

CHAPTER TWO

Syllable Stress

S ounds are the building blocks of language. They can combine and recombine in a multitude of patterns to accommodate the growing demand for a larger and more technical vocabulary required by an increasingly complex society.

The smallest combination of sounds is called a syllable. It is composed of one vowel sound and one or more consonants.

EXAMPLE: go   strike

A vowel can stand alone as a syllable (**a**lone, **a**go) but a consonant cannot. A vowel can stand alone as a word (**eve, I**) but a consonant cannot.

The vowel, therefore, forms the nucleus, or core, of the syllable. Without a vowel, there is no syllable. Without one or more vowels, there are no words.

A word can contain one or more syllables.

EXAMPLE:

Word	*Number of Syllables*
game	1
remain	2
register	3
abbreviate	4
constitutional	5

Combinations of syllables in a single word may result in variations and modifications of that word.

EXAMPLE: constitute

constitution, constitutional, constitutionally,
unconstitutional, reconstitute, constituency

Prefixes and suffixes add immeasurably to the flexibility of the language. In the words listed above, **remain** contains the syllable **re,** which is a prefix; **abbreviate** contains the prefix **ab-,** and the suffix **-ate,** both of which are also syllables; while **constitutional** contains the prefix **con-**, and the suffixes **-tion** and **-al**, all of which are syllables. The examples of word modification above also reveal the importance of prefixes and suffixes.

In the English language, one syllable is generally stressed more than other syllables within the word. The stressed syllable is longer, louder, and higher in pitch than any other syllable in the word. A stressed syllable can appear in the beginning, middle, or end of a word.

EXAMPLE: ′pi lot,   ap ′point ment,   ap ′pear*

The vowel sound in the stressed syllable is most important because it possesses the features of volume, duration, and pitch. If the vowel in the stressed syllable is not longer, louder, or higher in pitch than the vowel in the weaker, or unstressed, syllables, the English stress pattern is lost. Therefore, the accuracy of pronunciation is impaired. Non-native and nonstandard speakers must be particularly careful to stretch the vowel in the stressed syllable to maintain the English pattern of strong and weak beats within a word.

Syllable stress very often shifts as the form of a word changes.

EXAMPLE: i ′ma gine   i ma gi ′na tion

            ′pho to graph   pho ′tog ra phy

Another example of shift occurs when the same word is used as two different parts of speech.** If the word is a noun, the first syllable is stressed. When used as a verb, the second syllable is stressed.

EXAMPLE: ′converse (noun)   con ′verse (verb)

            ′ob ject (noun)   ob ′ject (verb)

The importance of the stressed/unstressed concept cannot be overemphasized. The two vowel sounds used to represent the unstressed syllables are / ɪ / and the schwa / ə /. Both are very short in duration.

What Is a Syllable?

A.   A syllable is a unit of sound that contains *one vowel sound.*

    EXAMPLE: c<u>o</u>me   r<u>e</u> t<u>u</u>rn   th<u>ou</u>ght f<u>u</u>l l<u>y</u>

A word with three vowel sounds has three syllables or beats.

    EXAMPLE: w<u>o</u>n d<u>e</u>r f<u>u</u>l   d<u>i</u>s <u>a</u>p p<u>oi</u>nt   ch<u>a</u>l l<u>e</u>n g<u>e</u>s

---

* The primary stress mark (′) in the phonetic alphabet is placed at the begining of the stressed syllable, above the first letter of the syllable This is in contrast to the dictionary system, where the stress mark appears at the end of the syllable.

    EXAMPLE: *IPA*   *Dictionary*
                ′pi lot   pi′ lot

** There are some exceptions to this rule, such as ′com fort (verb) and ′com fort (noun).

A word with four vowel sounds has four syllables or beats.

    EXAMPLE: m<u>a</u>g n<u>i</u> f<u>i</u> c<u>e</u>nt   d<u>i</u>s <u>a</u>p p<u>oi</u>n t<u>e</u>d   <u>e</u> l<u>e</u> tr<u>i</u> c<u>ia</u>n

B. The vowel sound (or the diphthong) in the syllable may

   ♦ stand alone.

     EXAMPLE: <u>a</u>   <u>eye</u>   <u>a</u> ble

   ♦ be preceded by one or more consonants.

     EXAMPLE: <u>r</u>ay   <u>tr</u>y   <u>str</u>i kers

   ♦ be followed by one or more consonants.

     EXAMPLE: de<u>sk</u>   ea<u>ch</u>   te<u>nts</u>

C. Syllables combine to form words.

   ♦ ap pen di ci tis   re mar ka ble   so ci o lo gy.

How Are Words Divided into Syllables?

A. Through the process of syllabication, words may be divided into syllables for aiding pronunciation, reading, and spelling.

   1. Our approach to syllabication combines dictionary and phonic rules. In this way, you can acquire listening and speaking skills more easily.

   2. Standard dictionaries show the two methods of syllabication. The number of syllables, however, remains the same.

Dictionary	*Phonic*
want ed	wan ted
com ing	co ming
choo ses	choo ses
teach er	tea cher
dan ger ous	dan ge rous

   3. In many instances, letters within a syllable are not pronounced.

     EXAMPLE: ar range   / ə ˈreɪndʒ /

                  oc ca sion   / ə ˈkeɪ ʒn /

                  op pose   / ə ˈpouz /

   4. Sounds do not always correspond with letters. The letter *a,* for example, may be pronounced / æ / as in **hat,** / eɪ / as in **day,** or / a / as in **dark.**

B. Rules for counting the number of syllables

1. Every syllable has only one vowel sound.

   EXAMPLE: ch<u>ee</u>se   st<u>o</u>pped   c<u>o</u>n d<u>u</u>c t<u>or</u>

2. Every syllable—where possible—begins with a consonant sound.

   EXAMPLE: <u>t</u>e <u>l</u>e <u>vi</u> <u>s</u>ion   lea <u>v</u>ing   <u>b</u>e <u>g</u>in <u>n</u>ing

3. Every syllable—where possible—ends with a vowel sound.

   EXAMPLE: c<u>a</u> me r<u>a</u>   ps<u>y</u> ch<u>o</u> l<u>o</u> g<u>y</u>   re l<u>i</u> a bl<u>y</u>

4. In words with double consonants, divide the consonants as follows:

   EXAMPLE: sig <u>n</u>al   o<u>c</u> <u>c</u>a sion   cha<u>n</u> <u>c</u>es

5. In words beginning with a prefix, the prefix stands alone.

   EXAMPLE: <u>re</u> duce   <u>de</u> cide   <u>pre</u> pare   <u>pro</u> fes sor

6. In words ending with a suffix, the suffix stands alone.

   EXAMPLE: slow <u>ly</u>   cu ri <u>ous</u>   go vern <u>ment</u>

7. Syllables ending in *-tle, -ble, -ton,* and *-ten* contain the short vowel sound / ə /, called the "schwa."

   EXAMPLE: bot <u>tle</u>   ca pa <u>ble</u>   but <u>ton</u>   of <u>ten</u>

   Note: There are two vowel sounds, and therefore two syllables, in the suffix **a ble,** as in **rea so na ble** and in **know ledge a ble.**

C. *Practice exercises:* How many syllables in a word?

1. Divide the following words into syllables using a slash between syllables. Write the number of syllables in each word in the space provided.

   EXAMPLE: e/qual __2__   im/por/tant __3__   in/tel/li/gent __4__

Word	*No. Syllables*	*Word*	*No. Syllables*
obey	_____	waited	_____
tutor	_____	vitamins	_____
signal	_____	cafeteria	_____
satisfy	_____	compare	_____
closet	_____	television	_____
terrible	_____	occupation	_____
climate	_____	danced	_____

Practice reading aloud to check your answers.

2. Every syllable has only one vowel sound, but not every vowel has a sound. Write the number of syllables in each word. Then practice reading aloud.

EXAMPLE: states ___1___   hated ___2___   jumped ___1___

Word	No. Syllables	Word	No. Syllables
come	_____	stops	_____
cheese	_____	stopped	_____
coming	_____	furious	_____
expensive	_____	sadly	_____
reply	_____	transportation	_____
chances	_____	evening	_____
teach	_____	offered	_____
teacher	_____	required	_____

What Is the Function of Stress in Syllables?

A. Stressed syllables

1. Stress is the major emphasis or force given to one syllable within the word. The other syllables are weak and unstressed.

   EXAMPLE: be <u>low</u>   <u>an</u> swer   di <u>vi</u> sion   com po <u>si</u> tion

2. The vowel or diphthong sound in the stressed syllable receives the major emphasis.

   EXAMPLE: r<u>a</u>ce   ho t<u>el</u>   pr<u>o</u> mised   at t<u>en</u> tion

3. The vowel sound in a stressed syllable tends to be longer than the vowel sound in an unstressed syllables within the word.

   EXAMPLE: pre <u>tend</u>   <u>syl</u> la ble   de <u>par</u> ture

B. Unstressed syllables

1. Unstressed syllables are weak and short in duration in comparison with the stressed syllables within the word. Below, the dash indicates a long syllable; the dot a short syllable.

   EXAMPLE: hōs pi tăl   rĕ mēm bĕr   ă grēe ă blĕ

2. The vowel sound in unstressed syllables tends to be short in duration and is usually represented by the schwa / ə / or the / ɪ /.*

---

* The / ɪ / may be a weak and short vowel in unstressed syllables, but it can also be the vowel sound in stressed syllables.

   EXAMPLE: / ɪ /   in stressed syllables: cŏn sī dĕr   clīck

   / ɪ /   in unstressed syllables: dĕ cīde   hŭn drĕd

3. Unstressed syllables may be found in the beginning, middle, or end of a word.

EXAMPLE: rē lȧ tïve   cȯn sī dėr   ün dėr stānd

What Are the Elements of Stress?

A. Duration

1. The vowel sound in the stressed syllable is lengthened or prolonged. Therefore the syllable is longer in duration than the other syllables within the word.

EXAMPLE: a <u>chieve</u> ment   si tu <u>a</u> tion   ar <u>ri</u> val

2. The vowel sound before a voiced consonant is prolonged; before a voiceless consonant, the vowel is shortened.

EXAMPLE: sad sat   bag back   cab cap   robe rope

B. Pitch

The vowel sound in the stressed syllable may be higher in pitch than the vowel sounds in the unstressed syllables within the word.

EXAMPLE: de ᶫⁱᵍʰᵗ ful   mar ve lous   cor ʳᵉᶜᵗ

C. Volume

The vowel sound in the stressed syllable may be louder than the vowel sounds in the unstressed syllables within a word.

Example: <u>ang</u> ry   a <u>dult</u>   im <u>me</u> di ate ly

Listening/Speaking: The Stressed Syllable

A. Which syllable receives the major stress?

In the following words, one syllable has been capitalized to indicate greater emphasis than the other syllables.

Listen carefully and repeat after your instructor.

1. fan TAS tic	7. FEA ture	13. RE gis ter
2. DOC tor	8. ma TURE	14. PUB lic
3. WON der ful	9. in di VI du al	15. pro TECT
4. ho TEL	10. ac COUN ting	16. PRO mise
5. RE la tive	11. tech NO lo gy	17. ex a mi NA tion
6. re LA tion	12. EVE ning	18. MI nutes

B. Circle the stressed syllable in the underlined words as your instructor reads each sentence aloud. Repeat each sentence following the teacher's model.

1. He was a <u>fantastic doctor</u>.

2. We stayed at a <u>wonderful hotel</u>.

3. We spent a pleasant <u>evening</u> with our <u>relatives</u>.

4. I don't believe in <u>public opinion</u> polls.

5. She <u>frequently missed</u> her <u>appointment</u>.

6. They drove <u>slowly</u> through the <u>village</u>.

7. There was a <u>terrible tropical</u> storm.

8. The <u>dinner</u> at the <u>restaurant</u> was excellent.

9. They <u>enjoyed</u> the warm southern <u>climate</u>.

10. She <u>promised</u> to meet him in fifteen <u>minutes</u>.

C. This exercise provides practice in phrasing questions. Compose five questions using five words from section A. Underline each selected word.

As you read your questions aloud, stress the major syllables in the underlined words.

Ask members of the class to respond to your questions using your selected words.

> **EXAMPLE:**   fantastic
>
> > Q: Why is he a <u>fantastic</u> doctor?
> >
> > A: He's <u>fantastic</u> because he is helpful.

D. Shift in Stress

The shift in stress may be related to the part of speech used. The first syllable is stressed in nouns; the second syllable is stressed in the verbs.

> **EXAMPLE:**   (in) sult (n)   in (sult) (v)

Listen carefully for the shift in stress as your instructor reads these two words aloud. Circle the stressed syllable. Repeat after the instructor.

1. Compare the stress pattrens of the nouns and the verbs in the following lists of words.

Noun	*Verb*
RE bel	re BEL
PRE sent	pre SENT
RE cord	re CORD

Noun	Verb
PER mit	per MIT
SUS pect	sus PECT
con duct	con duct
de sert	de sert
con flict	con flict
ex port	ex port
ob ject	ob ject

2. As your instructor reads aloud, circle the syllable you hear with the major stress or emphasis. Write N if the word is a noun, V if it is a verb.

	N/V			N/V
rebel	_____		suspect	_____
insult	_____		record	_____
survey	_____		conduct	_____
contest	_____		object	_____
present	_____		permit	_____
progress	_____		export	_____

3. Underline the two contrasting words in each sentence. Circle the stressed syllable in the underlined nouns and verbs as you read aloud.

   EXAMPLE: I refused to sur(vey) my neighbors for that (sur)vey.

   1. May I present you with this present?

   2. We could not record your voice on this broken record.

   3. They did not permit Harry to use this special permit.

   4. I suspect that John is a suspect in the murder case.

   5. Don't desert your friends in the desert.

   6. That rebel did not rebel as we had expected.

   7. I cannot estimate what his estimate of the damages will be.

   8. Although my classes did not conflict, I had a conflict with my exams.

9. While Dick did not join the protest march, he did protest in court.

10. Although he is in the export business, he doesn't export guns.

11. Your progress has inspired me to progress more quickly.

12. I did not contest the decision of the contest.

E. Stress in multisyllabic words

Circle the stressed syllable in each word as your instructor reads aloud. Repeat each word with the teacher or a tape as model.

1. Two-syllable words

   ◆ Stress the first syllable.

traffic	student	wallet
system	business	quiet
forest	sharpened	diamond
purchase	habit	market

   ◆ Stress the second syllable.

debate	career	dismiss
consult (v)	create	promote
allow	pretend	appear
disturb	exchanged	refer

2. Three-syllable words

   ◆ Stress the first syllable.

foreigner	influence	challenging
agency	anxiously*	difficult
interested	nervously	frequently
probably	excellent	furious

---

* The symbols of the IPA can be helpful in improving your pronunciation. *Anxiously* is pronounced / æŋkʃəslɪ /.

♦ Stress the second syllable.

election	arrival	refusal
prediction	decision	politely
statistics	embarrass	employment
accustomed	financial	inflation

♦ Stress the third syllable.

incorrect	disbelief	interact
interrupt	misbehave	disppoint
disappear	reinforce	introduced
understand	personnel	disagree

3. Four-syllable words

Make certain that you produce the last syllable even though it is unstressed.

historian	preferable	traditional
economics	compulsory	predictable
experience	electrician	appropriate
competition	permanently	philosophy
photography	application	naturally

4. Five-syllable words

sociology	examination	consideration
appendicitis	dictatorial	environmental
investigators	secretarial	determination
hypochondriac	psychological	extraordinary
vocabulary	organization	technological

5. Additional practice exercises

   a. Circle the stressed syllable in these multi-syllabic words as they are read aloud. Repeat after the instructor or the tape.

correct	planet	gesture
hostage	elect	collapse
arrest	angrily	liberal
nuclear	hesitated	impatiently
promises	available	technologies

   b. Prepare to read these sentences aloud in class. Circle the stressed syllables in the underlined words.

      1) The <u>electrician rewired</u> the <u>entire apartment</u>.

      2) He <u>entered</u> the <u>photography competition</u>.

      3) A <u>nuclear</u> war can <u>exterminate</u> an <u>entire population</u>.

      4) We live in an age of <u>technological discoveries</u>.

      5) <u>Liberal</u> arts <u>students usually</u> study <u>philosophy</u> and <u>sociology</u>.

Listening/Speaking: The Unstressed Syllable

A. The vowel sound in an unstressed syllable is short in duration and is represented by the schwa / ə / or / ɪ /.

a bi li ty	/ ə bɪ lɪ tɪ /	op po si tion	/ ɑ pə zɪ ʃən /
fu ri ous	/ fju rɪ əs /	hys te ri cal	/ hɪs tɛ rɪ kəl /
fo reig ner	/ fɑ rɪ nɚ /	sta tis tics	/ stə tɪs tɪks /
pre vi ous	/ pri vɪ əs /	a to mic	/ ə tɑ mɪk /

B. Unstressed syllables may be found at the beginning, middle, or end of a word. In the examples, the stressed syllables are underlined. The dots indicate the unstressed syllables.

1. a <u>loud</u>   con <u>si</u> der   ac <u>cus</u> tomed   ex <u>cuse</u>

2. <u>re</u> la tive   <u>re</u> a lize   <u>chal</u> len ges   <u>li</u> be ral

3. <u>em</u> pha sis   <u>for</u> tune   ca fe <u>te</u> ri a   un <u>con</u> scious

C. Prefixes and Suffixes

Prefixes and suffixes receive little or no stress and are very short in duration. Listen to your instructor or a tape and repeat each word accurately. Circle the stressed syllable in each word.

1. Prefixes

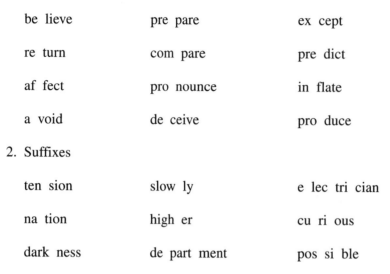

be lieve	pre pare	ex cept
re turn	com pare	pre dict
af fect	pro nounce	in flate
a void	de ceive	pro duce

2. Suffixes

ten sion	slow ly	e lec tri cian
na tion	high er	cu ri ous
dark ness	de part ment	pos si ble
go ing	high est	pre vi ous ly

3. Consonant + suffix*

ha ted	cou rage	run ner
tea chers	dan cing	tu tor
neigh bors	per for mance	ju dges
mee ting	fa ces	chur ches

Listening/Writing

A. Your instructor will read the following words aloud. Listen carefully for the unstressed syllables. Can you hear which syllables are short and unstressed? As your instructor reads aloud, write the schwa / ə / or / ɪ /** in the space provided.

> **EXAMPLE:** department / d____partm____nt /

1. reply   / r____plaɪ /   3. climate / klaɪm____t /

2. special / spɛʃ____l /   4. nation   / neɪʃ____n /

---

* See phonic rules for syllabication.

** The schwa / ə / and / ɪ / are often used interchangeably.

5. aloud   / ___laʊd /

6. different / dɪfr___nt /

7. oppose   / ___poʊz /

8. conscious / kɑnʃ___s /

9. pleasant   / plɛz___nt /

10. necklace   / nɛkl___s /

B. Your instructor will read the following words aloud. Listen carefully for the stressed syllables. Can you hear which syllables are lengthened and emphasized? As your instructor reads aloud, circle the stressed syllable. Repeat each word with the teacher as model. Indicate the number of syllables in each word using the space provided.

1. excellent   _____

2. available   _____

3. troubled   _____

4. appropriate   _____

5. technologies   _____

6. hesitated   _____

7. exclaimed   _____

8. appointment   _____

9. advertising   _____

10. portfolio   _____

NAME: _____ DATE: _____

Chapter 2 Homework Review

A. Write the number of syllables in each word. Be sure to stress the correct syllable as you practice pronouncing the words aloud.

1. beginning	_____	6. neighbor	_____	11. fuel	_____
2. information	_____	7. impatiently	_____	12. interested	_____
3. promised	_____	8. confused	_____	13. expire	_____
4. cases	_____	9. waved	_____	14. corresponds	_____
5. imagine	_____	10. embarrass	_____	15. mathematics	_____

B. Pronounce the following words aloud. Circle the stressed syllable or syllables in each word.

1. president	9. agency
2. experience	10. personnel
3. permanently	11. evidence
4. examination	12. financial
5. inflation	13. estimate (n)*
6. frequently	14. estimate (v)*
7. interrupt	15. associate (n)*
8. extraordinary	16. associate (v)*

C. Select the appropriate word from Exercise B and write it in the space provided. Circle the stressed syllable of the underlined word and practice reading the sentence aloud.

EXAMPLE: responsible   He was a res(pon)sible citizen.

_____

* Note the pronunciation of these words. There are two strong syllables in the verb form. The circle marks the stressed syllables.

estimate (n) / (ɛs)tɪ mɪt /   associate (n) / ə (sou) sɪ ɪt /
estimate (v) / (ɛs)tɪ (meɪt) /   associate (n) / ə (sou) sɪ (eɪt) /

1. He presented the jury with little _____ to convict the suspect.

2. Mary's _____ situation was good when she was employed.

3. That was an _____ concert I heard last night.

4. I decided not to _____ the meeting, so I waited outside for awhile.

5. I can't _____ the cost of this project.

6. We shall remain in this country _____.

7. My _____ is now the _____ of the company.

8. How much _____ have you had in this field?

9. My _____ situation is poor now because of the high _____ rate.

10. The _____ at the employment _____ were very helpful.

Reading Aloud

A. Your instructor may serve as your model for correct and fluent oral reading. Listen carefully for correct syllable stress* and accurate pronunciation in preparation for reading this dialogue aloud in class.

A Suspect

———◆———

1. Q: Is Tom a suspect in that murder case?

   A: Yes, he is a suspect in that murder case.

2. Q: Will the police conduct an investigation of the case?

   A: They will conduct an investigation soon.

3. Q: Did they record Tom's voice?

   A: No, they didn't record Tom's voice.

4. Q: Do you suspect his neighbor?

   A: I do suspect his neighbor.

5. Q: Did they permit Tom to carry a gun?

   A: The police did not permit Tom to carry a gun. But his neighbor has a permit.

6. Q: Why haven't they made any more progress on this case?

   A: They have begun to progress, but it is going very slowly.

7. Q: Has Tom's family objected?

   A: No, his family did not object.

8. Q: Does Tom have a record of any previous crime?

   A: No, he has no record of any previous crime.

9. Q: Did Tom's business associate present any new evidence?

   A: Tom's business associate did not present any new evidence.

10. Q: How long do you estimate this case will take?

    A: I estimate that it could take at least a year.

---

* In the noun form, the first syllable of the word is stressed. In the verb form, the second syllable is stressed.

B. As your instructor reads this passage aloud, circle the stressed syllable in each underlined word.

Your instructor may serve as your model for correct and fluent oral reading. Be prepared to read aloud in class using correct syllable stressing and accurate pronunciation.

Finding a Career

◆

Rita and Pablo opened the door to the employment agengy and stared at the <u>enormous</u> sign above the entrance that read: YOUR CAREER STARTS HERE!

"I'm scared," Rita <u>whispered nervously</u>. "I've never been to an employment agency before."

"You and me both!" Pablo tugged at his shirt collar. "I'm not <u>accustomed</u> to ties. This one's choking me!"

"My cousin warned me to look <u>professional</u>, so I wore a suit instead of jeans," Rita confessed.

A large, imposing woman advanced upon them, waving application forms. "I am Mrs. Sanders, a counselor. You both seem confused. Is it your first time here?"

"Yes, ma'am," Pablo said politely, while Rita nodded in agreement.

"Good. I trust you are <u>computer literate</u> and <u>technologically oriented</u>. <u>Genetic engineering</u> is a growing field."

Pablo held up his <u>portfolio</u>. "I'm interested in the graphic arts, and in drafting."

The counselor shook her head. "A very <u>inappropriate</u> choice."

"What about the paralegal field?" Rita asked.

"Excellent! Later, you could consider law school."

"Law school?" Rita echoed in disbelief.

"Think big," Mrs. Sanders urged. "Fill out the applications and then we can sit down and chat."

Both students <u>exchanged</u> glances and moved toward the door.

"You're right about our being confused," Pablo said. Then they both turned and fled.

"My friend Wang told me these counselors are called headhunters. Now I understand why," Pablo laughed.

Rita shook her head. "Law school! She's way ahead of me."

Once outside, they spotted a Japanese restaurant. They went in and ordered sushi.

"There are two agencies I want to check out," Pablo said, his mouth stuffed with sushi. "After all, we're <u>experienced</u> job hunters."

Rita snapped her fingers. "Paralegal to lawyer, just like that."

"Way to go," Pablo agreed. "So let's put our careers on hold and take time out for lunch."

CHAPTER THREE

Word Stress

As syllables combine to form words, so do words combine to form units of thought, or phrases, ending in the completed thought we call the sentence. A phrase is a series of related words without a subject or a verb.

EXAMPLE: to the store   from the house   into the water

A sentence must contain, at the very least, a subject and a verb.

EXAMPLE: John swims.   The dog barks.   She disappears.

Most sentences are far more complex than the examples given. The same pattern of strong and weak stresses that characterize syllable stress applies to word stress within the phrase or sentence. Syllables can be strong or weak, and so can words.

This chapter focuses on stressed and unstressed words. The parts of speech that tend to be stressed are words with content:

Nouns	chair	desk	child
Verbs	run	walk	remember
Adjectives	blue	happy	intelligent
Adverbs	slowly	terribly	accidentally

These words carry the meaning and emotion of the sentence. They are longer, louder, and higher in pitch than unstressed words. These factors constitute the elements of stress: duration, volume, and pitch.

Unstressed words are function words. They include the following categories:

Articles	the	a	an
Pronouns	she	whom	which
Prepositions	by	from	in
Conjunctions	but	or	and
Auxiliary verbs	should	have	were

37

Function words are weak; they connect the major ideas in the unit of thought or within a sentence.

A word can be composed of one syllable or many syllables. A sentence can be simple, a single unit of thought, or it can be complex, containing one or more independent clauses, modified by dependent clauses and phrases. But no matter how complex, the sentence can be analyzed in terms of the stressed and unstressed words.

EXAMPLE: 1. <u>Marie lost</u> her <u>English textbook</u>. / /

2. <u>Marie lost</u> her <u>English texbook</u> / in the <u>cafeteria</u>. / /

3. <u>Marie lost</u> her <u>English textbook</u> / in the <u>cafeteria</u> / because she was <u>careless</u>. / /

4. Although <u>Marie</u> was <u>usually careful</u>, / she lost her <u>English textbook</u> / in the <u>cafeteria</u> / because she left it under her <u>chair</u> / during <u>lunch</u> / and <u>completely forgot</u> about it / in her <u>rush</u> / to <u>get</u> to her <u>next class</u>. / /

Each of the sentences above is increasingly complex yet the words that are stressed are easy to select. You can see that the stressed words, those that are underlined, are nouns, verbs, adjectives, and adverbs, all of which carry meaning.

The single and double slash markers indicate a very important aspect of word stress. Every compound or complex sentence, composed of more than a single idea, is divided into phrases or thought units. The end of the phrase (incomplete thought) is marked by a single slash; the end of the completed thought (sentence) is marked by a double slash. You will find that the technique of phrasing and pausing between one idea and the next will help you to control the accuracy of your pronunciation and the clarity of your articulation. Ends of words can be completed more easily, greater attention can be paid to pitch variation and vocal projection, and the listener is given the time to absorb the meaning of the sentence. Appropriate pausing enables you to monitor and correct your speech patterns.

While pausing and phrasing are necessary, the linking or joining of the words within the phrase is equally important. Here, the strong-weak stress pattern is most obvious.

EXAMPLE: I'm <u>going</u> / for a <u>walk</u> / in the <u>park</u>. / /

        or

I'm <u>going</u> for a <u>walk</u> in the <u>park</u>. / /

It is the combination of pausing, linking, and stressing that gives English its unique melody pattern. American English swings from one phrase to the next, with a pause between the phrase and linking within the phrase. The phrase **in the park** has one stressed word, **park,** and two unstressed words, **in the. Park** is much longer and stronger than **in the.** The vowel in **park** is stretched, and the beat of the phrase is: short, short, long.*

The elements of stress have been isolated in this chapter through exercises and readings in each area. In speaking and reading, however, the elements of pitch, volume, and duration are fused so that the stressed word, which carries meaning to your listener, is longer, louder, and higher in pitch.

---

* Another way to indicate the duration of a word is to use dots and dashes, the dot for short duration and the dash for longer duration, as **ıṅ thė pār̄k.**

Stress in Words

A. What is a stressed word?

    1. It is longer than other words in the phrase or sentence.

    2. It is louder than other words in the phrase or sentence.

    3. It is higher in pitch than other words in the phrase or sentence.

    4. It receives the greatest emphasis or force within the phrase or the sentence.

B. What kinds of words are stressed?

    1. Nouns: The <u>girl</u> sat down.

    2. Verbs: He <u>dove</u> into the pool.

    3. Adjectives: She has <u>brown</u> hair.

    4. Adverbs: She walked <u>slowly</u>.

C. What is an unstressed word?

    1. It receives little or no emphasis within the phrase or sentence.

    2. It is usually a word of one syllable.

D. What kinds of words are unstressed?

    1. Articles: The boy bought an apple.*

    2. Prepositions: They went to the house from the store.

    3. Pronouns: She waved to her friend.

    4. Conjunctions: He and she left, but the others stayed.

    5. Auxiliary Verbs: They were going.

How Do We Make Use of Stressing?

A. Words are grouped together to express an idea or a thought in a unit called a phrase.

    EXAMPLE: He brought a book / that he liked. / /

B. Important words within the phrase are stressed to convey meaning.

    EXAMPLE: The <u>policeman</u> <u>raced</u> <u>quickly</u> / down the <u>street</u> / after the <u>thief</u>. / /**

---

* The dot indicates a short unstressed word.

** Can you find other ways to phrase this sentence?

C. Individual phrases are separated by a single slash marker.

> **EXAMPLE:**   Although he was late, / he made no excuses / to his friends. / /*

D. Words within a phrase are linked together.

> **EXAMPLE:**   A wealthy lady / in her position / would not be expected / to do the cooking / in the family. / /*

E. Phrases combine to form a completed thought, or sentence.

> **EXAMPLE:**   The bank was open for business / until six Friday / for the convenience / of its depositors. / /*

What Are the Three Elements of Stress?

A. Duration

  1. Duration is the length of the pause between one phrase and another or between sentences.

> **EXAMPLE:**   *Pause between phrases:*   He made two touchdowns / in the last half / of the game. / /
>
> *Pause between sentences:*   Snow began falling that evening. / / A snow alert was immediately issued. / /

Practice exercise: Divide each sentence into phrase units using single and double slashes. Remember to link the words within a phrase. Be prepared to read aloud in class.

  1) Several minutes before the crash the pilot talked to the control tower.

  2) Three grandchildren and two friends were killed in the fire.

  3) A number of students were upset to discover that some of their classes had been canceled at the last moment.

  4) The doctor and his nurse were sued for malpractice by two patients, but the other patients spoke highly of their services.

  5) Once outside in the street, Rita and Pablo spotted a Japanese restaurant. They decided to go in and have sushi for lunch.

  2. Duration is the amount of time given to the utterance of a word.

    a. A stressed word is longer than an unstressed word.

---

* Can you find other ways to phrase this sentence?

b. The vowel in a stressed word is longer than the vowel in an unstressed word.

> **EXAMPLE:**   *Stressed words:*   He <u>arrived</u> <u>home</u> in <u>time</u> to <u>study</u> his <u>notes</u>.
>
> *Unstressed words:*   S̈he r̈ushed tö catch thë train.

c. ***Practice exercise:*** Circle the stressed words that will make each sentence meaningful to your listeners. Remember to prolong the vowel sounds in content words such as nouns, verbs, adjectives, and adverbs. Be prepared to read aloud in class.

1) Now is the time to decide. Later it will be too late.

2) "My cousin told me to wear a suit instead of jeans," Rita confessed.

3) "I'm interested in graphic arts and drafting," Pablo said. "Here is my portfolio."

4) Mary didn't believe that she owed the government money.

5) Who are you?

3. ***Reading selections***

a. The following story has been divided into phrase units using single and double slashes. The capitalized words signify that the vowel sounds are stretched to emphasize the content words.

Listen carefully and repeat as your instructor reads each phrase. Notice how the use of the pause and the lengthening of the vowels increase intellibility.

The Man Who Was Full of Truth

———◆———

There was a MAN / who was a GREAT LIAR / the BIGGEST LIAR in the WHOLE TOWN. // Never in his LIFE / did anyone KNOW him / to tell the TRUTH. // So in the END / he DIED, / as ALL of us MUST. // And so they CAME / to BURY him. //

And the WIDOW, / when the COFFIN was going out the DOOR, / began to WEEP and YELL, / "You are LEAVING us, / oh LITTLE BODY, / so FULL of truth." //

Finally, / ONE of her FRIENDS, / who was her BEST friend, / asked her, / "LISTEN. // WHY do you keep CALLING it / a LITTLE BODY / full of TRUTH? // Wasn't my FRIEND / just a LITTLE BIT on the LYING side? //

"PLENTY," / she said. // "THAT's why he's LEAVING us / so FULL of ALL KINDS of TRUTHS. // He NEVER / let one OUT." //

b. Lenthening the vowels in the stressed words increases intelligibility.

Listen carefully and repeat as your instructor reads each phrase. Use slashes to indicate the appropriate pauses. Note the stretching of the vowels in the capitalized words, particularly in the word "ashamed." Not only intelligibility but meaning and feeling are increased through the lengthening of the vowels.

Therefore I Must Tell the Truth (Navajo)

◆

I am ASHAMED before the EARTH;

I am ASHAMED before the HEAVENS;

I am ASHAMED before the DAWN;

I am ASHAMED before the EVENING TWILIGHT;

I am ASHAMED before the BLUE SKY;

I am ASHAMED before the SUN;

I am ASHAMED before that STANDING within me which SPEAKS with me.

Some of these things are ALWAYS LOOKING at me.

I am NEVER out of SIGHT.

Therefore I MUST TELL THE TRUTH.

That is why I ALWAYS tell the TRUTH.

I HOLD my WORD TIGHT to my BREAST.

c. In the following selection, note how words have been shortened or omitted completely.

Listen as your instructor reads this passage aloud and observe the decreased intelligibility. Then translate the passage into standard English.

Pancakes for Two

◆

BEN: Watcha doin' tonigh'?

KEN: Dunno.

BEN: Ya hungry? Wanna bi'?

KEN: Cou' be. Where shou' I meetcha?

BEN: Salls sa' to me.

KEN: Zasso? Tell you wha'. Seeya in fi' minis at Pa's Panca' Pla'.

BEN: Grea' idea. I kin tas' 'em awready.

KEN: Wanna ta' in a movie too?

BEN:	Nuttin' goo' playin'.
KEN:	Wassa difference?
BEN:	Gotta tes'. Gotta study. Les sto' wastin' ti'. Salmos' eigh' o'clo'.
KEN:	Yerrigh'. Meetcha in fi'.

B. Volume

1. Volume is the use of a stronger or louder voice to emphasize words that convey added meaning in any given speaking situation.

   EXAMPLE: I <u>demand</u> that you open the door and let me in!

   <u>Never!</u> Do you <u>understand</u>? You and I are <u>finished</u>!

2. Volume is the selective use of a louder or softer voice in any given situation.

   a. Volume is diminished in a one-to-one situation.

   EXAMPLE: *Teacher to student:* "José, you forgot to hand in your homework."

   b. Volume is increased in a one-to-many situation.

   EXAMPLE: *Teacher to classroom of students:* "Please open your books to page 174."

   c. Volume is vastly increased in a large auditorium.

   EXAMPLE: *President addressing college students:* "May I please have your attention? We have many important matters to discuss."

3. *Practice exercise:* Circle the stressed words, which will help you to sound convincing and expressive. Remember to produce these words with a stronger voice. Be prepared to read aloud in class.

   a. "You're certainly late! Where have you been?"

   b. "Mr. Smith, we've had this leak in the kitchen for two whole weeks."

   c. "This is my book, not yours!"

   d. "Operator, there is an emergency in my home. We need an ambulance immediately!"

4. *Reading selection:* In the following story, the important words have been underlined and will be read in a louder voice. The capitalized words indicate that the vowels should be stretched. The pauses between phrases and sentences are marked with single and double slashes.

   Listen carefully and repeat as your instructor reads each phrase. Adding the element of volume or loudness to that of duration (vowel length and pausing) results in increased intelligibility and conveys meaning more easily.

The Fable of the Fox and the Fish (from Aesop)

A <u>FOX</u> saw a <u>FISH</u> / <u>DARTING</u> back and forth / near the <u>MIDDLE</u> of a river. / / He asked, / "<u>FRIEND</u> <u>FISH</u>, / why don't you swim <u>ONE</u> way / or the <u>OTHER</u>?" / /

The fish replied, / "If I go <u>ONE</u> way, / I shall be <u>SWEPT</u> over the waterfall / and <u>DIE</u>. / / If I swim the <u>OTHER</u> way, / a <u>FISHERMAN</u> with a <u>NET</u> / hopes to <u>CATCH</u> me." / /

"My <u>FRIEND</u>," / said the cunning fox. / / "Why not come <u>ASHORE</u> / and avoid <u>BOTH</u> dangers?" / /

"No, thank you," / answered the fish. / / "My mother <u>WARNED</u> me / that it is <u>ALWAYS</u> <u>SAFER</u> / to put up with <u>KNOWN</u> dangers / than to face <u>UNKNOWN</u> ones." / /

Moral: Do not <u>JUMP</u> / from the <u>FRYING</u> <u>PAN</u> / into the <u>FIRE</u>. / /

C. Pitch

1. Pitch is a tone on the musical scale that may be heard as high or low.

2. Pitch variation is a marked aspect of the English language.

3. Emotional, subjective reactions as well as grammatical structure affect the pitch patterns of English.

4. Pitch patterns in the English language have several characteristic patterns.

   a. The downward, or falling, inflection may be heard at the end of a sentence.

      1. At the end of a statement

         EXAMPLE: We're leaving. ⬇

      2. When giving a command

         EXAMPLE: Sit down! ⬇

      3. When asking questions beginning with an interrogative word

         EXAMPLE: Where is he going? ⬇
         What time is it? ⬇
         How are you feeling? ⬇

   b. The upward or rising inflection may be heard in the middle or at the end of a sentence in the following instances:

1. When questions require a simple yes or no answer

    EXAMPLE: Are you going? ↗

    Is it raining? ↗

2. To indicate significant emphasis

    EXAMPLE: I want to go but I can't go today. ↘

    Four people were killed last night on Main Street. ↘

3. To suggest doubt, uncertainty, or an incomplete thought

    EXAMPLE: Well, if you feel like that . . . ↗

4. To indicate a series of ideas within a sentence

    EXAMPLE: They couldn't decide if they wanted a dog, ↗ a cat, ↗ a parrot, ↗ or a hamster ↗ for a pet. ↘

5. *Practice exercise:* With your instructor as model, practice reading aloud and mark the various rising and falling inflection patterns in the following sentences.

    a. Use the falling inflection for declarative sentences, commands, and questions beginning with an interrogative word.

        1) We're leaving.

        2) I lost my book.

        3) Close that door!

        4) He ran to catch the bus.

        5) Where is the train?

        6) Turn out that light now!

        7) Why did he leave?

        8) How is Tom feeling?

        9) When is your class?

        10) It's too early to eat.

b. Use the rising inflection to suggest doubt, uncertainty, or an incomplete thought, with questions requiring a simple *yes* or *no* answer, and to emphasize an idea.

1) I'm not sure if I recognize the name of the street.

2) He bought apples, pears, a container of milk, and a pound of butter.

3) Are you ready to leave?

4) Is it snowing?

5) I don't know about that.

6) We plan to come, but . . .

7) Were your books found?

8) Did you get your ticket?

9) Did Mary meet your friends?

10) Is the movie over?

c. Compare the pattern in Column A with the pattern in Column B. Indicate the reason for the downward inflection in the first column and the upward inflection in the second.

Column A	*Column B*
1) This is important	1) Is this important?
2) This is an important matter.	2) Is this an important matter?
3) It's snowing.	3) Is it snowing?
4) I think so.	4) Do you think so?
5) You're late.	5) Am I late?
6) It's true.	6) Is it true?
7) The stores are crowded.	7) Were the stores very crowded?
8) We're leaving.	8) Are you leaving?
9) I want a cup of coffee.	9) Do you want a cup of coffee?
10) I'll vote later.	10) Will you vote later?

d. Use the upward arrow ⬈ and the downward arrow ⬊ in the sentences below to show rising or falling pitch, as appropriate.

    1) We saw him.

    2) Tom had a terrible accident.

    3) Are you coming?

    4) I'll be ready in a minute.

    5) Did he find his keys?

    6) The car turned completely over.

    7) Open the window!

    8) She bought shoes, a hat, and a coat.

    9) Did you remember to unplug the cofee maker?

    10) Don't tell me you want to go back now!

e. Read the following two passages aloud. Mark with appropriate arrows the rising or falling inflection used at the end of each phrase or sentence. Underline the specific words that you would emphasize by raising your vocal pitch to convey meaning and feeling.

WALTER: Hi, Joan, can you hear me? Yes, I know its a terrible connection. Look, I'm in a hurry. I just wanted to know if you could meet me for lunch. . . . Yes, today. At twelve o'clock. Can you make it? You can? Great! In front of the coffee shop. There goes my other phone. See you later.

JOAN: Walter, is that you? I can hardly hear you. What a terrible connection. Did you say lunch? It depends on the time. Yes, I can get away at twelve. I'll meet you in front of the coffee shop. See you later. Try to be on time for a change.

The Unstressed Word

A. Certain types of words in English receive little or no stress.

    1. Some one-syllable words have vowels of short rather than long durations.* Such words occur in informal and casual conversations.

---

* The unstressed vowel is usually represented by / ə / or / ɪ /.

2. These words are known as function words and include the following parts of speech. (The dot placed above the function word signifies a weak, short, or unstressed syllable.)

a. *Articles:*   a   an   the

   The girl ate an apple and a banana.

b. *Prepositions:*   to   of   in   from   by

   The letters to John were mailed from Spain

c. *Personal pronouns:*   I   me   he   him   she   her

   He gave her the book to read.

d. *Possessive pronouns:*   my   his   your   her   their   our

   My teacher found your book in her desk.

e. *Relative pronouns:*   who   that   which   whom

   The books that were left/were taken by Mary, who brought them to the library.

f. *Conjunctions:*   and   or   but   as   if

   She and I will go, but you must remain here.

g. *Auxiliary verbs:*   was   have   should   could   had

   I could have gone to the movies, but I was too tired.

B. In reading aloud and in speaking, the weak forms of these wordss are used. Observe the differences in the duration of the vowels in the strong and weak forms. In the strong forms, the vowel sounds are longer in duration than those in the weak forms.

EXAMPLE:*	*Strong*	*Weak*	*Phrase*
an	/ æn /	/ ən /	/ ən æpəl /
to	/ tu /	/ tə /	/ tə ðə bæŋk /
of	/ ɑv /	/ əv /	/ bæg əv plʌmz /
and	/ ænd /	/ ən /	/ brɛd ən bʌtɚ /
was	/ wɑz /	/ wəz /	/ ʃɪ wəz sæd /
from	/ frɑm /	/ frəm /	/ frəm speɪn /
he	/ hi /	/ hɪ /	/ hɪ sɔ mi /
as	/ æz /	/ əz /	/ hæpɪ əz ə lɑrk /

* The dictionary shows these words in the stressed or strong forms only.

C. *Practice exercise:* As you read aloud, make certain that the vowels in the unstressed words are short in duration.

Articles: the   a   an

1. The test is over.*

2. Wait a minute.

3. Meet you in half an hour.

4. Have an apple.

5. Bring the books back.

Prepositions: to   from   of   at   for   in

1. I want to see you now.

2. This is for you.

3. Rememer to write often.

4. He's from Spain.

5. He has lots of money.

6. See you at ten.

7. He worked for nothing.

8. Have a cup of coffee.

9. We'll meet in the store.

Pronouns: his   her   them   he   she   we   your   that   who

1. Let's see him now.

2. I saw them yesterday.

3. He went away.

4. She lost her book.

---

* In the word **the,** the final sound has two pronunciations. When it precedes a word beginning with a vowel, the / ɪ / is used. When it precedes a word beginning with a consonant, the / ə / is used.

EXAMPLE: The apple: / ðɪ æpəl /

The test: / ðə tɛst /

5. Here are your keys.

6. We'll meet you later.

7. The books that were needed were sent.

8. I met the salesman who was nasty.

Conjunctions: and or but if

1. Ham and eggs, please.

2. Which way, left or right?

3. He was sick, but glad to see us.

4. Is this picture too high or too low?

5. I'll go if you join me.

6. I bought some "wash and wear."

7. Will you take the trip if I do?

Verbs: to be (is was am are) to have (have has had)
Auxiliary verbs: have do will shall should can could may might must

These sentences illustrate the use of the forms of the verbs **to be** and **to have,** and the use of auxiliary verbs.

1. He is sick.

2. She was pretty.

3. They were happy.

4. The bank has one guard.

5. He has paid all his taxes.

6. Who is going with me?

7. We must wait for him.

8. I should have gone with you.

9. Tom should have been there.

10. We can see that it's too late now.

Characteristics of Stress Patterns in Conversational Speech

A. Conversational speech is informal and casual.

    1. The grammatical structure includes sentence fragments, incomplete ideas, and contractions.

    2. The language is idiomatic and informal.

B. Conversational speech is characterized by

    1. pauses that may be very long or very short.

    2. stress patterns that are very marked.

        a. Important words are strongly emphasized.

        b. Important words receive considerable pitch variations.

C. *Practice exercises:* These dialogues stress the conversational element without sacrificing clarity. Be sure to link the words within the phrases and stress the important words. Work for variety of pitch as you respond to your partner's words.

Divide each selection into phrase units, using single and double slashes, and underline the stressed words.

      EXAMPLE: <u>Well</u>, / you <u>finally</u> made it. / / I <u>thought</u> our <u>date</u> / was for <u>twelve</u>. / /

A tape or your instructor may serve as your model for correct and fluent oral reading.

A Lunch Date

———◆———

JOAN:	Well, you finally made it. I thought our date was for twelve.
WALTER:	Honey, I'm sorry, but I got tied up on the phone.
JOAN:	You're always tied up on the phone. Next time you say twelve, I'll get here at twelve-thirty.
WALTER:	Enough complaining. Let's get inside and take a look at today's special.
JOAN:	I'm on a diet. I just want some cottage cheese and fruit.
WALTER:	Good. A cheap lunch.
JOAN:	Another crack like that and I'll pay my own check.
WALTER:	You can't scare me.
JOAN:	One day, I'll go off my diet and I'll eat everything on the menu.
WALTER:	I'm safe. You're never off a diet.
JOAN:	You could stand losing a few pounds yourself. Take a look at that pot.

WALTER: What pot? I'm not standing straight. Take a look now.

JOAN: Relax. In another second, you'll explode. All right, Walter, you proved your point. You're turning purple.

WALTER: Come to think of it, I'm getting a little flabby. What about doing some jogging this weekend?

JOAN: You can jog. I'll stick to cottage cheese.

WALTER: All right. Cottage cheese it is! Let's go. I'm starved.

Burning the Midnight Oil

MOTHER: Bill, what are you doing up so late?

BILL: It's not late, it's early.

MOTHER: It's two o'clock in the morning!

BILL: That's early, isn't it?

MOTHER: In my language, that's late. Enough reading, get some sleep.

BILL: Are you for real? I've got three tests tomorrow.

MOTHER: How can you study for three tests in one night?

BILL: Easy—if you get me something to eat.

MOTHER: At two in the morning?

BILL: My stomach says, "Feed me!"

MOTHER: Well, there's cheescake and some of that meatloaf you like.

BILL: Fantastico! A pot of coffee would help, too.

MOTHER: Really, Bill, you've studied enough.

BILL: Mother, I leave the kitchen to you. You leave the studying to me.

MOTHER: It would be much simpler if—

BILL: Mother, please don't be a mother.

MOTHER: I get the message.

BILL: More important, get the food!

Chapter 3 Homework Review

A. This reading passage focuses on the use of appropriate word stress. Be sure to link the words within phrases and stress important words, while maintaining conversational tone. Work for variety in pitch, duration, and volume. Divide the sentence into phrase units, using single and double slashes, and underline the stressed words. Remember to pause between phrases.

> **EXAMPLE:** The bookstore was crowded with students / buying textbooks, / paper, / pens, / pencils, / and rulers. / /

Prepare to read aloud in class.

The Bookstore

—◆—

In was the beginning of the semester. The bookstore was crowded with students buying textbooks, pens, paper, pencils, markers, and folders.

"Thirty-five dollars for *this?*" a student asked, waving a thin book in the air. "What a rip-off! I'll get a used copy."

"Forget it," the cashier snapped. "The department ordered the new edition."

"What's wrong with the old edition?"

"How should I know?" the cashier answered. "Make up your mind."

The student dug into his jeans and pulled out a wallet.

"Get a move on up there," a voice called from the back.

"Take it easy," the student shot back as he grabbed the book and made for the exit.

Clerks kept rushing in and out of the stockroom, replenishing supplies and adding books to the shelves.

The manager came out of the stockroom, surveyed the scene, and said to the cashier, "Finish up in here. Then I'll close for fifteen minutes."

"Nobody comes in till I say so," he said to the student aide at the entrance.

There were angry howls from those standing in line outside.

The manager ran a hand over his bald head. "You want books? You wait!"

The casher looked up. "When can I get my stuff?"

Her boss sighed. "I'll take over till you get back. But make it snappy," he warned as she slid off the stool. "The madhouse starts again in fifteen minutes. You can deal with them better than I can."

B. List 10 words from the passage that are stressed and indicate next to each its grammatical function.

    EXAMPLE: semester (noun)

_____   _____

_____   _____

_____   _____

_____   _____

_____   _____

C. List 10 words from the passage that are unstressed and indicate next to each its grammatical function.

    EXAMPLE: it (pronoun)

_____   _____

_____   _____

_____   _____

_____   _____

_____   _____

Reading Aloud

A. As you read the following selections, practice all the elements of stressing that have been discussed. Be sure to

♦ analyze and discuss each selection to increase your understanding.

♦ use the single and double slashes to indicate the ends of phrases and completed thoughts.

♦ link the words within a phrase.

♦ stress the important words within a phrase by lengthening the vowel, increasing your volume, and raising your vocal pitch.

Incantation for Rain (Navajo)

◆

The corn grows up.

The waters of the dark clouds drop, drop.

The rain descends.

The waters from the plants drop, drop.

The corn grows up.

The waters of the dark mists drop, drop.

The corn grows up.

The waters of the dark mists drop, drop.

The Koran, Book XXXIII

◆

O Believers, remember God oft

And give Him glory at the dawn and in the evening.

It is He who blesses you and His Angels.

To bring you forth from the shadows into the light.

He is all compassionate to the believers.

Their greeting on the day that they shall meet Him

will be Peace.

The Twenty-Third Psalm

◆

The Lord is my shepherd; I shall not want.

He makes me lie down in green pastures;

He leads me beside the still waters.

He restores my soul;

He leads me in the paths of righteousness for his name's sake.

Yes, though I walk through the valley of the shadow of death,

I will fear no evil; for you are with me;

Your rod and your staff comfort me,

You prepare a table before me in the presence of my enemies;

You anoint my head with oil; my cup runs over.

Surely goodness and mercy shall follow me all the days of my life,

And I will dwell in the house of the Lord forever.

—*The King James Bible*

The Charge of the Light Brigade

◆

Cannon to right of them,

Cannon to left of them

Cannon in front of them

   VOLLEYED AND THUNDERED;

STORMED at with shot and shell,

BOLDLY they rode and well,

Into the JAWS OF DEATH,

Into the MOUTH OF HELL

Rode the six hundred.

—*Alfred, Lord Tennyson*

In Memoriam

———◆———

Ring out, wild bells, to the wild sky,
The flying cloud, the frosty light,
The year is dying in the night;
Ring out, wild bells, and let him die.

Ring out the old, ring in the new
Ring, happy bells, across the snow;
The year is going, let him go;
Ring out the false, ring in the true.

—Alfred, Lord Tennyson

Arabian Proverb

———◆———

He who knows, and know he knows, —
He is wise—follow him.
He who knows and knows not he knows, —
He is asleep—wake him.
He who knows not, and knows not he knows not, —
His is a fool—shun him.
He who knows not, and knows he knows not,—
He is a child—teach him.

syllable

vowels

Consonants

consonants

lateral and glides

diphthongs

Folktales

Haitian Folktale:

All the birds were flying from Haiti to New York, but Turtle could not go for he had no wings.

Pigeon said to Turtle: "Here's what we'll do. I'll hold in my mouth one end of the wood and you will hold the other end in your mouth. Do not let go or you will fall into the sea."

Pigeon and Turtle flew up into the air above the land toward the sea. When they came near the sea, they saw animals waiting to say goodbye.

"Look," the animals cried, "Turtle is going to New York!"

And Turtle was so pleased to hear everyone talking about him, that he called out the only word he knew in English,

"Bye-bye!"

Turtle had opened his mouth. He let go of the wood and fell into the sea. For that reason, there are many Pigeons in New York, but Turtle is in Haiti.

Russian Folktale:

A raven flew above the sea, looked down and saw a lobster. She grabbed him, intending to perch somewhere on a tree and eat a good meal. The lobster saw his end was coming and said, "O, raven, I knew your father and mother. They were fine people."

"Humph," said the raven without opening his mouth.

"And I know your brothers and sisters. What fine people they are."

"Humph."

"But they are not equal to you. In the whole world, there is no wiser than you."

"Aha," cawed the raven, opening his mouth wide, and dropped the lobster into the sea.

In the sentence, "The_ d_g r_n d_wn th_ str_ _t," the vowel sounds have been omitted. Yet, it's simple to fill in the gaps and reconstruct the sentence. If, however, you see this pattern: "_ _e _o_ _a_ _o_ _ _ _ _ee_," you will have some difficulty decoding the sentence. You can see, therefore, that consonants are necessary for speaker intelligibility. They also provide for accuracy of pronunciation and clarity of articulation. Substitutions, omissions, faulty placement and production of the consonants can interfere with effective communication.

The articulators play a very important part in consonant production, more so than in vowels. The shift from one consonant to the next is marked by many rapid and complex adjustments of the tongue, teeth, lips, and palate.

Consonants may occur in the initial position (**mo**re), the medial position (su**mm**er), or the final position (hi**m**). If a final consonant is omitted, the speaker's message can become unclear. Notice what happens when the final sound is left out in the following words:

EXAMPLE: light—lie   lied—lie   life—lie

No matter what message was intended, all three words will sound like "lie."

Consonants have specific characteristics.

1. They can be *voiced* or *voiceless*. For a voiced sound, the vocal cords approximate (come close together) and vibrate. For a voiceless sound, the vocal cords are apart and the breath stream moves freely through the vocal tract.

   EXAMPLE: *Voiced:*   / b / buy   / d / die   / g / gum

   Voiceless: / p / pie   / t / tie   / k / come

2. They can be *oral* or *nasal*. The sounds / m, n, ŋ / are relased through the nose; the rest of the consonants are oral, emitted through the mouth.

   EXAMPLE: / m / ram   / n / ran   / ŋ / rang

3. They can be *stop sounds* or *continuants*. In a stop sound, the airstream is completely blocked at the point of contact of the articulators, and the consonant sound is relatively brief.

   EXAMPLE: / p / pie   / t / tie   / k / come

   In a continuant sound, the airstream is partially blcoked at the point of contact of the articulators, and the consonant is long and sustained.

   EXAMPLE: / f / feel   / z / zeal   / m / meal

There are twenty-five consonant sounds: fifteen are voiced / b d g z ʒ l w r j ʤ ð v m n ŋ /. And ten are voiceless: / p t k s ʃ tʃ θ f h hw /.

Two consonant sounds that are produced the same way except for their voicing, are known as *cognates*. For example, the consonants / t / and / d / are produced in the same way. The tip of the tongue is pressed firmly on the gum ridge behind the upper front teeth and then released. But / t / is voiceless and / d / is voiced. Substitution of a voiceless sound for a voiced one may result in the production of a totally different word. If you unvoice the / d / in **dime,** you will be saying **time.**

Other pairs of cognates are

/ p /   / b /   pie—buy

/ k /   / g /   come—gum

/ f /	/ v /	fine—vine
/ s /	/ z /	sue—zoo
/ ʃ /	/ ʒ /	shoe—*
/ θ /	/ ð /	thin, them**
/ tʃ /	/ ʤ /	chin—gin

Consonants can also be described in terms of their acoustic and articulatory features. The six stop sounds in American English / p t k b d g / are known as plosives. All the other consonants are continuants and are classified as follows:

Fricatives: / f v s z ʃ ʒ θ ð h /

Affricates: / tʃ ʤ /

Nasals: / m n ŋ /

Glides: / l w r j hw /

These groups are discussed in later chapters.

Langauge is never static. Words and word usage change, and so do sounds. These changes occur slowly, almost imperceptibly, over a long period of time. When a sound is influenced by a neighboring sound so much that the original sound disappears, or is modified, *assimilation* has occurred. Some of these assimilated sounds have become incorporated into the language.

EXAMPLE: handkerchief / nd / has been replaced by / ŋ /

grandpa / nd / has been replaced by / m /

income / n / has been replaced by / ŋ /

Other substitutions and modifications are questionable and may be considered careless or even non-standard rather than assimilative.

EXAMPLE: *twenty* becomes *twenni*

want to becomes *wanna*

something becomes *sumpin*

---

* / ʒ / does not appear in initial position in English.

** / θ / and / ð / do not contrast.

CHAPTER FOUR

The Plosives

There are six plosive sounds in the English language:

/ p /	as in *pie*
/ b /	as in *buy*
/ t /	as in *tie*
/ d /	as in *die*
/ k /	as in *key*
/ g /	as in *guy*

There are two phases in the production of these sounds:

1. The air stream is blocked (imploded).

2. The air stream is released suddenly (exploded) with a burst of energy.

The plosives quite literally "stop" once they are produced. Compare the / p / with the / s /, which is not a plosive. To produce the / p /, the airstream is blocked by the lips, which close firmly and stop the air completely. This is not true of the / s /. Here, the airstream is only partially obstructed as it forces its way through a narrow opening between the tongue and teeth, and so the sound / s / *continues*. Plosives are known as stop, or noncontinuing, consonants, as opposed to other consonant groups. Plosives are oral sounds; they are emitted through the mouth or oral cavity.

The six plosive sounds are divided into pairs, known as cognates. The three pairs are / p / and / b /, / t / and / d /, and / k / and / g /. As you produce these sounds, you will notice that each pair uses the same articulatory placement.

/ p / and / b /	Both lips (bilabial)
/ t / and / d /	Tongue tip and upper gum ridge (lingua-alveolar)
/ k / and / g /	Back of tongue and soft palate (lingua-velar)

63

However, / p / is easily distinguished from / b /, / t / from / d /, and / k / from / g /. The / p /, / t /, and / k / sounds are *voiceless,* while / b /, / d /, and / g / are *voiced.*

There are other sounds similar in articulatory placement to the plosives. In addition to the / p / and / b / sounds, / m / and / w / also involve the use of the lips. The / n / and / l / sounds are produced with the tongue tip on the upper gum ridge, similar to the / t / and / d / sounds. The / ŋ / sound is produced with the elevated back section of the tongue touching the soft palate, similar to the / k / and / g / sounds. But there the similarity ends, for the / m /, / n /, and / ŋ / are nasal sounds using the nasal passages as the exiting chambers. The / l / sound is a lateral produced with air emitted over the lowered sides of the tongue; / w / is a glide requiring rounded lips which slide into the vowel sounds that follow.

In summary, then, the six plosives are all oral, they are stops, and they are paired into voiced and voiceless sounds.

Target Sounds: / p / and / b /

Distinctive Features

/ p / and / b / are bilabial oral plosives.
/ p / is voiceless; / b / is voiced.

How Are / p / and / b / Made?

The lips are pressed together, stopping the airstream briefly. As the lips are separated, these plosive sounds are released.

/ p / requires a tense or firm lip closure. When the / p / precedes a vowel in a stressed syllable, a strong puff of air is emitted. Thus / p / is an aspirated sound.

If you place your finger in front of your lips as you produce / p / in these words, you can feel the air as it is released.

EXAMPLE: pay   appear   appointment

The / p / sound is produced with less force and weaker aspiration in final position. However, there is still a light puff of air released as the lips separate.

EXAMPLE: map   up   top

/ b / requires a more relaxed or lax lip closure. There is no puff of air as the lips come together lightly and separate.

If you place your hand at your larynx and produce / b / in these words, you can feel the vibration of the vocal cords.

EXAMPLE: bay   about   cab

The / b / sound is produced with less force in final position as the lips gently come together.

EXAMPLE: lab   rib   robe

So in contrasting these sounds, there is no vibration at the larynx for the / p / sound and no air emitted for the / b / sound.

What Are the Problems in Spelling?

/ p / is silent in words with **pn, ps,** and **pt** spelling.

EXAMPLE: pneumonia   psychology   pteriodology

is represented by letters **p** and **pp***

EXAMPLE: stop   stopping   pepper   tapped

/ b / is silent in words with **mb** spelling.

EXAMPLE: numb   comb   plumber

is silent in **bt** spelling.

EXAMPLE: debt   doubt

is represented by letters **b** and **bb**

EXAMPLE: obey   robe   robbed

What Are the Problems in Pronuniation?

/ p / may be voiced and weakly aspirated and resemble the / b / sound.

EXAMPLE: *bay* instead of *pay*

may be weak or omitted in final position if there is insufficient force exerted on the lips or if the lips are not pressed together.

EXAMPLE: *row* instead of *rope*

/ b / may be followed by the weak (schwa) vowel / ə / if there is excessive pressure on the lips.

EXAMPLE: *caba* / kæbə / instead of *cab* / kæb /

may be weak or omitted in final position if the lips fail to come together.

EXAMPLE: *row* instead of *robe*

may resemble / v / if you place the upper front teeth on the lower lip and fail to bring the lips together.

EXAMPLE: *very* instead of *bury*

---

* The **ph** spelling represents the / f / sound, as in **physician.**

Note: Students who speak French, Italian, or Spanish do not aspirate or explode the voiceless / p /. Spanish-speaking students may need to work on / p / and / b /, and / b / and / v /.

Listening/Speaking

A. Compare the voiceless / p / and the voiced / b / in the *initial position*. When the voiceless / p / is produced, a strong puff of air is released. Are these words the same or different?

1	2	1	2
pair	bear	pat	bat
pie	buy	pen	Ben
pole	bowl	pay	bay
peas	bees	peak	beak

Can you *feel* the difference as you repeat after your instructor?

Can you *hear* the difference beween / p / and / b /?

Your instructor will say three words from columns 1 and 2 for each pair. Indicate the pattern that you hear.

> **EXAMPLE:**   If you hear *pair, bear, pair,* the pattern is 1 2 1.

B. Observe the / p / and / b / sounds in *final position*. Omission of the final consonants changes the pronunciation and meaning of the word.

> **EXAMPLE:**   row—rope   row—robe

1. Words with and without the final consonant / p /

1	2	1	2	1	2
row	rope	why	wipe	see	seep
ray	rape	ma	mop	mow	mope
key	keep	sew	soap	we	weep
rye	ripe	dough	dope	sue	soup

2. Words with and without the final consonant / b /

1	2	1	2
row	robe	too	tube
low	lobe	cue	cube
ma	mob	jar	job

3. Contrasting / p / and / b / in *final position*

1	2	1	2	1	2
rip	rib	pup	pub	mop	mob
cup	cub	cap	cab	tap	tab
ape	Abe	lap	lab	sop	sob
rope	robe	cop	cob	flap	flab

C. Observe the / p / and / b / sounds in *medial position.*

1	2	1	2
ample	amble	sopping	sobbing
rapid	rabid	ripping	ribbing
simple	symbol	capping	cabbing
staple	stable	repel	rebel

D. / b / and / v / may be confused.*

1	2	1	2	1	2
boat	vote	Lib	live	rabble	ravel
best	vest	robe	rove	robing	roving
berry	very	dub	dove	marble	marvel
biking	Viking	curb	curve	curbing	curving

E. Underline the contrastive words in each sentence. As you read aloud, remember to produce the final / p / and / b / sounds when they occur.

    EXAMPLE: Please <u>keep</u> my <u>key</u>.

1. He left his cap in the cab.

2. Who jumped through that hoop?

3. I want a tube of shampoo, too.

4. Kay lives on Cape May.

5. Mrs. Lapp works in a lab.

6. The cub played with the cup.

7. A pup is not allowed in a pub.

8. That cop likes corn-on-the-cob.

9. That ape was named Abe.

---

* Spanish students produce / b / and / v / as a bilabial fricative and therefore should work on placing the lips firmly together for / b /, as in **boat, robber,** and **tub.** To produce / v / as in **vote, have,** and **ever,** the upper front teeth touch lightly on the lower lip.

    EXAMPLE: That <u>berry</u> is very sweet.

Listening/Writing

A. Listen carefully for / p / and / b / as your instructor reads each word. Write these sounds when they occur in initial, medial, or final position using the symbols of the IPA. If / p / or / b / are not heard, write a dash in the space provided.

> **EXAMPLE:**   rob   /_____b__ /   pipe   /__p_____p_ /   leave   /_____—___ /

1. rope	_____	6. probably	_____	11. stable	_____
2. row	_____	7. baseball	_____	12. marvel	_____
3. rove	_____	8. buildup	_____	13. staple	_____
4. robe	_____	9. disturbed	_____	14. marble	_____
5. liberal	_____	10. curve	_____	15. available	_____

B. Circle the word read aloud by the instructor.

1. rip	rib	6. repel	rebel
2. cap	cab	7. staple	stable
3. pup	pub	8. rapid	rabid
4. plot	blot	9. ample	amble
5. pole	bowl	10. cups	cubs

C. Your instructor will select one of the words in parentheses and read the entire sentence aloud. Listen carefully and circle the word you hear. Practice reading each sentence aloud using either one of the words in parentheses.

1. Have you seen the (pub, pub)?

2. The baby played with the (cup, cub).

3. Where's your (cab, cap)?

4. We need a big (vote, boat).

5. Our (bay, pay) is very small.

6. Have you seen those terrible (bees, peas)?

7. The (pear, bear) was rolling on the ground.

8. That's a great (pie, buy).

9. Let's (soap, sew) this old rug.

10. Which (bowl, pole) are you talking about?

D. Circle the stressed syllable as each word is read aloud. Then write the number of syllables in each word.

1. liberal _____	6. camping _____	11. popular _____
2. appreciate _____	7. believe _____	12. appearance _____
3. president _____	8. anybody _____	13. politician _____
4. reply _____	9. opera _____	14. compliment _____
5. campaign _____	10. appointed _____	15. practicing _____

Chapter 4 Homework Review

A. Fill in the missing sounds using the symbols of the IPA. Then write the number of sounds in each word.

    EXAMPLE: bump / <u>b</u> ʌm <u>p</u> /   <u>4</u>

1. anybody / ɛnɪ___ɑ___ɪ / _____
2. remember / rə___ɛ___ ___ɚ / _____
3. public / ___ʌ___lɪk / _____
4. popcorn / ___ɑ___ ___ɔrn / _____
5. buildup / ___ɪl___ə___ / _____
6. cab / ___æ___ / _____
7. row / ___oʊ / _____
8. pie / ___aɪ / _____

9. pipe / ___aɪ___ / _____
10. rope / ___oʊ___ / _____
11. grab / ___ræ___ / _____
12. grabbed / ___ræ___d / _____
13. Bob's / ___ɑ___ ___ / _____
14. expect / ɪk___ ___ɛ___t / _____
15. pick you up / ___ɪ___ juʌ___ / _____

B. Circle the stressed syllable. Then write the number of syllables in each word.

1. everybody _____
2. campaign _____
3. compliment _____
4. supposed _____
5. available _____

6. practicing _____
7. president _____
8. appointment _____
9. impressed _____
10. property _____

11. probably _____
12. liberal _____
13. appeal _____
14. simple _____
15. blind _____

C. *Additional review: / p / and / b / in medial position.* Circle the stressed syllable. Practice saying each word aloud, making certain that the lips come together for / p / and / b /.

/ p /

oppose	approve	unemployment
capital	staple	opponent
impossible	popular	responsible
reply	republic	popcorn

71

/ b /

stable	liberal	baseball
probably	available	disturbed
cable	debate	absent
everybody	number	public

D. Select the appropriate word from exercise C for each sentence and write it on the line. Circle the stressed syllable in the underlined word and practice reading the sentence aloud.

> **EXAMPLE:**   compliment   I must (com)pliment you on your good work.

1. Henry decided not to _____ to that letter.

2. I canceled my _____ with the doctor.

3. Do you have _____ television?

4. I always have trouble beating my _____ in chess.

5. It's fun to eat _____ at the movies.

6. Peter majored in the _____ arts.

7. Nobody wanted to _____ the president.

8. The _____ is concerned about the _____ of crimes in this neighborhood.

9. We will _____ go to the _____ game at two o'clock.

10. The Pope is _____ with many people.

E. Select five words from the list in Exercise C and compose a sentence for each. Underline each selected word in the sentence and practice reading it aloud using correct pronunciation.

Reading Aloud

A. This dialogue focuses on the accurate production of / p / and / b /. Do not omit these sounds at the ends of words. Remember to link the words within phrases and stress the important words, while maintaining the conversational tone of the dialogue. Work for variety in pitch and clarity of articulation.

Divide the sentence into phrase units, using single and double slashes, and underline the stressed words.

> **EXAMPLE:**   His <u>parents</u> / had a <u>piece</u> of <u>property</u> / they <u>wanted</u> to <u>sell</u>. / /

Your instructor may serve as your model for correct and fluent oral reading. Prepare to enact this dialogue in class.

Peter and Barbara

———◆———

PETER:	Hello. Is Barbara home?
BARBARA:	This is Barbara.
PETER:	Hi, Barbara. This is Peter.
BARBARA:	Peter? I don't know anybody named Peter.
PETER:	Well, do you remember Bob Perez?
BARBARA:	Dear old Roberto. Sure I do, but he's dropped out of sight.
PETER:	He had to go to Puerto Rico. His parents had a piece of property they wanted to sell, so Bob went along to help.
BARBARA:	Is he back?
PETER:	Yes, but listen, I want to talk about us, not Bob.
BARBARA:	Us?
PETER:	You know what I mean. Bob spoke so highly of you. Besides, we're practically neightbors. I live just a couple of blocks away.
BARBARA:	I don't believe in blind dates, Peter.
PETER:	Look, if I'm Bob's buddy, how bad can I be?
BARBARA:	You might not be happy with my reply.
PETER:	Why don't I pick you up in about an hour?
BARBARA:	Don't push so hard.
PETER:	What do you expect, after Bob's buildup? He said we dig the same things— baseball, bebop, hip-hop, the big bands—not to mention buttered popcorn.
BARBARA:	You do put on a campaign!

PETER: I'm practicing running for president.

BARBARA: You're persistent, but tonight's impossible.

PETER: What about Saturday night? By now, we're pals, so I won't be a blind date.

BARBARA: If you put it that way, how can I refuse?

PETER: Perfect! Saturday night. Eight p.m. sharp.

BARBARA: It's a date!

Target Sounds: / t / and / d /

Distinctive Features

/ t / and / d / are tongue tip–alveolar oral plosives.
/ t / is voiceless; / d / is voiced.

How Are / t / and / d / Made?

The tongue tip rests against the upper (alveolar) gum ridge just behind the upper front teeth stopping the air stream briefly. As the tongue tip is quickly lowered, these plosive sounds are released.

/ t / requires firm contact between the tongue tip and the alveolar ridge. When the / t / sound precedes a vowel in a stressed syllable, a strong puff of air is emitted. Thus / t / is an aspirated sound.

If you place your finger in front of your lips and produce / t / in these words, you can feel the air as it is released.

EXAMPLE: time   attach   attention

The / t / sound is produced with less force and weaker aspiration in final position. As the tongue tip separates quickly from the upper gum ridge, a light puff of air is released.

EXAMPLE: mat   coat   cost

/ d / requires a more relaxed or lax contact between the tongue tip and the alveolar ridge. When the / d / is produced, there is no puff of air as the tongue tip is pressed against the upper gum ridge and then lowered.

If you place your hand at your larynx and produce / d / in these words, you can feel the vibration of the vocal cords.

EXAMPLE: dime   idea   hide

The / d / sound is produced with less force in final position. The tongue tip touches the upper gum ridge lightly and moves quickly away.

EXAMPLE: food   ride   said

So in contrasting these sounds, there is no vibration at the larynx for the / t / sound and no air emitted for the / d / sound.

What Are the Problems/Patterns in Spelling?

/ t / is silent in words with **-ten** endings.

EXAMPLE: listen   often   fasten

is represented by the letters **t, tt,** and **ed.***

EXAMPLE: tight   letter   write   locked

---

* When **ed** follows a voiceless sound, it is pronounced / t /. When **ed** follows a voiced sound, it is pronounced / d /. See Chapter 4 on the pronunciation of **-ed.**

/ d / is represented by letters **d, dd,** and **ed.***

EXAMPLE: dead   blade   ladder   grabbed

What Are the Problems in Pronunciation?

/ t / may be voiced, weakly aspirated and resemble the / d / sound.

EXAMPLE: *done* instead of *ton*

may be weak or omitted in final position or in consonant clusters** if insufficient force is exerted or if the tongue tip does not touch the alveolar gum ridge.

EXAMPLE: *lie*   instead of *light*

   can   instead of *can't*

   Tess instead of *test*

/ d / may be followed by the weak (schwa) vowel / ə / if there is excessive pressure on the upper gum ridge in final position.

EXAMPLE: *sada* / sædə / instead of *sad* / sæd /

may be weak or omitted in final position or in consonant clusters if the tongue tip does not touch the alveolar gum ridge.

EXAMPLE: *may*   instead of *made*

   can   instead of *canned*

   coal instead of *cold*

may resemble / t / if voicing is not produced.

EXAMPLE: *let* instead of *led*

---

* When **ed** follows a voiceless sound, it is pronounced / t /. When **ed** follows a voiced sound, it is pronounced / d /. See Chapter 4 on the pronunciation of **-ed.**

** Consonant cluster words are listed in Appendix B.

Note: Students who speak French, Spanish, Italian, and Greek tend to use the blade of the tongue instead of the tongue tip. They do not aspirate or explode the voiceless / t /.

Listening/Speaking

A. Compare the voiceless / t /* and the voiced / d / in the *initial position*. Are these words the same or different?

1	2	1	2	1	2
time	dime	to	do	tore	door
tip	dip	tick	Dick	toe	dough
too	due	Ted	dead	tie	die
ton	done	ten	den	town	down

Can you *feel* the difference as you repeat after your instructor?

Can you *hear* the difference beween / t / and / d /?

Your instructor will say three words from columns 1 and 2 for each pair. Indicate the pattern that you hear.

      EXAMPLE: If you hear *time, dime, time,* the pattern is 1 2 1.

B. Observe the / t / and / d / sounds in *final position*. Omission of the final consonants changes the pronunciation and meaning of the word.

      EXAMPLE: ray—rate   ray—raid

1. Words with and without the final consonant / t /

1	2	1	2	1	2
may	mate	tie	tight	why	white
sue	suit	lie	light	way	wait
lay	late	row	wrote	way	weight
high	height	fee	feet	see	seat
sigh	sight	buy	bite	cue	cute

2. Words with and without the final consonant / d /

1	2	1	2	1	2
may	made	tie	tide	see	seed
high	hide	lie	lied	why	wide
sue	sued	row	rowed	way	wade
sigh	sighed	fee	feed	cue	cued
lay	laid	buy	bide	way	weighed
cry	cried	toe	toad	crew	crude

---

* Aspirate or release a strong puff of air when the / t / is produced.

3. Contrasting / t / and / d / in *final position*

1	2	1	2	1	2
coat	code	seat	seed	set	said
height	hide	suit	sued	right	ride
hat	had	white	wide	hurt	heard
mate	made	sat	sad	feet	feed
root	rude	bit	bid	rate	raid

C. Observe the / t / and / d / sounds in *medial position*.

1	2	1	2
latter	ladder	grating	grading
rattle	raddle	waited	waded
metal	meddle	rating	raiding
bitter	bidder	tenting	tending

D. Underline the contrasting words in each sentence. As you read aloud, remember to produce the final / t / and / d / sounds in the underlined words.

   EXAMPLE: The <u>sad</u> child <u>sat</u> quietly.

   1. Sy sighed when he saw that beautiful sight.

   2. Yesterday, I found the right person to ride with.

   3. I heard he was hurt in an accident.

   4. You can wait for me if you stay out of my way.

   5. I live in that wide white building.

   6. Ted said, "Set the tables at five o'clock."

   7. Don't tie your tie too tight.

   8. Sue sued her landlord.

   9. Ted was dead when we arrived.

   10. That red bead resembles a beet.

E. Compare the full, or formal, verb form and the contraction form below. When the auxiliary verb **had** or **would** follows a noun or pronoun, **'d** is used in the shortened form.

   EXAMPLE: We would go. ⟶ We'd go.

   Mary had gone away. ⟶ Mary'd gone away.

The **'t** contraction represents the auxiliary verbs **will not, cannot, would not,** and **could not.**

> **EXAMPLE:** will not ———→ won't
> cannot ———→ can't
> could not ———→ couldn't
> would not ———→ wouldn't

Read the formal and the contracted forms aloud and listen for the differences.

1.	I would like it.	I'd like it.
2.	You had better come.	You'd better come.
3.	I cannot go there.	I can't go there.
4.	Who would meet us?	Who'd meet us?
5.	He would like a job.	He'd like a job.
6.	We would not like it.	We wouldn't like it.
7.	She would not see us.	She wouldn't see us.
8.	Mary will not find us.	Mary won't find us.
9.	I will not tell them.	I won't tell them.
10.	Will you not come with us.	Won't you come with us?

Listening/Writing

A. Listen carefully for / t / and / d / as your instructor pronounces each word. Write these sounds when they occur in initial, medial, or final position using the symbols of the IPA. If / t / or / d / is not heard, write a dash in the space provided.

> **EXAMPLE:** tight /_t_____t_/   tied /_t_____d_/   castle /_____—_____/

1. Tess	_____	7. great	_____	13. heard	_____
2. try	_____	8. grades	_____	14. hurt	_____
3. tried	_____	9. test	_____	15. twenty	_____
4. trite	_____	10. why	_____	16. tutor	_____
5. late	_____	11. wide	_____	17. missed	_____
6. elevators	_____	12. white	_____	18. wanted	_____

B. Circle the word read aloud by the instructor.

1.	may	mate	made
2.	rye	write	ride

3.	ray	rate	raid
4.	her	hurt	heard
5.	fee	feet	feed
6.	tie	tight	tied
7.	bee	beat	bead
8.	sue	suit	sued
9.	why	white	wide
10.	cue	cute	cued

C. Your instructor will select one of the words in parentheses and read the entire sentence aloud. Listen carefully and circle the word you hear. Practice reading each sentence aloud using either one of the words in parentheses.

1. The rug is very (white, wide).

2. He (heard, hurt) his dog yesterday.

3. I forgot to bring the (coat, code).

4. Do you want a (dip, tip)?

5. We can use the (time, dime).

6 The police (raided, rated) the restaurant.

7. I'd like a (rye, ride).

8. Don't (wait, wade) there.

9. Were you (hurt, heard) at the meeting?

10. I like to (ride, write) every day.

D. Circle the stressed syllable as each word is read aloud. Then write the number of syllables in each word.

1. absent	_____	6. crowded	_____	11. admit	_____
2. continuing	_____	7. attempted	_____	12. deserve	_____
3. realized	_____	8. fourteen	_____	13. identify	_____
4. expecting	_____	9. attended	_____	14. outline	_____
5. elevators	_____	10. submit	_____	15. planned	_____

Chapter 4 Homework Review

A. Fill in the missing sounds using the symbols of the IPA. Then write the number of sounds in each word.

      EXAMPLE: write / raɪ_t_ / __3__

1. crowded / kraʊ___ɪ___ / _____
2. failed / feɪ___ ___ / _____
3. wanted / wɑn___ɪ___ / _____
4. trite / traɪ___ / _____
5. helped / hɛlp___ / _____
6. tried / traɪ___ / _____
7. rated / reɪ___ɪ___ / _____
8. he'd / hi___ / _____

9. raided / reɪ___ɪ___ / _____
10. admit / ə___mɪ___ / _____
11. I'd / aɪ___ / _____
12. won't / woʊn___ / _____
13. missed / mɪs___ / _____
14. couldn't / kʊ___n___ / _____
15. toward / tɔr___ /* _____
16. can't / kæn___ / _____

B. Circle the stressed syllable. Then write the number of syllables in each word.

1. tutor _____
2. expensive _____
3. consider _____
4. where'd _____
5. secret _____

6. understand _____
7. hotel _____
8. elevators _____
9. makeup _____
10. answered _____

11. antique _____
12. outline _____
13. continuing _____
14. records _____
15. suppose _____

C. Fill in the missing consonant sounds using the symbols of the IPA.

1. great / ___eɪ___ /
2. grade / ___eɪ___ /
3. debt / ___ɛ___ /
4. dead / ___ɛ___ /

5. said / ___ɛ___ /
6. passed / ___æ___ /
7. past / ___æ___ /
8. Ted / ___ɛ___ /

_____

* In some dialectal areas, the / r / is omitted.

D. *Additional review: / t / and / d / in medial position.* Circle the stressed syllable. Practice saying each word aloud, making certain that / t / and / d / are produced clearly.

/ t /

attempted	attorney	certainly
twenty-five	protect	attended
detach	maintain	midterm
attached	retired	waited

/ d /

addicted	edit	recommended
additional	decided	identify
adopt	advertise	idea
admit	advised	attendance

E. Select the appropriate word from Exercise D for each sentence and write it on the line. Circle the stressed syllable in the underlined word and practice reading the sentence aloud.

    EXAMPLE: We had ad(di)tional work this weekend.

1. He had taken so many drugs he had become _____.

2. The application says to _____ the lower half of the sheet.

3. _____ students _____ their classes yesterday.

4. American businesses like to _____ their products and services.

5. Many _____ people need their social security.

6. We'll _____ do as you _____.

7. My _____ refused to _____ he was wrong.

8. Harry's teacher _____ him for the job.

9. The victim could not _____ his attacker.

10. We _____ for the train for thirty minutes.

F. Write the appropriate contraction for the auxiliary verb in parentheses.

    EXAMPLE: He had given me his pen.   <u>He'd</u> given me his pen.

1. I (will not) _____ have the time to practice.

2. I (cannot) _____ see you before 12:00.

3. (She would) _____ go with you if she had time.

4. (Who would) _____ like to see a movie?

5. They (will not) _____ visit their cousins this week.

6. (We would) _____ want to hire a lawyer.

7. We (could not) _____ afford a lawyer.

8. (They would) _____ rather visit Washington.

9. (Will not) _____ he help you?

10. We (would not) _____ be able to study during the day.

G. Contractions are used often in conversational and informal speech. Underline the contracted forms in the dialogue below. Then practice reading the dialogue aloud.

Tess and Dick

◆

TESS: Why don't you meet us Saturday night? There's a great jazz trio at Sweet Basil. They've gotten terrific reviews. Dimitri's tending bar and we're getting a discount.

DICK: I'm exhausted. There's a convention at the hotel.

TESS: Why don't you change careers? You're ruining your social life.

DICK: Right now, I'm too tired to think.

TESS: I'll talk to my counsin. He's got lots of connections. At the moment, though, he's out of the country.

DICK: Doing what?

TESS: Top secret. Wouldn't breathe a word to me.

DICK: Couldn't even give you a hint?

TESS: He can't talk about it to anyone. So Saturday night's out?

DICK: I can't see my way clear. Uh-oh, here comes Alvarez. He's a tyrant. Management's brought him in from Madrid. I'll get back to you.

TESS: I'll be waiting.

Reading Aloud

A. This dialogue focuses on the accurate production of the plosives / t / and / d /. Make sure the tongue tip touches the upper gum ridge, not the teeth, and do not omit these sounds at the ends of words. Remember to link the words within a phrase and stress the important words, to maintain the conversational tone of the dialogue. Work for variety in pitch and clarity of articulation.

Divide the sentences into phrase units, using single and double slashes, and underline the stressed words.

> **EXAMPLE:**   I <u>finally</u> <u>decided</u> / to <u>walk</u> up. / /

Your instructor may serve as your model for correct and fluent oral reading. Prepare to enact this dialogue in class.

Ted and His Teacher

◆

TEACHER:	Come in, Ted. I've been expecting you.
TED:	Sorry to be late, but I couldn't get into the elevators. They were too crowded. I finally decided to walk up.
TEACHER:	Well, sit down, and let me get out your records.
TED:	I bet you want to talk about my bad grades.
TEACHER:	I must admit your grades aren't great. What happened to you?
TED:	Is is trite to say I tried?
TEACHER:	Not trite, but is it quite true that you tried hard?
TED:	I didn't understand the first test. Then I got a tutor and he helped me.
TEACHER:	But you failed the exam.
TED:	Yes, I did.
TEACHER:	You were absent for the second test.
TED:	I had a bad cold.
TEACHER:	Why didn't you take a makeup?
TED:	I was afraid it would be too difficult.
TEACHER:	Now we come to the mid-term. You received a D+.
TED:	I was sure I deserved a C. I answered all the questions.
TEACHER:	Yes, but only fourteen answers were correct out of twenty-five.
TED:	I'd hate to fail.
TEACHER:	I realize that. That's why I wanted to talk to you. If you study hard, I think you can pass.

TED: I'm certainly going to try.

TEACHER: There are two more tests to take, and a final paper to write.

TED: I already have a topic in mind.

TEACHER: Good. Suppose you hand me an outline and we can go over it together.

TED: Thank you. I'm continuing to meet with my tutor.

TEACHER: Excellent. He should clear up any points you missed in class.

TED: I'll get my outline together and submit it to you next week. Thank you and good-bye.

TEACHER: See you in class.

Pronunciation of the -ed Suffix

The past tense and past participles of verbs present problems for the non-native and nonstandard speaker. The non-native speaker must learn a set of grammatical and phonic rules, while the nonstandard speaker must unlearn incorrect forms and acquire correct ones.

Verbs can be divided into two categories, regular and irregular. An irregular verb changes its form in the past tense.

EXAMPLE:

Present Tense	*Past Tense*
fight	fought
run	ran
go	went

The past tense and past participle forms of a regular verb are made by adding the suffix **-ed** to the verb stem.*

EXAMPLE:

Present Tense	*Past Tense and Past Participle***
stop	stopped
love	loved
wait	waited

The grammatical structure of the English language can be complex and puzzling, but the construction of the past tense of regular verbs is logical and straightforward. However the pronunciation of the suffix **-ed** can vary. Here are some examples.

1. The **-ed** in **stopped** is pronounced / t /, using a voiceless plosive.

2. The **-ed** in **loved** is pronounced / d /, using a voiced plosive.

3. The **-ed** in **waited** and **ended** is pronounced / ɪd / and consists of two sounds, the vowel / ɪ / and the voiced plosive / d /.

Thus there are three possible pronunciations for the **-ed** suffix: / t /, / d /, and / ɪd /.[†]

The rules that govern the pronunciation of the past tense and the past participle of regular verbs are phonic in nature. Unless you understand, learn, and practice the different **-ed** endings, you will find yourself making errors both in speaking and in writing.

EXAMPLE: The **-ed** in **checked** may be incorrectly pronounced as / ɪd /, resulting in a two-syllable word **chec ked** / tʃɛkɪd /, instead of as one-syllable word, **checked** / tʃɛkt /.

Loved may be incorrectly pronounced as a two-syllable word, **lo ved** / lʌvɪd /, instead of a one-syllable word, **loved** / lʌvd /.

---

* **EXAMPLE:**   I <u>waited</u> for him. (past tense)   I <u>have waited</u> for a long time. (past participle)

** The past participle is often used as an adjective.

    EXAMPLE: the <u>frightened</u> child;   the <u>corrected</u> paper

[†] The / ɪd / may also be transcribed as / əd /, using the weak vowel known as the schwa.

On the other hand, consider the past tense or past participle of the verb **want.** If you pronounce the two-syllable word **wan/ted** / wantɪd / as a one-syllable word, **want** / want /, you omit the past tense completely.

These problems may carry over into written English and result in faulty sentence structure. If you do not pronounce the endings of past tense or past participle verbs correctly, or if you omit them completely, you will tend to write inaccurately.

It is important, therefore, to understand both the grammatical and phonological rules, to hear and reproduce the different endings in context, and to integrate them into your daily conversation. Only then will you have control of the past tense and past participle of the regular verbs in both oral and written communication.

To determine the correct number of syllables, remember these two general rules.

1. When the **-ed** suffix is pronounced / t / or / d /, the number of syllables in the verb does not change.

   EXAMPLE:
talk	(one vowel sound, one syllable)
talked	(one vowel sound, one syllable)
move	(one vowel sound, one syllable)
moved	(one vowel sound, one syllable)

2. When the **-ed** ending is pronounced / ɪd /, another syllable is added.

   EXAMPLE:
hate	(one vowel sound, one syllable)
hated	(two vowel sounds, two syllables)

Rules for the Pronunciation of the -ed Suffix

-ed endings may be pronounced / t /, / d /, or / ɪd ~ əd /.

1. When **-ed** is added to any verb ending in a *voiceless* sound* (except the sound / t /), the **-ed** is pronounced / t /.

   EXAMPLE:
hope	/ houp /	hoped	/ houpt /
race	/ reɪs /	raced	/ reɪst /
cook	/ kʊk /	cooked	/ kʊkt /
wish	/ wɪʃ /	wished	/ wɪʃt /
reach	/ ritʃ /	reached	/ ritʃt /

2. When **-ed** is added to any verb ending in a *voiced* sound** (except the sound / d /), the **-ed** is pronounced / d /.

   EXAMPLE:
name	/ neɪm /	named	/ neɪmd /
happen	/ hæpɔn /	happened	/ hæpɔnd /
call	/ kɔl /	called	/ kɔld /
rob	/ rɑb /	robbed	/ rɑbd /
judge	/ ʤʌʤ /	judged	/ ʤʌʤd /

---

* The voiceless sounds are / p t k f s θ ʃ tʃ /.

** The voiced sounds are / b d g v j l m n ŋ r z ð ʒ ʤ / plus all vowels and dipththongs.

3. When **-ed** is added to any verb ending in a *vowel,* or a *diphthong,* the **-ed** is pronounced / d /.

EXAMPLE:	reply	/ rəplaɪ /	replied	/ rəplaɪd /
	interview	/ intɚvju /	interviewed	/ intɚvjud /
	free	/ fri /	freed	/ frid /
	row	/ roʊ /	rowed	/ roʊd /
	stay	/ steɪ /	stayed	/ steɪd /

4. When the verb ends in / t / or / d /, the **-ed** is pronounced either / ɪd / or / əd /.

EXAMPLE:	want	/ wɑnt /	wanted	/ wɑntɪd /	or	/ wɑntəd /
	land	/ lænd /	landed	/ lændɪd /	or	/ lændəd /
	wait	/ weɪt /	waited	/ weɪtɪd /	or	/ weɪtəd /
	rent	/ rɛnt /	rented	/ rɛntɪd /	or	/ rɛntəd /
	yield	/ jild /	yielded	/ jildɪd /	or	/ jildəd /

Listening/Speaking

A. Compare the verb stem and its past tense. Listen carefully and repeat as your instructor reads each pair of words aloud.

Your instructor will say three words from columns 1 and 2 for each pair. Indicate the pattern that you hear.

   EXAMPLE: If you hear *cap, capped, cap,* the pattern is 1 2 1.

1. Pronunciation of / t /

   The verbs in column 1 end in voiceless consonants. The final sound in each word in column 2 is therefore the voiceless / t /.

1	2	1	2
hope	hoped	watch	watched
hop	hopped	wish	wished
ask	asked	cough	coughed
laugh	laughed	reach	reached
lock	locked	escape	escaped
work	worked	notice	noticed

2. Pronunciation of / d /

   a. The verbs in column 1 end in voiced consonants. The final sound in each word in column 2 is therefore the voiced / d /.

1	2	1	2
rob	robbed	plan	planned
beg	begged	change	changed
dial	dialed	observe	observed
refuse	refused	raise	raised
rain	rained	bathe	bathed
climb	climbed	judge	judged

b. The verbs in column 1 end in vowels or diphthongs, which are voiced. The final sound in each word in column 2 is therefore the voiced / d /.

1	2	1	2
identify	identified	flow	flowed
cry	cried	agree	agreed
show	showed	enjoy	enjoyed
tie	tied	crow	crowed
play	played	annoy	annoyed

3. Pronunciation of / ɪd ~ əd /

a. The verbs in column 1 end in / t /. The final sounds in each word in column 2 are therefore / ɪd /or / əd /.

1	2	1	2
lift	lifted	correct	corrected
want	wanted	consist	consisted
rent	rented	hesitate	hesitated
doubt	doubted	rest	rested
suggest	suggested	expect	expected

b. The verbs in column 1 end in / d /. The final sounds in each word in column 2 are therefore / ɪd /or / əd /.

1	2	1	2
need	needed	recommend	recommended
end	ended	attend	attended
decide	decided	fade	faded
hand	handed	applaud	applauded
depend	depended	aid	aided

B. Underline the contrastive words in each sentence. As you read aloud, remember to produce the final endings of the underlined words.

   EXAMPLE: Before I could <u>rent</u> the apartment, it was already <u>rented</u>.

1. I believe he believed me.

2. Ask him if he asked her for a date.

3. I doubt if he doubted her word.

4. People need to know they're needed.

5. I expected you to call, even though I didn't expect you to come.

6. I dialed the wrong number, so I had to dial again.

7. He could never talk as fast as she talked.

8. Joe telephoned last night, but he won't telephone tonight.

9. Although she blamed me, I didn't blame her.

10. Tom and Dick didn't escape, but Harry escaped.

11. Our friends departed last night, but we'll depart next week.

12. I don't have to persuade you, since you've already been persuaded.

13. She had to crowd into the crowded* elevator.

14. I didn't have to work as hard this term as I had worked last term.

15. I had recommended him for the job, but I won't recommend him again.

Listening/Writing

A. Listen carefully for the / t /, / d /, and / ɪd ~ əd / pronunciation of the **-ed** endings in the following words. As your instuctor reads aloud, write the appropriate sound when it occurs at the end of the word, using the synmbols of the IPA.

EXAMPLE: *jumped* / t /   *mugged* / d /   *stated* / ɪd / or / əd /

1. gambled	_d_	7. requested	_ɪd_	13. interviewed	_d_
2. interested	_ɪd_	8. continued	_d_	14. distinguished	_t_
3. advertised	_d_	9. increased	_t_	15. accepted	_ed_
4. applauded	_d_	10. pressured	_d_	16. wished	_t_
5. hesitated	_ɪd_	11. persuaded	_əd_	17. published	_t_
6. faded	_ɪd_	12. agreed	_d_	18. managed	_d_

---

* Note the use of the past participle of the verb as an adjective.

B. Circle the stressed syllable as the instructor reads each word aloud. Then write the number of syllables in each word.

1. scheduled _____
2. intended _____
3. provided _____
4. realized _____
5. departure _____

6. delayed _____
7. continued _____
8. wired _____
9. remembered _____
10. participated _____

11. checked _____
12. collapsed _____
13. expected _____
14. served _____
15. recommended _____

C. This exercise focuses on the pronunciation of the past tense and the past participle of regular verbs. Your instructor will read each sentence aloud using one of the words in parentheses. Circle the word you hear. Decide if your instructor used the correct verb form.

> **EXAMPLE:** You have (convince, convinced) me to leave now.   *Incorrect*
> The past participle form should be pronounced / t /.

1. The agency (offer, offered) me a job this morning. _____

2. You (advertise, advertised) in yesterday's paper. _____

3. Mary (remember, remembered) to lock the trunk. _____

4. Who (checked, check) the baggage? _____

5. We had (expect, expected) to leave earlier. _____

6. The plane will be (delay, delayed). _____

7. Ted was (involve, involved) in gambling. _____

8. My friends (registered, register) last week. _____

9. We are (convince, convinced) that you should come. _____

10. I am (interesting, interested) in a new job. _____

D. Your instructor will say three words from columns 1 and 2 for each pair. Write the pattern you hear.

> **EXAMPLE:** If you hear *hope, hoped, hope,* write 1 2 1.

1	2	*Pattern*
1. call	called	
2. expect	expected	
3. check	checked	

	1	2	Pattern			
4.	intend	intended				
5.	plan	planned				
6.	offer	offered				
7.	remain	remained				
8.	gamble	gambled				
9.	involve	involved				
10.	continue	continued				

E. This exercise focuses on the past tense and the past participle of the verb. Listen carefully as your instructor reads each sentence aloud. Some are correct; some are incorrect. Write C for correct; I for incorrect.

C/I

1. My boss plan to close his business.   C   I
2. The police assured me that I was free.   C   C
3. We were urge to contribute more money.   C   C
4. They vote in the last election.   C   I
5. The chairperson approve my program change.   C   I
6. Tom's work had improve before he became sick.   C   I
7. We all watch the news last night.   C   I
8. The unhappy man jump from the bridge.   C   I
9. The police identified him as a detective.   C   C
10. The student laugh at the joke told by the teacher.   C   I
11. I hesitated to take that job.   C   C
12. The papers were distributed last week.   C   C
13. Several people have been mug near the train station.   C   C
14. I decided not to go.   C   C
15. I have been offer several jobs.   C   C

F. Read each question aloud and respond in a complete sentence, using the correct form of the past tense or the past participle of the verb. Underline the verb and write the sound you used for the **-ed** suffix: / t /, / d /, or / ɪd or əd /.

> **EXAMPLE:** *like*   Q: Did you _____ her?
>
> A: Yes, I <u>liked</u> her.   / t /

1. publish   Was the paper _____ on time?

    _____

2. crowd   Was the train very _____ ?

    _____

3. work   Did he _____ last week?

    _____

4. schedule   Did the registrar _____ exams for Saturday?

    _____

5. judge   Did she feel the jury _____ her unfairly?

    _____

6. interest   Are you _____ in applying for this job?

    _____

7. expect   Did you _____ to get an A in your science course?

    _____

8. fix   Did John _____ the television set?

    _____

9. convince   Did she _____ the jury?

    _____

10. hire   Did the hospital _____ people last week?

    _____

G. Answer each question in a complete sentence using the past tense of the underlined verb.

1. How long <u>did</u> you <u>jog</u> yesterday.

    _____

2. What time <u>did</u> the plane <u>land</u>?

    _____

3. When <u>did</u> your lawyer <u>call</u>?

   _____

4. Why <u>did</u> you <u>fire</u> your secretary?

   _____

5. Why <u>did</u> you <u>stop</u> going out with me?

   _____

6. <u>Did</u> you <u>report</u> the accident to the police?

   _____

7. How much money <u>did</u> your brother <u>need</u>?

   _____

8. Why <u>did</u> they <u>laugh</u> during the interview?

   _____

9. <u>Did</u> your friend <u>repeat</u> his writing course?

   _____

10. Why <u>did</u> they <u>vote</u> for that man?

   _____

Chapter 4 Homework Review

A. Each verb stem below ends in a voiced or voiceless sound. Write the past tense of the verb. Then write the pronunciation of the **-ed** ending using the symbols of the IPA.

EXAMPLE:	look	looked	/ t /
	learn	learned	/ d /
	support	supported	/ ɪd ~ əd /
	round	rounded	/ ɪd ~ əd /

Verb Stem	*Past Tense*	/ t / / d / / ɪd ~ əd /
1. stop	_____	_____
2. end	_____	_____
3. need	_____	_____
4. rob	_____	_____
5. turn	_____	_____
6. repeat	_____	_____
7. crash	_____	_____
8. report	_____	_____
9. agree	_____	_____
10. employ	_____	_____
11. laugh	_____	_____
12. announce	_____	_____
13. occupy	_____	_____
14. command	_____	_____
15. change	_____	_____
16. elect	_____	_____
17. involve	_____	_____

18. add _____   _____

19. discourage _____   _____

20. watch _____   _____

B. Select five words from the list in Exercise A. On a separate sheet of paper, write a sentence for each using the past tense or the past participle of the verb. Underline the verb.

Convert your declarative sentence into a question.

Be prepared to answer the questions asked by other members of the class.

> **EXAMPLE:** *elect*   Tom <u>was</u> <u>elected</u> president of the class.
>
>   Q: Why <u>was</u> he <u>elected</u>?
>
>   A: He <u>was elected</u> because he is very popular.

C. Fill in the missing sounds using the symbols of the IPA. Then write the number of sounds in each word.

> **EXAMPLE:** *decided* / dəsaɪ<u>d</u> <u>ɪ</u> <u>d</u> /   <u>7</u>

1. wanted   / wɑntɪ___ ___ /   _____
2. objected   / əbdʒɛk_ ___ ___ /   _____
3. phoned   / fou_ ___ ___ /   _____
4. blamed   / bleɪ___ ___ /   _____
5. interested / ɪntrɪst___ ___ /   _____

6. needed   / ni_ ___ ___ /   _____
7. begged   / bɛ_ ___ /   _____
8. aided   / eɪ___ ___ ___ /   _____
9. applauded / əplɔd___ ___ /   _____
10. changed   / tʃeɪndʒ___ /   _____

D. Write the last two sounds of each word, using / t /, / d /, or / ɪd ~ əd / to indicate the correct **-ed** pronunciation.

> **EXAMPLE:** *wanted* / ɪd /   *imagined* / nd /   *discussed* / st /

1. locked   / _____ /
2. typed   / _____ /
3. combed   / _____ /
4. developed / _____ /
5. loaned   / _____ /
6. collapsed   / _____ /
7. asked   / _____ /
8. crowded   / _____ /

9. grabbed   / _____ /
10. explained   / _____ /
11. attended   / _____ /
12. arrived   / _____ /
13. excited   / _____ /
14. convinced / _____ /
15. landed   / _____ /
16. waited   / _____ /

E. Circle the stressed syllable. Then write the number of syllables in each word.

1. earlier _____
2. stayed _____
3. pronounced _____
4. promised _____

5. provided _____
6. required _____
7. wired _____
8. baggage _____

9. occupied _____
10. suggested _____
11. scheduled _____
12. interviewed _____

F. Underline the correct word in parentheses. Be prepared to read aloud in class using accurate pronunciation.

1. The ambulance's siren (disturbed, disturb) the neighborhood.

2. We were all (oppose, opposed) to the war.

3. The payroll office (distribute, distributed) checks last Friday.

4. The doctor (suggest, suggested) I take a vacation.

5. The trains are very (crowded, crowd) at noon.

6. My sister has (attend, attended) every class this term.

7. The number of divorces has (increase, increased) in the past five years.

8. The apartment was (occupied, occupy) when I (arrive, arrived).

9. I (start, started) working last week.

10. My uncle (retired, retire) last year.

G. Complete the following sentences using the past tense or past participle of the regular verb. Practice reading aloud.

1. advise   This morning, my lawyer _____

2. schedule   The registrar in this college _____

3. employ   Although I was _____

4. agree   My landlord _____

5. interest   I am _____

6. retire   My uncle _____

7. object   The class _____

8. intend   We _____

9. suggest   My teacher _____

10. introduce My friend _____

H. Study the pronunciation given for each word. If the pronunciation is correct, write C. If incorrect, write I and show the correct pronunciation using the symbols of the IPA.

EXAMPLE: needed   / nid /   ___I___   ___/ nidɪd /___

		C/I	Correction
1. decided	/ dəsaɪd /	_____	_____
2. realized	/ riəlaɪzt /	_____	_____
3. convinced	/ kənvɪnst /	_____	_____
4. offered	/ ɔfɚd /	_____	_____
5. mugged	/ mʌgɪd /	_____	_____
6. provided	/ prəvaɪdət /	_____	_____
7. checked	/ tʃɛkəd /	_____	_____
8. waited	/ weɪtd /	_____	_____
9. intended	/ ɪntɛnd /	_____	_____
10. tried	/ traɪt /	_____	_____
11. planned	/ plænd /	_____	_____
12. expected	/ ɪkspɛktɪd /	_____	_____

I. *Additional review:* Form the past tense or past participle of these words ending in / t / and / d / by adding / ɪd / or / əd /. Practice aloud and produce the additional syllable needed for correct pronunciation.

report	direct	defend	admít
disgust	invest	attend	respónd
respect	instruct	remind	descénd
complicate	interpret	reprimand	dístribute
concentrate	irritate	comprehend	pópulate
contemplate	interrupt	correspond	condescend
originate	capitulate	prevaricate	participate
eliminate	experiment	incorporate	corróborate
appreciate	interrogate	deteriorate	améliorate

Reading Aloud

A. This dialogue concentrates on the past tense of the regular verb. Be sure to pronounce the **-ed** suffix using the correct ending, / t /, / d /, or / ɪd ~ əd /. The sentence will be grammatically incorrect if the past tense is omitted. Remember to link the words within phrases and stress the important words, while maintaining the conversational tone of the dialogue. Work for variety in pitch and clarity of articulation.

Divide the sentences into phrase units, using single and double slashes, and underline the stressed words.

> **EXAMPLE:**   I <u>tried</u> to get you <u>earlier,</u> / but there was <u>no</u> <u>answer.</u> / /

Your instructor may serve as your model for correct and fluent oral reading. Be prepared to enact this dialogue in class.

Preparing for a Plane Trip

◆

SID:	I tried to get you earlier, but there was no answer. Did you reach the airport on time?
PAT:	Yes, I reached the airport on time.
SID:	Did you park the car in the airport lot?
PAT:	Yes, I parked the car in the airport lot.
SID:	Did you remember to lock the trunk of the car?
PAT:	Yes, I remembered to lock the trunk of the car.
SID:	Did you check your baggage?
PAT:	Yes, I checked my baggage.
SID:	Did you cash the check I gave you?
PAT:	Yes, I cashed the check you gave me.
SID:	Did you ask for the number of your departure gate?
PAT:	Yes, I asked for the number of my departure gate.
SID:	Did you call your mother before you left?
PAT:	Ye, I called my mother before I left?
SID:	Your *mother,* not *my* mother.
PAT:	I called *both* mothers, all right?
SID:	Did you expect the plane to be delayed?
PAT:	Yes, I expected the plane to be delayed.
SID:	Did something happen?

PAT: Yes, something happened to one of the wheels and it had to be checked out.

SID: Did they serve you lunch on the flight?

PAT: Yes, they served us lunch.

SID: Did you decide how long you'll be staying with your friend?

PAT: Yes, I decided to stay forever if you don't stop asking me questions!

SID: How can I get an answer if I don't ask a question?

PAT: Good question. Anyway, I intended to return in a week.

SID: I had intended to ask you to return in a week. I'll see you then. Good-bye.

PAT: So long.

B. Read carefully and fill in the correct form of the past tense or past participle of the regular verb. Read aloud for accurate pronunciation and fluency.

1. Ted was becoming very _____.
   to discourage

2. For eight months he had _____ that opportunities for jobs were very scarce.
   to realize

3. He had _____ a position as an assistant manager in a hotel.
   to want

4. He had _____ as a clerk in his uncle's hotel from the time he was sixteen.
   to work

5. When his uncle _____ and _____, the small business _____.
   to collapse   to die   to fold

6. He _____ from one city to another.
   to move

7. Sometimes he _____ for hours to be _____.
   to wait   to interview

8. No one _____ him a job in a hotel.
   to offer

9. He _____ to write to a few hotels in Alaska.
   to decide

10. While waiting for answers, he _____ at some employment agencies.
    to register

11. They _____ him jobs as a dishwasher or a clerk.
    to offer

12. His aunt _____ to lend him money.
    to continue

13. Ted _____ one hundred dollars from his girlfriend.
    to borrow

C. This exercise is a continuation of Ted's story. Read each sentence carefully. If the past tense or past participle of the verb is correct, write C. If incorrect, write I. Practice reading aloud for accuracy of pronunciation and fluency.

C/I

1. Ted got involved in OTB (off track betting).　　_____

2. He had gamble away all the money his girlfriend had given him.　　_____

3. He lost twenty-eight dollars, a gift from his aunt.　　_____

4. Everything seem hopeless.　　_____

5. Finally he receive a postcard from Alaska.　　_____

6. It advised him to leave the following Saturday.　　_____

7. If Ted wanted a job, he could be a pipeline worker connecting pipes to oil wells.　　_____

8. He would receive $500 a week, if he remain and could survive the cold weather and long hours. Ted waste no time.　　_____

9. He immediately wire back his answer.　　_____

D. Complete the underlined word using the correct form of the past tense or past participle verb. Write the correct pronunciation of the **-ed** ending in the appropriate space: / t /, / d /, or / ɪd /.

　　　EXAMPLE:　Kim was <u>interested</u> / ɪd / in the job.

Practice reading this passage aloud for accuracy of pronunciation and fluency.

The Future of Kim Lee

　　　Kim Lee told his English teacher, Mr. Hadid, that he <u>want</u>___ /　/ to work on a newspaper. Mr. Hadid was <u>amuse</u>___ /　/ until he <u>realize</u>___ /　/ Kim was serious. The teacher <u>explain</u>___ /　/ that Kim had <u>limit</u>___ /　/ writing experience. Kim <u>look</u>___ /　/ so <u>disappoint</u>___ /　/ that Mr. Hadid <u>relent</u>___ /　/ and <u>ask</u>___ /　/ his friend, Jim Ramirez, who <u>edit</u>___ /　/ a local paper, to see Kim.

　　　Mr. Ramirez was <u>impress</u>___ /　/ with the young man's earnestness. Kim <u>point</u>___ /　/ out that he was an <u>experience</u>___ /　/ computer operator. Mr. Ramirez <u>look</u>___ /　/ thoughtful. "If I <u>hire</u>___ /　/ you, you'd get no salary but lots of experience." Kim would have <u>liked</u>___ /　/ a paying job and <u>hesitate</u>___ /　/ for a moment. He <u>realize</u>___ /　/ he <u>owe</u>___ /　/ a debt of gratitude to his English teacher for his help. He <u>decide</u>___ /   / to accept the offer. "When can I start?" he <u>ask</u>___ /   /.

Mr. Ramirez <u>turn</u>___ /   / on the computer. "Right now. I've <u>want</u>___ /   / to write an article encouraging young people like you to become <u>involve</u>___ /   / in local politics. I want to hear your ideas on the subject." Kim's face <u>brighten</u>___ /   /. "Just what I'm <u>interested</u>___ /   / in," he said and <u>seat</u>___ /   / himself at the computer.

Target Sounds: / k / and / g /

Distinctive Features

/ k / and / g / are back tongue–velar oral plosives.
/ k / is voiceless; / g / is voiced.

How Are / k / and / g / Made?

The back section of the tongue is raised and pressed against the soft palate, or velum, stopping the airstream briefly. As the back of the tongue is lowered, these plosive sounds are released. The tongue tip is anchored behind the lower front teeth.

/ k / requires firm contact between the rear section of the tongue and the velum (soft palate). When the / k / sound precedes a vowel in a stressed syllable, a strong puff of air is emitted. Thus / k / is an aspirated sound.

If you place your finger in front of your lips as you produce / k / in these words, you can feel the air as it is released.

EXAMPLE:　coal　　require　　accustomed

The / k / sound is produced with less force and weaker aspiration in the final position. However, a light puff of air is released as the back section of the tongue moves away from the soft palate.

EXAMPLE:　kick　　back　　take

/ g / requires a more relaxed or lax contact between the back of the tongue and the soft palate. There is no puff of air as the back section of the tongue is pressed against the velum and then moves down.

If you place your hand at your larynx and produce / g / in these words, you can feel the vibration of the vocal cords.

EXAMPLE:　goal　　legal　　leg

The / g / sound is produced with less force in final position as the back section of the tongue lightly touches the soft palate.

EXAMPLE:　fog　　bag　　egg

So in contrasting these sounds, there is no vibration at the larynx for the / k / sound and no air emitted for the / g / sound.

What Are the Problems in Spelling?

/ k / is silent in words with **kn** spelling.

EXAMPLE:　knock　　knee　　know

is represented by letters **c, k, ch, cc,** and **x** before voiceless consonants.

EXAMPLE:　cost　　fact　　kite　　character　　accident　　expense

/ g / is silent in words with **gn** spelling.

EXAMPLE: gnat   gnarl   sign

is represented by letters **g, gg,** and **x** before voiced sounds.

EXAMPLE: gone   legal   begged   exam

What Are the Problems in Pronunciation?

/ k / may be voiced, weakly aspirated, and resemble the / g / sound.

EXAMPLE: *goat* instead of *coat*

may be weak or omitted in final position if there is insufficient force exerted or if the back section of the tongue does not press against the velum.

EXAMPLE: *sew* instead of *soak*

may be omitted in words containing **x** before voiceless sounds.*

EXAMPLE: *expense* / ɪspɛns / instead of / ɪkspɛns /

/ g / may be followed by the weak (schwa) vowel / ə / if there is excessive pressure on the lips.

EXAMPLE: *egga* / ɛgə / instead of *egg* / ɛg /

may be weak or omitted in final position if the back of the tongue fails to rest against the velum.

EXAMPLE: *fa(r)* instead of *fog*

may resemble / k / if voicing is not produced.

EXAMPLE: *lock* instead of *log*

may be omitted in words containing **x** before voiced sounds.**

EXAMPLE: *exam* / ɪzæm / instead of / ɪgzæm /

---

* When **x** is followed by a voiceless sound, the pronunciation is / ks /.

    EXAMPLE: extra   expect   exhale

** When **x** is followed by a vowel in a stressed syllable, the pronunciation is / gz / in most instances.

    EXAMPLE: exam   exist   executive

Note: Students who speak French, Spanish, Italian, and Greek do not aspirate or explode the voiceless / k /, thereby producing a sound resembling / g /.

Listening/Speaking

A. Compare the voiceless / k /* and the voiced / g / in the *initial position*. Are these words the same or different?

1	2	1	2	1	2
cut	gut	cold	gold	call	gall
coat	goat	come	gum	cape	gape
coast	ghost	Kate	gate	came	game
could	good	cap	gap	coal	goal

Can you *feel* the difference as you repeat after your instructor?

Can you *hear* the difference between / k / and / g /?

Your instructor will say words from columns 1 and 2 for each pair. Indicate the pattern that you hear.

EXAMPLE: If you hear *coat, goat, coat,* the pattern is 1 2 1.

B. Observe the / k / and / g / sounds in *final position*. Omission of the final consonants changes the pronunciation and meaning of the word.

EXAMPLE: Kay—cake   we—weak   play—plague

1. Words with and without the final consonant / k /.

1	2	1	2	1	2
Lee	leak	Fay	fake	bee	beak
ray	rake	sea	seek	bay	bake
we	weak	lay	lake	tea	teak
sew	soak	weigh	weak	stow	stoke

2. Words with and without the final consonant / g /.

1	2	1	2	1	2
few	fugue	play	plague	collie	colleague
hay	Hague	Lee	league	row	rogue

3. Contrasting / k / and / g / in *final position*.

1	2	1	2	1	2
leak	league	rack	rag	sack	sag
pick	pig	tuck	tug	buck	bug
back	bag	duck	dug	tack	tag
brick	brig	lack	lag	luck	lug

---

* Aspirate or release a strong puff of air when the / k / is produced.

C. Observe the / k / and / g / sounds in *medial position.*

1	2	1	2	1	2
backing	bagging	tinkle	tingle	backed	bagged
lacking	lagging	ankle	angle	whacking	wagging
stacker	stagger	tacking	tagging	meeker	meager
tucking	tugging	locker	logger	flocking	flogging

D. Underline contrasting words in each sentence. As you read aloud, remember to produce the / k / and / g / sounds in the underlined words.

> **EXAMPLE:** Here's a <u>tag</u> and a <u>tack</u>.

1. The league's office has several leaks.

2. Why did he pick a pig for a pet?

3. Hang the rag on the rack.

4. A brick was thrown into the brig.

5. Put your bag back on your desk.

6. Will you lug this heavy chain for luck?

7. The duck dug his way out of the lake.

8. Close the gate, Kate.

9. That bill is a fake, Fay.

10. Don't gape at the odd cape.

Listening/Writing

A. Listen carefully for / k / and / g / as your instructor pronounces each word. Write these sounds when they occur in initial, medial, or final position using the symbols of the IPA. If / k / or / g / are not heard, write a dash in the space provided.

> **EXAMPLE:** kick / <u>k</u>   <u>k</u> /   graphic / <u>g</u>   <u>k</u> /   judge / <u>   —   </u> /

1. income	_____	5. ankle	_____	9. damage	_____
2. legal	_____	6. college	_____	10. examined	_____
3. taxes	_____	7. recognized	_____	11. requested	_____
4. angle	_____	8. occasional	_____	12. expensive	_____

13. accountant _____   15. x-rays _____   17. dialogue _____

14. deduct _____   16. injury _____   18. fractured _____

B. Circle the word read aloud by the instructor.

1. rack   rag   6. back   bag

2. tack   tag   7. stack   stag

3. pick   pig   8. luck   lug

4. snacked   snagged   9. crate   great

5. lacked   lagged   10. ankle   angle

C. Your instructor will select one of the words in parentheses and read the entire sentence aloud. Listen carefully and circle the word you hear. Practice reading each sentence aloud using either one of the words in parentheses.

1. We need a (rag, rack) for the car.

2. Don't put a (tag, tack) on that chair.

3. Have you seen the (league, leak)?

4. Her (bag, back) was damaged in the accident.

5. Let's (see, seek) the money now.

6. Did you (sew, soak) your torn sock?

7. Let's (weigh, wake) those heavy dogs.

8. There's no (lag, lack) in this office.

9. Who needs a (buck, bug)?

10. Take your (pick, pig).

D. Circle the stressed syllable as each word is read aloud. Write the number of syllables in each word.

1. accident _____   6. ankle _____   11. fractured _____

2. deductions _____   7. recognized _____   12. court _____

3. awkward _____   8. extra _____   13. examined _____

4. backache _____   9. occasional _____   14. medical _____

5. collect _____   10. taxi _____   15. argument _____

Chapter 4 Homework Review

A. Fill in the missing sounds using the symbols of the IPA. Then write the number of sounds in each word.

        EXAMPLE: backed / bæ <u>k</u> <u>t</u> / <u> 4 </u>

1. x-rays   / ɛ____ ____reɪz /   ____   9. awkward / ɔ____wɚd /   ____

2. deduct   / dədʌ____ ____ /   ____   10. collect / ____əlɛ____t /   ____

3. taxi   / tæ____ ____ɪ /   ____   11. backache / bæ____eɪ____ /   ____

4. expenses / ɪ____ ____pɛnsɪz /   ____   12. accident / æ____ ____ɪdɪnt /   ____

5. ankle   / æŋ____əl /   ____   13. request / rə____wɛs____ /   ____

6. lucky   / lʌ____ɪ /   ____   14. extra / ɛ____ ____trə /   ____

7. exam   / ɪ____ ____æm /   ____   15. recognized / rɛ____ə ____ naɪzd /   ____

8. angle   / æŋ____əl /   ____   16. call / ____ɔl /   ____

B. Circle the stressed syllable. Then write the number of syllables in each word.

1. examined ____   6. requested ____   11. several ____

2. cousin ____   7. fractured ____   12. responsible ____

3. injury ____   8. occasional ____   13. insurance ____

4. dialogue ____   9. damage ____   14. accurate ____

5. college ____   10. doctor's ____   15. community ____

C. Fill in the missing consonant sounds using the symbols of the IPA.

1. tack / ____ æ ____ /   5. x-rays / ɛ ____ eɪ ____ /

2. taxi / ____ æ ____ /   6. backache / ____ æ ____ eɪ ____ /

3. taxes / ____ æ ____ ɪ ____ /   7. examine / ɪ ____ æ ____ ɪ ____ /

4. extra / ɛ ____ ____ ə /   8. legal / ____ ɪ ____ ɔ ____ /

D. *Additional review: / k / and / g / in medial position.* Circle the stressed syllable. Practice saying each word aloud, making certain that / k / and / g / are produced clearly.

/ k /

pictures	accidentally	architect
picnic	accustomed	practice
suitcase	accurate	occasion
fixed	fractions	expired

/ g /

hungry	eager	degree
agreement	exactly	aggravated
exhausted	agriculture	finger
exaggerate	ungrateful	language

E. Select the appropriate word from Exercise D for each sentence and write it on the line. Circle the stressed syllable in the underlined word and practice reading the sentence aloud.

    EXAMPLE: Let's take a picnic lunch.

  1. Mary's story was not completely _____.

  2. Has your driver's license _____?

  3. Those _____ at the museum are colorful.

  4. After three hours of classes, I was _____.

  5. Tom and Henry have a business _____ to share all expenses.

  6. We don't know _____ where he lives.

  7. I didn't understand the _____ used by the _____ of the building.

  8. Everyone was _____ to get a college _____.

  9. Anne's birthday was a special _____.

10. Dick likes to _____ when he tells a story.

F. Select five words from the list in Exercise D and compose a sentence for each. Underline each selected word in the sentence and practice reading it aloud using the correct pronunciation.

Reading Aloud

A. This dialogue focuses on the accurate production of / k / and / g /. Be sure to differentiate between the voiceless / k / and voiced / g /, and pay particular attention to the / k / in words such as **taxi, deduct,** and **accident.** Remember to link the words within phrases and stress the important words, while maintaining the conversational tone of the dialogue. Work for variety in pitch and clarity of articulation.

Divide the sentences into phrase units, using single and double slashes, and underline the stressed words.

> **EXAMPLE:**   A <u>taxi</u> <u>hit</u> my <u>car</u> / while I was <u>waiting</u> for my <u>cousin</u> / to <u>check</u> into a <u>hotel</u>. / /

Your instructor may serve as your model for correct and fluent oral reading. Prepare to enact this dialogue in class.

Peg and Mike

◆

PEG: Mike, it's great to see you.

MIKE: Must be close to a year.

PEG: Correct. So you couldn't have known about my fractured ankle. The x-rays indicated a break at an awkward angle. I was on crutches for eight weeks.

MIKE: Did you trip on the sidewalk?

PEG: No, it was an accident. A taxi hit my car while I was waiting for my cousin to check in at the Courtyard Hotel.

MIKE: Did you have adequate legal counsel?

PEG: Yes. My cousin recommended Max Corwin. Expensive, but with an excellent track record.

MIKE: Did you have to go to court?

PEG: Of course, but I was in luck. The judge recognized me. We were students together at Colgate Community College.

MIKE: That was a lucky break.

PEG: He moved the trial along at a fast clip. The taxi company was willing to settle out of court.

MIKE: And the cab driver?

PEG: Poor guy! He was from Pakistan—scared to death they'd take away his green card. Kept saying how sorry he was. He lives in Rego Park with his wife and two kids. His record was excellent. I hope he gets off easy.

MIKE: How come you're not angry with him?

PEG: I was, in the beginning, but now I just want to forget it.

MIKE: Well, it could have been worse.

PEG: The settlement was very generous, so I can't complain. I count myself lucky.

Reviewing the Plosives / p b t d k g /

A. Divide the following words from the passages in Sections D and E into syllables. Circle the stressed syllables and indicate the number of syllables in each word.

1. accidentally _____
2. apologized _____
3. contemptuous _____
4. considerate _____
5. sympathetic _____
6. license _____
7. attorney _____

8. expired _____
9. appealed _____
10. leaking _____
11. promised _____
12. apartment _____
13. medical _____

14. bumped _____
15. kitchen _____
16. appointment _____
17. technician _____
18. pipe _____
19. considered _____

B. Select the appropriate word from Exercise A to complete each sentence. Practice reading aloud for accuracy and fluency.

1. The plumber had to repair the _____ pipe in my _____.

2. I _____ to the judge when I _____ bumped into him.

3. I _____ firing the _____ when I received his bill.

4. My driver's _____ _____ last month.

5. I _____ my friend I'd meet her at her _____.

C. Write five sentences of your own, using the vocabulary listed above.

D. This reading passage focuses on the three voiceless aspirated plosive sounds: / p /, / t /, and / k /. Be sure to produce these sounds with a puff of air when they occur before a vowel in a stressed syllable. Although the sounds are weaker at the end of a word, try to produce these sounds, closing off the words completely.

Divide the selection into phrase units, using single and double slashes, and underline the stressed words.

EXAMPLE: Of <u>course</u>, / as you would <u>expect</u>, / I got a <u>ticket</u>. / /

A tape or your instructor may serve as your model for correct and fluent oral reading.

Dear Peter

◆

After I dropped you off at the corner of Fourteenth Street and Main, I made a left turn. I wanted to go uptown to shop and take back to my aunt a special wine that she likes. I backed up my car and accidentally bumped a police car behind me. Of course, as you would expect, I got a ticket. I apologized to the cop and appealed for another chance. I told him it was a mistake. I had a headache and was a bit sick. The cop got nasty and told me to take my case to court. I told Kate, my attorney, about the contemptuous attitude of the cop. We decided to take the cop's advice. However, Kate arrived late to our appointment. The judge, Judge Hoop, considered letting us go. He seemed considerate and even sympathetic when he wished me luck. I, too, had become contemptuous, and both Kate and I are now serving twenty-two days in a small jail in upstate New York. Can you pick us up at the end of August? My driver's license has expired.

E. This reading passage concentrates on all six plosive sounds. Be sure to produce the final sounds at the end of a word. Pay particular attention to the past tense and past participle of regular verbs, remembering to complete the **-ed** suffix using / t /, / d /, or / ɪd /.

Divide the selection into phrase units, using single and double slashes, and underline the stressed words.

EXAMPLE: I had just <u>lost</u> my <u>job</u> / as a <u>part-time</u> <u>medical</u> <u>lab</u> <u>technician</u>. / /

One of Those Days

◆

It was a cold, gray December morning and the weather reflected my mood exactly. I had just lost my part-time job as a medical lab technician. No more grant money they told me at the hospital. My tuition is due and I'm afraid to look at the balance in my checkbook.

I could do some errands. My boots need to be repaired. I wanted to buy eggs and chocolate. I promised to bake Paul a cake for his birthday next week. What else? I neglected to return my books to the library, and I'm quite sure my card has expired.

And I'm disgusted with the state of this apartment. The superintendent never repaired the leaking pipe in the kitchen or the broken radiator. I cut my hand on a splintered pane of glass in my bedroom. What a lot of blood. Life is such a mess.

It's snowing hard now. Forget the errands. Forget the checkbook. The best thing to do is to crawl back into bed. For better or worse tomorrow will take care of itself!

CHAPTER FIVE

Fricatives and Affricates

There are nine fricatives in the English language:

/ f /	as in **fee**
/ v /	as in **vie**
/ s /	as in **see**
/ z /	as in **zoo**
/ ʃ /	as in **shoe**
/ ʒ /	as in **beige***
/ θ /	as in **theme**
/ ð /	as in **the**
/ h /	as in **he****

The affricates / tʃ / and / ʤ / are also included in this chapter but will be discussed separately (see pages 171–183).

Unlike the plosives, the fricatives are not stopped completely as they are produced. They are stopped partially, and the air is pushed through a narrow opening. If you place your hand against your mouth for the production of / f /, / s /, / ʃ /, / θ /, and / h /, you will feel a steady stream of air. However, because the air is forced through very narrow openings, the air particles push against each other, causing rubbing, or friction—thus the term *fricatives*. The sounds are sometimes referred to as "spirants," from the Latin verb *spirare* (to blow).

---

* / ʒ / appears only in medial and final positions in English.

** / h / is also referred to as a fricative glide.

Eight of the nine fricatives are divided into pairs, known as cognates. The four pairs are / f / and / v /, / s / and / z /, / ʃ / and / ʒ /, and / θ / and / ð /. The / h /, which is voiceless, is not paired with another sound, and is not a cognate.

As you produce these sounds, you will notice that each pair has the same articulatory placement:

/ f / and / v /	labio-dental (upper teeth, lower lip)
/ s / and / z /	lingua-alveolar (tongue tip and the upper gum ridge section of the palate)
/ ʃ / and / ʒ /	lingua-palatal (tongue blade and roof of the mouth or palate)
/ θ / and / ð /	lingua-dental (tongue tip and upper and lower teeth)
/ h /	glottal fricative (the opening between the vocal bands)

Although these nine sounds share a particular type of production, they differ sharply in their placement.

♦ In the production of / f / and / v /, the friction is created at the lips and teeth. The upper teeth rest against the lower lip, and the air is forced through the opening.

♦ In the production of / s / and / z /, the air is forced through a narrow passageway between the tongue and the alveolar ridge (the ridge can be felt as a bump on the roof of the mouth behind the upper front teeth).

♦ In the production of / ʃ / and / ʒ /, the friction or noise that occurs results from the airstream rushing past the tongue and the roof of the front of the mouth.

♦ In the production of / θ / and / ð /, the tongue protrudes slightly between the upper and lower front teeth, almost totally blocking the breath stream.

♦ In the production of / h /, the glottis (the space between the vocal bands) is open. The vocal bands do not vibrate but are held open in a state of tension.

Of the four pairs of cognates, / f /, / s /, / ʃ /, and / θ / are voiceless, while / v /, / z /, / ʒ /, and / ð / are voiced. The ninth fricative, / h /, is voiceless. Two pairs of fricatives, / s / and / z /, and / ʃ / and / ʒ /, are also known as *sibilants*. The friction created as a result of producing these sounds causes a hissing or buzzing quality. The voiceless members of the fricative group appear more frequently than the voiced members, running the gamut from the very frequently used / s / to the infrequently used / ʒ /.

Target Sounds: / s / and / z /

Distinctive Features

/ s / and / z / are tongue-tip alveolar oral fricatives.*
/ s / is voiceless; / z / is voiced.

---

* / s / and / z / fricative sounds are also known as sibilants because of their hissing and buzzing acoustic qualities.

How Are / s / and / z / Made?

The tip, or blade, of the tongue is raised toward the upper gum, or alveolar, ridge, touching this section of the roof of the mouth very lightly.* Remember to keep the tongue tip away from the upper front teeth. The biting edges of the upper and lower front teeth are close together, while the sides of the tongue are in contact with the upper back teeth. Both sounds are long in duration, unlike the stop consonants, which are brief explosions.

/ s / is made by tensing and grooving the tongue tip, enabling the airstream to be released against the upper and lower front teeth. When the tongue is placed in proper position, a hiss, not a whistle, is produced.

If you place your finger in front of your lips as you produce / s / in these words, you can feel the air as it is emitted.

EXAMPLE: sip   us   asleep

When / s / is produced in final position, the sides of the tongue maintain contact with the upper side teeth. The upper and lower front teeth remain close together.

EXAMPLE: fuss   race   mouse

/ z / is made when the tongue tip touches the upper gum ridge. A buzz, not a hiss, is produced.

If you place your hand at your larynx and produce / z / in these words, you can feel the vibration of the vocal cords.

EXAMPLE: zoo   easy   his

When / z / is produced in final position, it is weaker than at the beginning of the word. The sides of the tongue maintain contact with the upper back teeth. The upper and lower front teeth remain close together.

EXAMPLE: does   raise   quiz

So in contrasting these sounds, there is no vibration at the larynx for the / s / sound and no air released for the / z / sound.

What Are the Problems or Patterns in Spelling?

/ s / may be represented by the letters **ce, ci, x,**** **psy, se,** and **ss.**

EXAMPLE: ice   accept   accident   fix   expire   psychology   course   lessons

/ z / may be represented by the letters **se, s, x,**** **z, zz,** and **es.**

EXAMPLE: raise   does   examine   zipper   puzzle   wishes

---

* Some speakers use other positions for the production of / s / and / z /. The tongue tip may lie flat in the back of the lower front teeth, with the blade of the tongue slightly elevated. The tongue tip may lie in a central position, neither up nor down, behind the upper and lower front teeth. The airstream is directed over the tongue tip.

** **x** followed by a voiceless sound is pronounced / ks / as in **expense** and **extend.**
   x followed by a vowel sound in a stressed syllable is pronounced / gz /, as in **example** and **executive.**

What Are the Problems in Pronunciation?

/ s / may be omitted after a voiced consonant.

EXAMPLE: *ten* instead of *tense*

sin instead of *since*

may be omitted at the end of plural and possessive nouns and third-person singular of present tense verbs and contractions.

EXAMPLE: *cat* instead of *cats*

talk instead of *talks*

my wife cat instead of *my wife's cat*

it late instead of *it's late*

may be omitted in consonant clusters / ts /.

EXAMPLE: *chess* instead of *chests*

guess instead of *guests*

may be produced as voiceless **th** when the tongue tip is place between the upper and lower front teeth.*

EXAMPLE: *think* instead of *sink*

faith instead of *face*

may be produced as a whistle when the tongue tip is placed too far back in the mouth or the upper and lower front teeth are separated.

/ z / may be replaced by / s / after a voiced sound.

EXAMPLE: *hiss* instead of *his*

loss instead of *laws*

may be omitted at the end of plural nouns, third-person singular of present tense verbs, posessive nouns, and contractions.

EXAMPLE: *pen* instead of *pens*

ride instead of *rides*

sister child instead of *sister's child*

he late instead of *he's late*

may be produced as a voiced **th** when the tongue tip is placed between the upper and lower front teeth.*

EXAMPLE: *breath* instead of *breeze*

---

* This is known as an interdental lisp and may be a problem for a non-native or a native speaker.

Note: Students who speak German, Spanish, and Asian languages may need to work on distinguishing and producing / s / and / z / phonemes.

Listening/Speaking

A. Compare the voiceless / s / and the voiced / z / in the *initial position*. Are these words the same or different?

1	2	1	2
sue	zoo	sip	zip
see	zee	sap	zap
seal	zeal	sink	zinc
sing	zing	seek	Zeke

Can you *feel* the difference as you repeat after your instructor?

Can you *hear* the difference between / s / and / z /?

Your instructor will read the words from columns 1 and 2 for each pair. Indicate the pattern that you hear.

> **EXAMPLE:**   If you hear *sue, zoo, sue,* the pattern is 1 2 1.

B. Observe the / s / and / z / sounds in *final position*. Omission of the final consonants changes the pronunciation and the meaning of the word.

> **EXAMPLE:**   knee—niece   tea—tease

1. Words with and without the final consonant / s /.

1	2	1	2	1	2
pea	piece	Fay	face	purr	purse
pay	pace	doe	dose	play	place
knee	niece	ray	race	I	ice
pry	price	you	use (n)	rye	rice
lie	lice	pea	peace	tray	trace

2. Words with and without the final consonant / z /.

1	2	1	2	1	2
pea	peas	Fay	phase	lay	lays
pay	pays	doe	doze	play	plays
knee	knees	ray	raise	I	eyes
pry	prize	you	use (v)	rye	rise
lie	lies	may	maze	tray	trays

3. Observe / s / and / z / contrasts in the *final position.*

1	2		1	2		1	2
peace	peas		face	phase		loose	lose
pace	pays		dose	doze		lace	lays
price	prize		race	raise		ice	eyes
lice	lies		use	use		rice	rise
place	plays		bus	buzz		trace	trays

C. Observe / s / and / z / contrasts in the *medial position.*

1	2		1	2
racer	razor		fussy	fuzzy
facing	phasing		ceases	seizes
looser	loser		doses	dozes
prices	prizes		uses (n)	uses (v)
lacy	lazy		busing	buzzing

D. Underline the contrastive words in each sentence. As you read aloud, remember to produce the / s / and / z / sounds when they occur.

EXAMPLE: The student could not <u>face</u> the last <u>phase</u> of the exam.

1. Your ring is so loose that you may lose it.

2. I heard a strange buzz on the bus.

3. Her eyes were the color of ice.

4. Raise the flag after the race.

5. His niece broke both knees in a skiing accident.

6. There wasn't a trace of food left on the tray.

7. I bought a new key chain for my keys.

8. Rye is a grain and so is rice.

9. The study notes you use are of no use to me.

10. Try not to doze after your final dose of medicine.

11. This place is too small for presenting plays.

12. It pays to pay your bills on time.

E. Compare the full form of the verb in column 1 with the contraction in column 2. When a noun or a pronoun is followed by the verb **is** or **has,** the shortened form is represented by **'s.**

	EXAMPLE:	She is here.	She's here.
		He has been there.	He's been there.

1.	He is here.	He's here.
2.	She is pretty.	She's pretty
3.	The boy is tall.	The boy's tall.
4.	The teacher has been ill.	The teacher's been ill.
5.	Mary is late.	Mary's late.
6.	What is going on?	What's going on?
7.	How is your family?	How's your family?
8.	Ted has been away.	Ted's been away.
9.	Who is speaking?	Who's speaking.
10.	That is true.	That's true.

Listening/Writing

A. Listen carefully for / s / and / z / as your instructor pronounces each word. Write these sounds when they occur in the initial, medial, or final position using the symbols of the IPA. If / s / or / z / is not heard, write a dash in the space provided.

EXAMPLE: expects / _s_____ _s_ / business / _z_____ _s_ / biology / ____—____ /

1. science _____	8. there's _____	15. reason _____
2. psychology _____	9. students _____	16. exact _____
3. statistics _____	10. mistake _____	17. chemistry _____
4. music _____	11. what's _____	18. cards _____
5. course _____	12. island _____	19. six _____
6. relax _____	13. Wednesday _____	20. says _____
7. closed _____	14. means _____	21. register _____

B. Circle the word read aloud by your instructor.

1. loss   (laws)   law
2. (place)   plays   play
3. use (n)   use (v)   (you)
4. race   raise   (ray)
5. (noose)   news   new

6. rice   rise   rye
7. niece   knees   knee
8. ice   eyes   eye
9. spice   spies   (spy)
10. (price)   prize   pry

C. Your instructor will select one of the words in parentheses and read the entire sentence aloud. Listen carefully and circle the word you hear. Practice reading each sentence aloud using either one of the words in parentheses.

1. Your (niece, knee) seems to be hurt.

2. Who wants another (race, raise)?

3. Susan found the (play, place) delightful.

4. Aren't those (lies, lice) horrible?

5. Sergei was amazed at the (price, prize).

6. Did you hear about the (laws, loss)?

7. That is an exciting (face, phase).

8. Who saw the (razor, racer)?

9. Tom's (pace, pay) at the office is poor.

10. The police found the (trace, trays) they were looking for.

D. Circle the stressed syllable as these words are read aloud. Write the number of syllables in each word.

1. roster   _____
2. psychology   _____
3. necessary   _____
4. statistics   _____
5. procedure   _____

6. registration _____
7. composition   _____
8. recognize   _____
9. lazy   _____
10. places   _____

11. closed   _____
12. tests   _____
13. courses   _____
14. raises   _____
15. resign   _____

E. *Additional review:* Listen carefully for / s / and / z / as your instructor pronounces each word. Write these sounds when they occur in the initial, medial, or final position using the symbols of the IPA. If / s / or / z / is not heard, write a dash in the space provided.

1. example   _____

2. raise   _____

3. race   _____

4. these   _____

5. isn't   _____

6. expense   _____

7. shoe   _____

8. escape   _____

9. sue   _____

10. consists   _____

11. does   _____

12. first   _____

13. hesitate   _____

14. leash   _____

15. lease   _____

F. Your instructor will read three words from columns 1 and 2 for each pair. Write the pattern that you hear.

   EXAMPLE: If you hear *phase, face, phase*, write 1 2 1.

1	2	Pattern
1. phases	faces	1 2 1
2. raise	race	1 2 2
3. test	tests	2 1 2
4. use (n)	use (v)	2 1 2
5. buzzing	busing	1 1 1
6. mates	maids	1 1 2
7. it	its	2 2 1
8. peas	piece	2 2 2
9. lose	loose	1 2 2
10. racer	razor	2 1 2

Chapter 5 Homework Review

A. Fill in the missing sounds using the symbols of the IPA. Then write the number of sounds in each word.

EXAMPLE: business / bɪ_z_n_ə_s / __6__

1. relax / rəlæ___ ___ / _____
2. exact / ɪg___æ___t / _____
3. example / ɪ___ ___æmpəl / _____
4. times / taɪ___ ___ / _____
5. explain / ɪ___ ___pleɪn / _____

6. sensible / ___ɛn___ə___əl / _____
7. music / mju___ɪ___ / _____
8. psych / saɪ___ / _____
9. Thursday / θɜˆ___deɪ / _____
10. closed / kloʊ___ ___ / _____

B. Circle the stressed syllable. Then write the number of syllables in each word.

1. chemistry _____
2. mistake _____
3. island _____
4. roster _____

5. composition _____
6. statistical _____
7. social _____
8. morning _____

9. hospital _____
10. courses _____
11. weekends _____
12. recognize _____

C. Write the following words using the symbols of the IPA.

1. piece / /
2. peas / /
3. says / /
4. Wednesday / /

5. niece / /
6. knees / /
7. plays / /
8. place / /

D. *Additional review: / s / and / z / in the medial position.* Circle the stressed syllable in each word. Practice saying each word aloud, making certain that the / s / and / z / are produced clearly.

/ s /

assign	buses	defenses	procedure
assist	risk	expected	chemistry
participate	statistics	places	expense
consists	mistake	assassinate	necessary

/ z /

		ガヂ executive	
easy	resign	ヂ	isn't
lazy	business	physical	present
doesn't	Wednesday	closed	because
razor	raises ｴｽ	physics	physician

E. Select the appropriate word from Exercise D to complete each sentence. Circle the stressed syllable in the underlined word and practice reading the sentence aloud.

   Example: It is (ne)cessary to study.

   1. Betty John decided to _____ in the anti-war demonstration.

   2. The _____ positions in this company are the president, vice-president, and the manager.

   3. My _____ specializes in cardiology.

   4. I am studying here at my own _____ .

   5. Send mail to my home, not my _____ address.

   6. My computer class _____ of theory and practice.

   7. The teacher didn't _____ any homework over the weekend.

   8. We _____ to study at the library, but it was closed.

   9. What is the new _____ for enrolling in this program?

   10. None of the workers at the factory received _____ this year.

F. Select five words from the list in Exercise D and compose a sentence for each. Underline the selected word in the sentence and practice reading aloud using correct pronunciation.

Reading Aloud

A. This dialogue focuses on the accurate production of the fricatives / s / and / z /. Make sure the tongue tip lightly touches the upper gum ridge, not the teeth, and do not omit these sounds at the end of a word. Remember to link the words within phrases and stress the important words, while maintaining the conversational tone of the dialogue. Work for variety in pitch and clarity of articulation.

Divide the sentence into phrase units, using single and double slashes, and underline the stressed words.

> **EXAMPLE:**   I'm so <u>lazy</u> / that I do <u>everything</u> / at the last <u>moment</u>. / /

A tape or your instructor may serve as your model for correct and fluent oral reading. Prepare to enact this dialogue in class.

Registration? Simple as A, B, C!

◆

CÉSAR: Rosa, I didn't expect to see you in the late registration line. I thought you registered early.

ROSA: I did. I saw my advisor; we selected the courses I needed. I'm in my second year of nursing and I must have sociology, psychology, advanced Spanish, and English composition.

CÉSAR: That's a stiff schedule! But I still don't understand why you're standing here.

ROSA: Because at the last moment the Spanish class was canceled. The psychology section I wanted was also canceled. I'm so upset! I slaved over that schedule. Morning classes on Tuesday, Wednesday, and Thursday. Monday and Friday I would work at the hospital. How could they do this to me? I could scream.

CÉSAR: Take it easy. Be like me. I'm so lazy that I do everything at the last moment. You expect too much.

ROSA: Sometimes I wish I had your disposition. Next time I'll follow your advice and register by phone.

CÉSAR: Not so fast! I was closed out of a class. My name wasn't on the roster. So I decided to take an elective.

ROSA: I have no choice. My courses are required. I'll just explain that to the person handling registration.

CÉSAR: Don't waste your breath. No place, no space. That's what they'll say. You can't beat the system. Resign yourself. Take the elective The History of Jazz. Meets Tuesday and Thursday mornings. It fits right into your schedule.

ROSA: I suppose I must be sensible. The History of Jazz?

CÉSAR: We'll explore New Orleans–style jazz and the Preservation Band and all the great blues singers, like Bessie Smith—

ROSA: You make it sound interesting. I haven't taken a single elective. I was saving them for my senior year.

CÉSAR: Well, here's your chance. Just step up to the desk and register.

ROSA: César, you've convinced me.

Target Sounds: The -s and -es Suffixes

When the letters **-s** or **-es** are added to the end of a word, you are seeing any one of three possible grammatical constructions: a plural noun, a possessive noun, or the third-person singular of the present tense of a verb. Knowing how and when to use these endings, both grammatically and phonologically, will add immeasurably to your command of the English language. Most native speakers were using these suffix endings correctly by the time they entered first grade. But many second-language English speakers and some native speakers have found this linguistic feature so troublesome that it has interfered with their ability to speak and write English accurately.

We are dealing here with two parts of speech—nouns and verbs. Let's talk about the nouns first. What does plural mean? Simply more than one person, object, idea or event. To convey the concept of plurality, the letters **-s** or **-es** is added to the singular noun.

EXAMPLE: *Singular Noun*   *Plural Noun*

girl	girls
book	books
disk	dishes
class	classes
opinion	opinions

A possessive noun expresses the idea of *belonging*. Something belongs to someone, or someone belongs to something. The thing may be an object, a person, an idea, or a concept. The **'s** is added to the singular or plural noun to signal possession or belonging. The listener or reader is informed that a particular object, attitude, or event belongs to a particular person, group, or organization.

EXAMPLE: *What*   belongs to   *Whom*   *Possessive Noun*

book	friend	friend's book
pens	students	student's pens
coat	judge	judge's coat
coats	judges	judges' coats
opinion	nurse	nurse's opinion

The **'s** is a concise way of expressing possession that eliminates extra words and brings the possessor and the thing possessed closer together.

EXAMPLE:

the book of my friend	=	my friend's book
the pens of the students	=	the students' pens
the coat of the judge	=	the judge's coat
the coats of the judges	=	the judges' coat
the opinion of the nurse	=	the nurse's opinion

Now let's turn to the verbs—specifically, the third-person singular of the present tense of a verb. The present tense indicates action taking place now. In conjugating the present tense, nothing is added to the root of the verb except in the *third-person singular,* that is, when the verb follows **he, she,** or **it.** Listed below are conjugations of some common verbs.

EXAMPLE:	I go	I like	I wish	I stand
	you go	you like	you wish	you stand
	he goe<u>s</u>	she like<u>s</u>	he wish<u>es</u>	it stand<u>s</u>
	we go	we like	we wish	we stand
	you go	you like	you wish	you stand
	they go	they like	they wish	they stand

The third-person singular of a present-tense verb may also be used with proper names, common nouns, and interrogative and relative pronouns.

EXAMPLE:
1. John goe<u>s</u> to the movies often.
2. That student wish<u>es</u> to change his program.
3. The hospital stand<u>s</u> firm in its policy.
4. Who like<u>s</u> coffee with milk?
5. An employee who speak<u>s</u> clearly is respected.

As you can see, the third-person singular is formed by adding either **-s** or **-es** to the root of the verb.

The use of these suffix endings is complicated by the fact that there are three possible pronunciations for **-s** or **-es.**

1. The **-s** suffix is pronounced / s /, as in the plural noun **tapes** / s / and the third-person singular of the verb **walks** / s /.

2. The **-s** suffix is pronounced / z /, as in the plural noun **names** / z / and the third-person singular of the verb **blames** / z /.

3. The **'s** ending may be pronounced / s / or / z /, as in the possessive nouns **ship's** / s / and **teacher's** / z /.

4. The **-es** and **'s** endings are pronounced / ɪz /, as in the plural noun **wishes,** the verb **catches,** and the possessive nouns **judge's** and **Alice's.** The phonemes in this suffix are the vowel / ɪ / and the voiced fricative / z /.

When **-s, -es,** or **'s** is pronounced / s / or / z /, the number of syllables in the word does not change.

EXAMPLE: state (one vowel sound, one syllable)
states (one vowel sound, one syllable)
names (one vowel sound, one syllable)
cat (one vowel sound, one syllable)
cat's (one vowel sound, one syllable)

However, when **-es** is pronounce / ɪz /, the number of syllables in the word does change.

EXAMPLE: class (one vowel sound, one syllable)
classes (two vowel sounds, two syllables)
church (one vowel sound, one syllable)
churches (two vowel sounds, two syllables)

The rules that govern the pronunciation of the **-s** and **-es** are essentially phonic. If you omit **-s, -es,** or **'s** when indicating plurality, possession, or the third-person singular of a present-tense verb, you will confuse your listeners and your readers. See if you can recognize which statements you tend to produce when you speak, or write or even read aloud in the examples listed below

Incorrect	*Correct*
1. He tape his voice often.	1. He <u>tapes</u> / teɪps / his voice often.
2. Two judge reviewed the case.	2. Two <u>judges</u> / ʤʌʤɪz / reviewed the case.
3. The judge book was misplaced.	3. The <u>judge's</u> / ʤʌʤɪz / book was misplaced.
4. The judges books were lost.	4. The <u>judges'</u> ʤʌʤɪz / books were lost.
5. John misjudge me.	5. John <u>midjudges</u> / mɪsʤʌʤɪz / me.
6. She always blame me.	6. She always <u>blames</u> / bleɪmz / me.

It is necessary to understand both the grammatical and phonological rules and to hear and reproduce the different endings in context. Look for these forms in the newspaper, practice reading them aloud, and observe the use of these suffixes by newscasters on radio and television. Work on your exercises every day. You will find them helpful. Try to integrate correct patterns into your everyday conversation. Control over your pronunciation will also help your writing. Both speaking and writing skills are important in your public communications in your business and professional careers.

Rules for the Pronunciation of the -s and -es Suffixes

The **-s** and **-es** ending may be pronounced / s /, / z /, or / ɪz ~ əz /.

1. When the **-s** suffix appears after a voiceless sound* (except after / s /, / ʃ /, / ʧ /), the **-s** is pronounced / s /.

EXAMPLE:	tape	/ teɪp /	tapes	/ teɪps /
	laugh	/ læf /	laughs	/ læfs /
	take	/ teɪk /	takes	/ teɪks /
	month	/ mʌnθ /	months	/ mʌnθs /

2. When the **-s** suffix occurs after a voiced sound** (except after / z /, / ʒ /, / ʤ /), the **-s** is pronounced / z /. These voiced sounds include all vowels and diphthongs.

EXAMPLE:	phone	/ foun /	phones	/ founz /
	observe	/ əbzɝˆv /	observes	/ əbzɝˆvz /
	agree	/ əgri /	agrees	/ əgriz /
	stay	/ steɪ /	stays	/ steɪz /

---

* The voiceless sounds are / p t k f θ /.

** The voiced sounds are / ð ŋ b d g v l m n r / plus all vowels and diphthongs.

3. When the **-s** or **-es** suffix occurs after / s /, / z /, / ʃ /, / ʒ /,* / tʃ /, or / ʤ /, the **-s** or **-es** is pronounced / ɪz / or / əz /.

EXAMPLE:	glass	/ glæs /	glasses	/ glæsɪz /**
	raise	/ reɪz /	raises	/ reɪzɪz /
	church	/ tʃɝˆtʃ /	churches	/ tʃɝˆtʃɪz /
	judge	/ ʤʌʤ /	judges	/ ʤʌʤɪz /

Listening/Writing

A. Parts of speech

These rules are used to form plural nouns (cat, cats), possessive nouns (John, John's), and the third-person singular, present-tense verbs (ask, asks). Observe these parts in the words below. Listen carefully and produce the appropriate / s /, / z /, or / ɪz / or / əz / pronunciation.**

1. Pronunciation / s /

Verbs	*Plural Nouns*	*Possessive Nouns*
takes	students	student's book
hopes	breaths	earth's surface
laughs	chiefs	wife's child
marks	checks	Jack's friend
tapes	shops	shop's windows

2. Pronunciation / z /

Verbs	*Plural Nouns*	*Possessive Nouns*
brags	eggs	egg's size
sells	plans	plane's pilot
moves	problems	king's gift
fires	countries	country's flag
loathes	teachers	cave's rocks

3. Pronunciation / ɪz / or / əz /

Verbs	*Plural Nouns*	*Possessive Nouns*
dresses	dresses	judge's decision
changes	nieces	niece's wedding
watches	beaches	beach's lifeguard
causes	classes	class's teacher
praises	garages	garage's mechanic

---

* The sibilants are / s z ʃ ʒ /.

** / ɪz / is interchangeable with / əz /.

B. The lists below compare the base word with the forms of plural and possessive nouns and the third-person singular of present-tense verbs.

Listen carefully and repeat as your instructor reads each pair of words aloud.

Your instructor will say three words from columns 1 and 2 for each pair. Indicate the pattern that you hear.

> **EXAMPLE:** If you hear *type, types, type,* the pattern is 1 2 1.

1. Pronunciation of / s /

   a. The words in column 1 end in a voiceless consonant. The final sound in each word in column 2 is therefore the voiceless / s /.

1	2	1	2
dentist	dentists	breath	breaths
escape	escapes	laugh	laughs
type	types	think	thinks
strike	strikes	guest	guest's
graph	graph's	tap	taps
wife	wife's	visit	visits

   b. Fill in the missing sounds in the following words using the symbols of the IPA. Then practice reading them aloud.

   1. minutes / mɪnɪ___ ___ /

   2. wolf's / wʊl___ ___ /

   3. ship's / ʃɪ___ ___ /

   4. months / mʌn___ ___ /

   5. checks / tʃɛ___ ___ /

   6. dentist's / dɛntɪ___ ___ /

   7. tips / tɪ___ ___ /

   8. coughs / kɔ___ ___ /

   9. chief's / tʃɪ___ ___ /

   10. lacks / læ___ ___ /

   11. faiths / feɪ___ ___ /

   12. picnics / pɪknɪ___ ___ /

2. Pronunciation of / z /

   a. The words in column 1 end in voiced consonants. The final sound in each word in column 2 is therefore the voiced / z /.

1	2	1	2
plan	plans	rule	rules
job	jobs	game	game's
sing	sings	lab	lab's
obtain	obtains	brag	brags
find	finds	love	loves
cave	cave's	reason	reasons

b. The words in column 1 end in a vowel or diphthong sound, which is always voiced. The final sound in each word in column 2 is therefore the voiced / z /.

1	2	1	2
go	goes	require	requires
agree	agrees	fare	fares
sue	sues	doctor	doctor's
window	windows	annoy	annoys
spy	spy's	law	laws

c. Fill in the missing sounds in the following words using the symbols of the IPA. Then practice reading them aloud.

1. rugs   / rʌ___ ___ /

2. guards   / gɑr___ ___ /

3. songs   / sɔŋ ___ /

4. jobs   / mʌn___ ___ /

5. hires   / haɪɚ___ /

6. teacher's / titʃɚ___ /

7. enjoys   / ɪndʒɔɪ___ /

8. agrees   / əgr___ ___ /

9. wears   / wɛɚ___ /

10. train's   / treɪn___ /

11. says   / s___ ___ /

12. dimes   / daɪ___ ___ /

3. Pronunciation of / ɪz–əz /

a. The words in column 1 end in / s /, / z /, / ʃ /, / ʒ /, / tʃ /, and / dʒ /. The final sound in each word in column 2 is therefore pronounced / ɪz / or / əz /.

1	2	1	2
class	classes	experience	experiences
prize	prizes	stage	stages
wish	wishes	lose	loses
speech	speeches	garage	garage's
course	courses	office	office's
orange	oranges	church	church's

b. Fill in the missing sounds in the following words using the symbols of the IPA. Then practice reading them aloud.

1. races   / reɪ___ ___ ___ /

2. causes   / kɔ___ ___ ___ /

3. refuses   / rəfju___ ___ ___ /

4. watches   / wɑtʃ___ ___ /

5. manages   / mænɪdʒ___ ___ /

6. courses   / kɔr___ ___ ___ /

7. purchases / pɝˆtʃəsɪ___ /

8. messages / mɛsɪdʒ___ ___ /

9. services   / sɜˆvɪ___ ___ ___ /

11. college's   / kɑlɪʤ___ ___ /

10. raises   / reɪ___ ___ ___ /

12. massages   / məsɑʒ___ ___ /

C. Underline the contrastive words in each sentence. As you read aloud, remember to produce the final endings of the underlined words.

> **EXAMPLE:**   Tom <u>manages</u> the store well but his brother hates to <u>manage</u> it.

1. The cop's gun was found by another cop.

2. We all sing well, but Susan sings the best.

3. Our class, along with two other classes, visited Washington, D.C.

4. All the phones are tied up except this phone.

5. Who will judge those judges' actions?

6. The corner office is larger than the other offices on the floor.

7. Our country has sent medical supplies to many other countries.

8. I tend to refuse invitations, but my friend never refuses.

9. My two eldest nieces live in Utah, but my youngest niece prefers Florida.

10. I never watch television, but my brother watches it all the time.

11. Those banks were bought by another bank.

12. I don't have a driver's license, but my brothers have licenses.

13. This course is a lot easier than my other courses.

14. We prefer this shop to the other shops in the neighborhood.

15. How does this college differ from other colleges?

Listening/Writing

A. Listen carefully for the / s /, / z /, or / ɪz ~ əz / pronunciation of the -s and -es endings in the following words. As your instructor reads aloud, write the appropriate sounds when they occur at the end of the word, using the symbols of the IPA.

> **EXAMPLE:**   caps / s /   cabs / z /   dishes / ɪz ~ əz /

1. climbs   _____

3. judge's   _____

5. offices   _____

2. thinks   _____

4. calls   _____

6. dislikes   _____

7. ship's	_____	11. believes	_____	15. hates	_____
8. states	_____	12. nurses	_____	16. finds	_____
9. problems	_____	13. gags	_____	17. pages	_____
10. refuses	_____	14. sneezes	_____	18. recognizes	_____

B. Circle the word read aloud by the instructor.

1. absence	absences		6. page	pages
2. conduct	conducts		7. gag	gags
3. glass	glasses		8. package	packages
4. United State	United States		9. opinion	opinions
5. dislike	dislikes		10. find	finds

C. Circle the stressed syllable as the instructor reads these words aloud. Then write the number of syllables in each word.

1. happens	_____	7. courses	_____	13. hires	_____
2. recalls	_____	8. salaries	_____	14. licenses	_____
3. costs	_____	9. absences	_____	15. college's	_____
4. realizes	_____	10. divorces	_____	16. invitation	_____
5. problems	_____	11. experiences	_____	17. shouts	_____
6. course	_____	12. strikes	_____	18. stuffed	_____

D. This exercise focuses on the pronunciation of the **-s** and **-es** suffixes.

Your instructor will select one of the words in parentheses and read the entire sentence aloud. Listen carefully and circle the word you hear.

Practice reading each sentence aloud using the correct word in parentheses.

1. All of my friends have their (license, licenses).

2. Who (recognize, recognizes) this man?

3. Have you traveled through all the (states, state)?

4. How many (nieces, niece) do you have?

5. Several (student, students) complained.

6. What happened to (César, César's) leg?

7. There are many (problems, problem) in the (suburb, suburbs).

8. I saw him a couple of (month, months) ago.

9. Nearly all (countries, country) belong to the United (Nation, Nations).

10. Is (Alice, Alice's) friend ill?

E. This exercise highlights the proper endings of plural and possessive nouns and the third-person singular of present-tense verbs.

Listen carefully as your instructor reads the following sentences aloud. Some are correct; some are incorrect. Write C for correct; I for incorrect. Practice reading each sentence aloud using accurate pronunciation.

	C/I
1. Those prices are too high.	C
2. There are fifty-one state in the United States.	C
3. Was the cop gun found?	C
4. These dresses are old-fashioned.	C
5. Do you know any good lawyers?	C
6. Is the dentist office open late?	I
7. Several dishes were broken.	C
8. The tutor help him once a week.	C
9. Is the beach's life guard alert?	C
10. His wife ideas were practical.	C
11. The author's publisher helped him.	C
12. Tim dislike work.	C
13. The manager agrees with me.	C
14. Ann's daughter dress well.	C
15. Some garage are open on Sunday.	C

Check over your answers in class. Rewrite the incorrect sentences.

Chapter 5 Homework Review

A. Fill in the missing sounds using the symbols of the IPA. Then write the number of sounds in each word.

    EXAMPLE: glasses / glæsɪz /   <u>6</u>

1. believes	/ bəli___ ___ /	_____	9. courses	/ kɔr___ ___ ___ /	_____
2. gags	/ gæ___ ___ /	_____	10. causes	/ kɔ___ ___ ___ /	_____
3. calls	/ kɔ___ ___ /	_____	11. becomes	/ bəkʌ___ ___ /	_____
4. patients'	/ peɪʃɪn___ ___ /	_____	12. raises	/ reɪ___ ___ ___ /	_____
5. faces	/ feɪ___ ___ ___ /	_____	13. lawyer's	/ lɔjɚ___ /	_____
6. Susan's	/ ___u___ən___ /	_____	14. states	/ steɪ___ ___ /	_____
7. holds	/ hoʊl___ ___ /	_____	15. pages	/ peɪʤ___ ___ /	_____
8. refuses	/ rəfju___ ___ ___ /	_____	16. coughs	/ kɔ___ ___ /	_____

B. Write the ending of each word using the symbols of the IPA. The final sound may be / s /, / z /, or / ɪz ~ əz /.

    EXAMPLE: times / z /   wishes / ɪz /   costs / s /

1. escape	/	/	9. taxes	/	/
2. physics	/	/	10. months	/	/
3. rings	/	/	11. divorces	/	/
4. statistics	/	/	12. lunches	/	/
5. stays	/	/	13. suburbs	/	/
6. glasses	/	/	14. cruises	/	/
7. changes	/	/	15. costs	/	/
8. garages	/	/	16. cashes	/	/

C. Circle the stressed syllable. Then write the number of syllables in each word.

1. happened _____
2. united _____
3. personnel _____
4. complained _____
5. interviews _____

6. ridiculous _____
7. organizes _____
8. interference _____
9. secretary _____
10. experiences _____

11. licenses _____
12. cashes _____
13. lenses _____
14. headaches _____
15. waitresses _____

D. Underline the correct word in parentheses. Be prepared to read aloud in class using accurate pronunciation.

1. My (job, job's) location is good.

2. Lettuce (cost, costs) too much these days.

3. Where did you put the (waiter, waiter's) tip?

4. Several (phone, phones) were bugged.

5. Have you seen any good (play, plays)?

6. We've had a few good (experience, experiences) with some (judge, judges).

7. The bank (cash, cashes) all my checks.

8. John (cough, coughs) a lot.

9. The masseuse gives good (massage, massages).

10. Tom (refuse, refuses) to take any more (course, courses).

11. My (lawyer, lawyer's) (opinion, opinions) are well-informed.

12. The United (State, States) has many (problem, problems).

13. Our (license, licenses) were renewed.

14. The (waitress, waitresses) refuse to leave.

15. According to his eye doctor, Tom (need, needs) new (glass, glasses).

C. Write the following words using the symbols of the IPA.

1. classes   /   /   2. dentists   /   /

3. dentist's   /   /   6. nieces   /   /

4. states   /   /   7. tests   /   /

5. places   /   /   8. raises   /   /

F. Study the pronunciation given for each word. If it is correct, write C. If incorrect, write I and show the correct pronunciation using the symbols of the IPA.

      EXAMPLE: lose / lus /   __I__   _____ / luz / _____

                                         C/I   *Correction*

1. college   / kɑlɪʤɪz /   _____   / _____ /

2. niece's   / nizɔz /   _____   / _____ /

3. states   / steɪt /   _____   / _____ /

4. Charles's   / tʃɑrlzɪz /   _____   / _____ /

5. judge's   / ʤʌʤɪz /   _____   / _____ /

6. judges   / ʤʌʤɪz /   _____   / _____ /

7. beaches   / bitʃz /   _____   / _____ /

8. beach's   / bitʃz /   _____   / _____ /

9. costs   / kɔst /   _____   / _____ /

10. bombs   / bɑms /   _____   / _____ /

11. recognizes   / rɛkəgnaɪz /   _____   / _____ /

12. refuses   / rəfjusəz /   _____   / _____ /

G. The following exercise focuses on possessive nouns. Change the underlined words into the possessive form using the **'s** at the end of the proper or common noun. Indicate the pronunciation of the **'s:** / s /, / z /, or / ɪz ~ əz /.

      EXAMPLE: The decisions of the judge were fair.

                   The judge's decisions were fair.   / ɪz / or / əz /

1. Did Henry lose the book that belongs to Alice?

_____

2. The uniforms of the waitresses are blue and white.

_____

3. <u>The experiences of Tom</u> at the dentist were unpleasant.

4. <u>The mother of Carlos</u> dislikes her daughter-in-law.

5. <u>Does the daughter of your sister</u> have many problems?

6. <u>The son of my boss</u> is a pleasant person.

7. Who can solve <u>the problems of this country</u>?

8. <u>The family of the victim</u> and <u>the family of the criminal</u> met in church.

9. <u>The keys of my brothers</u> were stolen yesterday.

10. Did you meet <u>the secretary of Dr. Diggs</u>?

H. Read each question aloud. Then write an answer in a complete sentence using the correct form of the third-person singular of the persent-tense verb. Indicate the pronunciation of the ending of the verb as / s /, / z /, or / ɪz ~ əz /.

   EXAMPLE: Q: Why does Mary take a bus to school?

   A: Mary <u>takes</u> a bus because it is a pleasanter ride than the train.   / s /

1. Why does Tom believe his sister?

2. Who hires the personnel in this department store?

3. Who tries to convince the jury in the courtroom?

4. What does the college catalogue say about required English courses?

5. How does your uncle feel about going to live in Florida?

_____

6. What does your teacher suggest for improving study habits?

_____

7. Why does your brother object to your taking an apartment?

_____

8. What does Mary know about that case?

_____

9. How much does your employer pay you?

_____

10. How much does his dentist charge?

_____

Reading Aloud

A. This dialogue focuses on the accurate pronunciation of the **-es** and **-s** suffixes. Be sure to use the correct ending for plural and possessive nouns and the third-person singular of present-tense verbs: / s /, / z /, or / ɪz ~ əz /. The sentence will be grammatically incorrect if these endings are omitted.

Circle the correct word in parentheses as you read aloud. Remember to link the words within phrases and stress the important words, while maintaining the conversational tone of the dialogue. Work for variety in pitch and clarity of articulation.

Divide the sentences into phrase units, using single and double slashes, and underline the stressed words.

> **EXAMPLE:** Sergei (want, wants) to bring his mother / to the (United State, United States). //

Your instructor may serve as your model for correct and fluent oral reading. Prepare to enact this dialogue in class.

Sergei's Mother

◆

AUNT:	You've heard me speak of my niece, Susan.
FRIEND:	Yes, she's your (sister, sister's) daughter. (Susan, Susan's) husband is Russian.
AUNT:	Sergei (work, works) as a nurse in the (hospital, hospital's) orthopedic clinic. He (want, wants) to be a doctor. Susan (work, works) in administration.
FRIEND:	She (seem, seems) very happy.
AUNT:	Until now.
FRIEND:	What's the matter?
AUNT:	Sergei (want, wants) to bring his mother to the (United State, United States).
FRIEND:	And Susan (think, thinks) that's a mistake?
AUNT:	Her mother-in-law (speak, speaks) no English and (prefer, prefers) to remain in Moscow with her two older (sister, sisters). Sergei (say, says) he (miss, misses) his mother very much.
FRIEND:	I hope Susan (find, finds) a solution.
AUNT:	She (hope, hopes) she can. She is the one who (plan, plans) the medical conventions. The next convention (meet, meets) in Russia, and medical personnel can attend.
FRIEND:	In that way, Sergei (visit, visits) his mother and then (come, comes) back with Susan and (continue, continues) his medical studies.
AUNT:	I only hope she (convince, convinces) Sergei.
FRIEND:	I'm betting on Susan—and her mother-in-law. A smart woman usually (get, gets) her way!

B. Complete the underlined word by using the correct ending of the third-person singular of the present-tense verb. Write the correct pronunciation of the **-s** or **-es** ending in the appropriate space: / s /, / z /, or / ɪz ~ əz /.

      EXAMPLE: Tom <u>hates</u> / s / dentists.

Practice reading this passage aloud for accuracy of pronunciation and fluency.

Tom and His Dentists

      Tom <u>hate</u> / / dentists. He always <u>think</u> / / of his terrible experiences with them. He <u>remember</u> / / Dr. Hodges, the dentist who <u>sneeze</u> / / in his patients' faces. Tom <u>gag</u> / / as he <u>recall</u> / / how Dr. Diggs placed his dental mirror too far back in Tom's mouth. He still <u>hate</u> / / Dr. Pages, who disappeared to work on another patient, leaving Tom alone with packs of cotton stuffed in his mouth. Tom's girlfriend, Tanya, <u>sympathize</u> / / with him and <u>feel</u> / / guilty because her teeth are perfect. She <u>brush</u> / / and <u>floss</u> / / morning and night. She always <u>come</u> / / with Tom when he <u>visit</u> / / a new dentist. Now she <u>wait</u> / / while Tom <u>see</u> / / Dr. Miller.

      Suddenly, the door <u>open</u> / / and Tom <u>rush</u> / / out. He <u>hold</u> / / something in his hand. "A perfectly healthy tooth!" he <u>yell</u> / / at her. "He extracted the wrong one!"

      Tanya <u>shake</u> / / her head and <u>follow</u> / / Tom out of the office. "There <u>go</u> / / dentist number four," she <u>think</u> / / to herself. "When I get home, I must remember to brush my teeth."

C. In the following exercise, one student asks the question, then selects a classmate to answer the question by defining and/or describing each of the terms. Remember to produce the fricative sounds / s / and / z / clearly as you ask or answer each question.

1. What's a mouse?
2. Where's the Office Assistant?
3. Where's the Wizard?
4. What can the Page Setup do?
5. What's the difference between Save and Save As?
6. What are icons?
7. How can you change margins?
8. What's the purpose of the recycle bin?
9. What does Times New Roman mean?
10. What's your worst experience with a computer?

Target Sound: 's *Contraction*

The 's contraction appears at the end of a noun or a pronoun replacing the full form of the verb **is** or the auxiliary verb **has.**

EXAMPLE: He is early.   He's early.
              The boy has gone away.   The boy's gone away.

's may be pronounced / s / or / z /.
The following rules can help you determine which pronunciation to use.

1. When an 's occurs after a voiceless consonant (except / s /, / tʃ /, or / ʃ /), it is pronounced / s /.

    EXAMPLE: *Noun/Pronoun + Verb*   *Contraction*

                  It is late.   It's late.
                  What is going on?   What's going on?
                  His wife has been ill.   His wife's been ill.
                  Jack has disappeared.   Jack's disappeared.

2. When an 's occurs after a voiced sound (except / z /, / dʒ /, or / ʒ /), it is pronounced / z /.

    EXAMPLE: *Noun/Pronoun + Verb*   *Contraction*

                  He is busy.   He's busy.
                  Tom is late.   Tom's late.
                  Who is there?   Who's there?
                  She has been away.   She's been away.

3. When a noun ends in / s /, / z /, / ʃ /, / ʒ /, / tʃ /, or / dʒ / the 's suffix may be pronounced / ɪz ~ əz /. This contraction form is not heard often.

    EXAMPLE: The class is large.   The class's large.
                  The church is closed.   The church's closed.

Listening/Speaking

A. Compare the full verb form and the contraction form below. Be sure to pronounce the 's ending using / s / or / z /.

1. Pronunciation of / s /

    The nouns and pronouns in column 1 end in voiceless consonants. Therefore the 's is pronounced / s /.

1	2
It is true	It's true
What is happening?	What's happening?
That is too bad.	That's too bad.

1	2
His wife is ill.	His wife's ill.
The booth is closed	The booth's closed.
The clinic is open.	The clinic's open.
It is late.	It's late.
The clock is broken.	The clock's broken.
The rope is torn.	The rope's torn.
His cough is better.	His cough's better.

2. Pronunication of / z /

The nouns and pronouns in column 1 end in voiced sounds. Therefore the **'s** is pronounced / z /.

1	2
The teacher is pleased.	The teacher's pleased.
Our team has been good.	Our team's been good.
Her child is sad.	Her child's sad.
Who is going?	Who's going.
The boy is bright.	The boy's bright.
Where is he going?	Where's he going?
Susie is here.	Susie's here.
Our cab is damaged.	Our cab's damaged.
How is your father?	How's your father?
The jogger is tired.	The jogger's tired.

B. Underline the full form and the contraction form of the verb **'s** or the auxilary verb **has.** Be sure to pronounce the **'s** correctly as you read aloud.

1	2
1. It is rather early.	It's rather early.
2. How is the weather in Florida?	How's the weather in Florida?
3. The team is losing.	The team's losing.
4. Henry has been writing to everyone.	Henry's been writing to everyone.
5. Tony's lawyer is helping him.	Tony's lawyer's helping him.
6. Inflation is affecting everybody.	Inflation's affecting everybody.
7. Tom is unhappy with his job.	Tom's unhappy with his job.
8. Where is his sister?	Where's his sister?
9. My experiment is finished.	My experiment's finished.
10. Your report is well written.	Your report's well written.

Listening/Writing

A. Listen carefully for / s / or / z / endings in the contractions as your instructor reads the following sentences aloud. Write the correct sound for the **'s** using the symbols for the IPA.

EXAMPLE: It's late / s /   The food's bad. / z /

1. That's good.   _____
2. Who's coming?   _____
3. She's here.   _____
4. When's he coming?   _____
5. He's been there.   _____

6. His eye's bleeding.   _____
7. That's nonsense.   _____
8. It's better.   _____
9. The student's early.   _____
10. How's he feeling?   _____

B. Your instructor will select one of the words in parentheses and read the entire sentence aloud. Listen carefully and circle the word you hear. Practice reading each sentence aloud using the contraction forms.

1. (It is, It's) too late.

2. (Who is, Who's) coming?

3. (There is, There's) nothing left.

4. The (problem has been, problem's been) settled.

5. (Where is, Where's) he going?

6. My (book is, book's) lost.

7. (That is, That's) for sure.

8. (Why is, Why's) he leaving now?

9. The (president is, president's) here.

10. (What is, What's) the reason?

C. Circle the stressed syllable as each word is read aloud. Then write the number of syllables in each word.

1. lessons   _____
2. compromise   _____
3. influence   _____
4. Sagittarius   _____
5. beginning   _____

6. astrology   _____
7. meditation   _____
8. circulation   _____
9. hamburgers   _____
10. meant   _____

Chapter 5 Homework Review

A. Fill in the missing sounds using the symbols of the IPA. Then write the number of sounds in each word.

    EXAMPLE: let's / lɛt_s_ / __4__

1. says / sɛ___ / _____
2. he's / h___ ___ / _____
3. yoga's / joʊ___ə___ / _____
4. vitamins / vɑɪtə___ɪ___ ___ / _____
5. what's / wɑ___ ___ / _____
6. who's / hu___ / _____

7. what've / wɑtə___ / _____
8. stomach / stʌ___ɪ___ / _____
9. meant / m___ ___ ___ / _____
10. food's / fu___ ___ / _____
11. pizza / pi___ ___ə / _____
12. reason / ri___ə___ / _____

B. Circle the stressed syllable. Then write the number of syllables in each word.

1. stars _____
2. nutritionist _____
3. astrology _____
4. suddenly _____
5. influence _____

6. Sagittarius _____
7. compromise _____
8. it's _____
9. waitresses _____
10. nutritious _____

C. Underline the subject noun or pronoun and the following verb in each sentence. Then write these words in the form of a contraction. In the last column, write the last two sounds of the contraction using the symbols of the IPA. Practice reading aloud.

    EXAMPLE: <u>Ben is</u> late. ____Ben's____ / nz /

	Contraction	Ending
1. Dick has disappeared.	_____	/ /
2. What is the matter?	_____	/ /
3. The cat is sick.	_____	/ /
4. She is sorry.	_____	/ /

	Contraction	*Ending*	
5. Her husband is traveling.	_____	/	/
6. Registration is hectic.	_____	/	/
7. Everyone is coming.	_____	/	/
8. The apartment is occupied.	_____	/	/
9. The child has been ill.	_____	/	/
10. How is the family?	_____	/	/

D. Write one sentence using the contraction form of each phrase below.

      EXAMPLE: That is   <u>That's</u> too easy.

1. That is   _____

2. Where is   _____

3. How is   _____

4. Who is   _____

5. What is   _____

6. She is   _____

7. Our friend is   _____

8. My employer is   _____

9. That teacher is   _____

10. The lawyer is   _____

11. The radio is   _____

12. It is   _____

E. Write the underlined words using the symbols of the IPA. Practice reading aloud.

1. The <u>tape's</u> broken.   /   /

2. <u>It's</u> the end.   /   /

3. The <u>food's</u> great.   /   /

4. <u>Let's</u> go.   /   /

5. <u>He's</u> tired.   /   /

6. The <u>dog's</u> sick.   /   /

7. <u>Dick's</u> late   /   /

8. Her <u>husband's</u> better.   /   /

F. Read each question aloud. Then write an answer in a complete sentence using the contraction form. Indicate the pronunciation of the **'s** using / s / or / z /.

    EXAMPLE: Q: Why has Sara written to you?

                A: Sara<u>'s</u> written to me because she needs money.

                The **'s** is pronounced / z /.

1. Where is Carol working?

_____

2. Why has she continued to study?

_____

3. Why is Tom leaving his job?

_____

4. What has John been doing lately?

_____

5. How is your father?

_____

6. Where has his secretary been?

_____

7. Why is he always late?

_____

8. How is your cousin?

_____

9. Where has Betty traveled lately?

_____

10. What has Ted told you about his job?

_____

Reading Aloud

A. This dialogue focuses on the contraction form of a verb following a noun or pronoun. Be sure to produce / s / or / z / when **'s** appears. The sentence will be grammatically incorrect if the sound is omitted.

Remember to link the words within phrases and stress the important words, while maintaining the conversational tone of the dialogue. Work for variety of pitch and clarity of articulation.

Divide the sentence into phrase units, using single and double slashes, and underline the stressed words.

> **EXAMPLE:** It's <u>better</u> to <u>break</u> up <u>now</u>, / before it's <u>too</u> late. //

Your instructor may serve as your model for correct and fluent reading. Prepare to enact this dialogue in class.

The Stars

———◆———

SALLY: It's the end. It's all over between us.

SAM: What's wrong.

SALLY: It's no use. It's dead. Finished. Over.

SAM: What's the reason? I know—it's because I'm late.

SALLY: It's not that.

SAM: I walk in the door—and suddenly I'm the man you hate the most.

SALLY: That's not true.

SAM: What's not true?

SALLY: I don't hate you at all.

SAM: Then what's going on?

SALLY: We're just not meant for each other.

SAM: Who say's so?

SALLY: The stars.

SAM: What stars?

SALLY: It's this book I've been reading. It's all about the stars and how they influence our lives. You're a Virgo and I'm a Sagittarius. We're no good for each other. So it's better to break up now, before it's too late.

SAM: So that's it. You're on an astrology kick. Let's talk it over later. After we've had dinner.

SALLY: Dinner! Seaweed and soybean hamburgers? That's dinner?

SAM: That food's nutritious.

SALLY: And what about those yoga lessons you took?

SAM: Yoga's good for the circulation.

SALLY: Astrology's more fun.

SAM: Let's compromise. No more astrology, and let's have pizza for dinner.

SALLY: That's more like it, Virgo.

SAM: I'm Sam, remember?

SALLY: How could I forget? Let's go, Sam. It's time for pizza.

Target Sounds: / ʃ / and / ʒ /

Distinctive Features

/ ʃ / and / ʒ / are lingua-palatal oral fricatives.*
/ ʃ / is voiceless; / ʒ / is voiced.

How Are / ʃ / and / ʒ / Made?

The blade of the tongue is raised and curled behind the alveolar ridge *without touching the hard palate.* The sides of the tongue are in contact with the upper side teeth. The lips protrude slightly; the biting edges of the upper and lower front teeth are close together. Both sounds are long in duration unlike the stop consonants, which are brief explosions.

/ ʃ / is produced by directing the airstream over the blade of the tongue against the closed upper and lower front teeth.

If you place your finger in front of your lips as you produce / ʃ / in these words, you can feel the air as it is released.

EXAMPLE: sure   ocean   cash

When / ʃ / is produced in final position, the blade of the tongue remains curled back toward the hard palate. The sides of the tongue maintain their contact with the upper side teeth.

EXAMPLE: rush   finish   crash

/ ʒ / is produced when the blade of the tongue, raised toward the hard palate, is accompanied by voice. There is no release of air. A buzzlike quality is a feature of the / ʒ / phoneme, which does not appear in the initial position in English.

EXAMPLE: beige   usual   conclusion

When / ʒ / is produced in final position, the sides of the tongue maintain contact with the upper side teeth. The upper and lower front teeth remain close together.

EXAMPLE: rouge   garage   massage

So in contrasting these sounds, there is no vibration at the larynx for the / ʃ / sound and no air released for the / ʒ / sound.

What Are the Problems or Patterns in Spelling?

/ ʃ / is represented by the letters **sh, su, ss, ti, ci, ce, ch, sci, xi,** and **si.**

EXAMPLE: shoe   sugar   tissue   mention   social   ocean

machine   conscious   anxious   tension

---

* These sounds are also known as sibilants because of the acoustic qualities.

Note: Students who speak French, Spanish, German, or Asian languages may need to work on distinguishing and producing / s /, / ʃ /, / z /, and / ʒ /.

/ ʒ / is represented by the letters **ge, si, sure,** and **su.**

EXAMPLE: corsage   vision   leisure   casual

What Are the Problems in Pronunciation?

/ ʃ / may be replaced by / s /.

EXAMPLE: *sip* instead of *ship*

mass instead of *mash*

may be confused with / ʧ /.

EXAMPLE: *watch* instead of *wash*

/ ʒ / may be replaced by / ʃ /.

EXAMPLE: *leisure* / liʃɚ / instead of / liʒɚ /

may be replaced by / ʤ /.

EXAMPLE: *garage* / gərɑʤ / instead of / gərɑʒ /

may be replaced by / z /.

EXAMPLE: *vision* / vɪzən / instead of / vɪʒən /

Listening/Speaking

A. Listen to your instructor and repeat: / ʃ /   / ʃ /   / ʃ /

Repeat the following syllables with / ʃ /:   / ʃi /   / ʃeɪ /   / ʃu /

B. Listen to your instructor and repeat: / ʒ /   / ʒ /   / ʒ /

Repeat the following syllables with / ʒ /:   / eɪʒ /   / ɑʒ /   / uʒ /

C. Repeat after your instructor. Be sure that your tongue tip is raised but does not touch the roof of your mouth.

1. The / ʃ / sound

   a. Initial position

shoe	sheet	show
sheep	ship	shower
short	share	shot
shop	shine	shell
shell	shoot	shield

b. Final position

wish	cash	plush
dish	rash	bush
wash	crash	flash
rush	crush	slash

c. Medial position

vacation	passion	notion
fashion	issue	dictation
mission	relation	tension
session	depression	intention
pressure	conscience	conscious

2. The / ʒ / sound

a. Final position

beige	barrage	triage
rouge	garage	camouflage
corsage	massage	mirage

b. Medial position

vision	conclusion	confusion
usual	pleasure	Asia
casual	collision	invasion
leisure	occasion	decision

D. Problems with / ʃ /

1. / ʃ / and / s / may be confused.

Compare / ʃ / and / s / in the initial, medial, and final position.

Can you *feel* and *hear* the differences as you repeat after the instructor? Your instructor will say three words from columns 1 and 2 for each pair. Indicate the pattern that you hear.

    EXAMPLE: If you hear *shoe, sue, shoe,* the pattern is 1 2 1.

a. Initial position

1	2	1	2
shoe	sue	shoot	suit
she	see	sheep	seep
shore	sore	short	sort
shell	sell	shave	save
shower	sour	shy	sigh

b. Final position

1	2	1	2
mash	mass	plush	plus
gash	gas	clash	class
leash	lease	crash	crass
brash	brass	lash	lass

a. Medial position

1	2	1	2
gashes	gases	clashes	classes
lashes	lasses	mashes	masses
leashes	leases	meshes	messes

2. Underline the contrastive words in each sentence. As you read aloud, remember to produce / ʃ / and / s / in the underlined words.

   EXAMPLE: Don't lay the <u>sheet</u> on the <u>seat</u>.

   a. He took some sort of medicine for a short time.

   b. Let's have a sip of water on the ship.

   c. I'm planning to sue the shoe store.

   d. I was sore because I didn't go the shore.

   e. She didn't see me.

   f. They didn't shoot a photo of the man in the black suit.

   g. According to my lease, every dog must have a leash.

   h. There was a clash between two students in the class.

   i. Sy seems very shy.

   j. Show me how well you can sew.

E. Problems with / ʒ /

Repeat each word after your instructor, noting the differences in the production of / ʒ / and / z /.

Although these words are not as alike in sound or appearance, it is helpful to read them aloud to feel and hear the differences between these phonemes.

1. / ʒ / and / z / may be confused.

    a. Medial position

1	2
vision	visible
pleasure	pleasant
glazier	glazing
composure	composer

    b. Final position

1	2
beige	bays
rouge	rues
loge	lows

2. / ʒ / and / dz / may be confused.

    In the final position, the single phoneme / ʒ / and the consonant cluster / dz / may sound the same, but the articulatory movements are quite different.

1	2
Bruges	broods
liege	leads
loge	loads

3. Underline the words with / ʒ / and / z / in the following sentences. Read them aloud using accurate pronunciation.

    EXAMPLE: His vacation in <u>Asia</u> was <u>pleasant</u>.

    a. The light was not visible to John, who has poor vision.

    b. It is a pleasure to meet such a pleasant person.

    c. The glazier who repaired my window also glazed this bowl.

    d. As usual, I am using your pen.

    e. What is your version of the story?

    f. Our conclusions were wrong.

    g. The barrage of bullets terrified the villagers.

    h. Bill decided to postpone his decision.

    i. That car collision was serious.

Listening/Writing

A. Listen carefully for / ʃ / and / ʒ / as your instructor pronounces each word. Write these sounds when they occur in initial, medial, or final position using the symbols of the IPA. If / ʃ / or / ʒ / is not heard, write a dash in the space provided.

EXAMPLE: beige /____3____/   ashes /_____ʃ__/   edge /_____—_____/

1. vision	_____	6. shopping	_____	11. corsage	_____
2. charge	_____	7. sues	_____	12. sure	_____
3. wish	_____	8. mention	_____	13. legion	_____
4. machine	_____	9. massage	_____	14. shoes	_____
5. measure	_____	10. sore	_____	15. collision	_____

B. Circle the word spoken by the instructor.

1. seep	sheep	6. class	clash
2. sue	shoe	7. mass	mash
3. seat	sheet	8. bass	bash
4. sore	shore	9. lass	lash
5. sip	ship	10. lease	leash

C. Your instructor will select one of the words in parentheses and read the entire sentence aloud. Listen carefully and circle the word you hear. Practice reading each sentence aloud using either one of the words in parentheses.

1. Stanley broke the (lease, leash).

2. Who saw the (clash, class)?

3. This is your (sheet, seat).

4. She (shows, sews) those dresses every Tuesday.

5. Let's not (ship, sip) this lemonade.

6. Did you (shell, sell) the peas?

7. We didn't know about those (gases, gashes).

8. Did you (sock, shock) him?

9. How do you feel about your (self, shelf)?

10. Where are those (leashes, leases)?

D. Circle the stressed syllable as each word is read aloud. Write the number of syllables in each word.

1. mention	_____	6. pajamas	_____	11. invasion	_____
2. machine	_____	7. usual	_____	12. garage	_____
3. shudder	_____	8. pleasure	_____	13. sensational	_____
4. shoemaker	_____	9. collision	_____	14. decision	_____
5. massage	_____	10. conscience	_____	15. relationship	_____

Chapter 5 Homework Review

A. Fill in the missing sounds using the symbols of the IPA. Write the number of sounds in each word.

EXAMPLE: shorts / __ʃ__ɔrts / __5__

1. occasion	/ əkeɪ___ən /	_____		8. massage	/ mə___ɑ___ /	_____
2. measure	/ mɛ___ɚ /	_____		9. leisure	/ li___ɚ /	_____
3. visual	/ vɪ___uəl /	_____		10. assorted	/ ə___ɔrtɪd /	_____
4. decision	/ dɪ___ɪ___ən /	_____		11. danish	/ deɪ___ɪ___ /	_____
5. shopping	/ ___ɑ___ɪŋ /	_____		12. sugar	/ ___ugɚ /	_____
6. conclusion	/ kənklu___ən /	_____		13. shirts	/ ___ɜ˺ts /	_____
8. cash	/ ___æ___ /	_____		14. soles	/ ___ou___ ___ /	_____

B. Circle the stressed syllable. Then write the number of syllables in each word.

1. mention	_____	5. decision	_____	9. finished	_____
2. explanation	_____	6. corsage	_____	10. pajamas	_____
3. vanish	_____	7. moustache	_____	11. unusual	_____
4. shoemaker	_____	8. constitutional	_____	12. conclusion	_____

C. Write the following words using the symbols of the IPA.

1. sheet	/	/	5. vanish	/	/
2. beige	/	/	6. vision	/	/
3. finished	/	/	7. shave	/	/
4. flesh	/	/	8. invation	/	/

D. Study the pronunciation given for each word. If it is correct, write C. If incorrect, write I and show the correct pronunciation using the symbols of the IPA.

EXAMPLE: wish / wɪs / ___I___ ___/ wɪʃ /___

		C/I	Correction
1. decisions	/ desɪzənz /	_____	/ _____ /
2. mention	/ mɛnsən /	_____	/ _____ /
3. moustache	/ mʌstæʃ /	_____	/ _____ /
4. flesh	/ flɛs /	_____	/ _____ /
5. corsage	/ kɔrsaʤ /	_____	/ _____ /
6. massage	/ məsɑdz /	_____	/ _____ /
7. shouting	/ ʃaʊtɪŋ /	_____	/ _____ /
8. sure	/ ʃuɚ /	_____	/ _____ /
9. machine	/ mətʃin /	_____	/ _____ /
10. confusion	/ kənfjuʒən /	_____	/ _____ /

E. *Additional review: / ʃ / and / ʒ / in medial position.* Circle the stressed syllable. Practice saying each word aloud, making sure / ʃ / and / ʒ / are produced clearly.

1	2	1	2
conscious	intention	version	lesion
issue	relaxation	camouflaged	illusions
pressure	position	unusually	fusion
tension	machinery	casual	leisure

F. Select the appropriate word from Exercise E to complete each sentence. Circle the stressed syllable in the underlined word and practice reading the sentence aloud.

EXAMPLE: There is no time for relaxation.

1. My _____ of the accident differs from yours.

2. What kind of a _____ are you looking for?

3. John was very _____ about his work.

4. What do you do in your _____ time?

5. I was not _____ during the operation.

6. I have no _____ about life in California.

7. His _____ was to finish school.

8. High blood _____ may result from excessive _____ .

9. The tank was _____ to avoid recognition.

10. Many people are concerned about the _____ of global warming.

G. Complete the following sentences and practice reading them aloud using accurate pronunication.

1. The collision _____ .

2. I should mention that _____ .

3. I usually _____ .

4. My garage _____ .

5. Your decision _____ .

Reading Aloud

A. The following dialogues *focus* on the production of / ʃ / and / ʒ /. Make sure that the tongue tip is raised and does *not* touch the palate or the roof of the mouth. Remember to link the words within phrases and stress important words, while maintaining the conversational tone of the dialogue. Work for variety in pitch and clarity of articulation.

Divide the sentences into phrase units, using single and double slashes, and underline the stressed words.

> **EXAMPLE:**   When the <u>bills</u> come in, / I'll be in a <u>state</u> of <u>shock</u>. / /

A tape or your instructor may serve as your model for correct and fluent oral reading. Prepare to read aloud in class.

Shira's Shopping Spree

◆

SHIRA:	What a pleasure it is to shop! I wish I were really rich!
ASHLEY:	You surely act as if you were.
SHIRA:	The decisions I had to make! Look at this smashing beige blouse—and this Parisian scarf.
ASHLEY:	Is it really from Paris?
SHIRA:	Well, a good copy, anyway. The cutest salesman helped me choose these shoes.
ASHLEY:	Those heels must measure three inches!
SHIRA:	I even had a massage.
ASHLEY:	Doesn't your conscience disturb you?
SHIRA:	No. Look at this marvelous makeup kit. It's called Precious Treasures. And I love these silk pajamas.
ASHLEY:	I'm ashamed of you.
SHIRA:	Today's a special occasion—my birthday.
ASHLEY:	That was two weeks ago, Shira.
SHIRA:	Are you sure? Maybe you're right.
ASHLEY:	You're too casual about money.
SHIRA:	I know. When the bills come in, I'll be in a state of shock. But until then, what can I say? I confess I have a passion for fashion!

Shawn and His Mother

◆

SHAWN: Mother, where've you been?

MOTHER: Out shopping.

SHAWN: It's about time you got back. Look at this. I just want you to look at this!

MOTHER: Why, Shawn, you're shaking. I believe you're upset.

SHAWN: My shirts. They're all gone. Even my T-shirts. Not a single shirt!

MOTHER: Imagine that! No shirts.

SHAWN: And where are my shorts? Tell me that. Where are my shorts?

MOTHER: No shorts either? My, my.

SHAWN: My jeans are gone, too. Not to mention my shoes.

MOTHER: Strange, very strange.

SHAWN: Things don't suddenly vanish, Mother.

MOTHER: You're sure, dear?

SHAWN: I demand an explanation!

MOTHER: Simple, Shawn, simple. Your shirts and shorts as well as jeans are in the washing machine. Your shoes are at the shoemaker.

SHAWN: At the shoemaker!

MOTHER: Except for the sneakers with holes in the soles. They're in the garbage.

SHAWN: I won't stand for this.

MOTHER: Stop shouting and listen. Your clothes had to be cleaned. Your shoes had to be fixed. Since you refused to do anything, I had to do something.

SHAWN: Am I supposed to go out in my pajamas?

MOTHER: Not at all. However, I suggest that you take a shower and shave. Trim that moustache and by the time you're finished, everything will be back in place.

SHAWN: My moustache! Blackmail, sheer blackmail! I won't do it! I stand on my constitutional rights!

MOTHER: Shawn, is it a deal?

SHAWN: Stabbed in the back by my own flesh and blood!

MOTHER: Well, Shawn?

SHAWN: Very well, mother, it's a deal.

Affricates

An affricate is a combination of a stop and a fricative. The stop sound slides into the fricative in the same area of the mouth. Depite the fact that it has two phonetic symbols, the affricate is recognized as a single sound, a phoneme in its own right.

There are two affricates in the English language: / tʃ /, which is voiceless, and / dʒ /, which is voiced. / tʃ / is composed of the stop plosive / t / and the fricative / ʃ /.

EXAMPLE: <u>ch</u>ew   tou<u>ch</u>   rea<u>ch</u>es

Similarly, the / dʒ / is composed of the stop plosive / d / and the fricative / ʒ /.

EXAMPLE: <u>j</u>ump   pa<u>ge</u>   ad<u>j</u>ust

To produce these sounds, the tongue moves from the stop position for / t / or / d / into the fricative position for / ʃ / or / ʒ /.

The two affricates are sometimes confused with / ts / and / dz /. However, / ts / and / dz /, in **cats** and **pads,** for example, are recognized as two distinctive sounds comprising a sound cluster, and therefore two separate phonemes, while / tʃ / and / dʒ / in **chew** and **jaw,** for example, are single entities.

Note: / ts / does exist as a phoneme in other languages, such as German.

   EXAMPLE: *Zeit* / tsaɪt / meaning "time" in German.

Target Sounds: / tʃ / and / dʒ /

Distinctive Features

/ tʃ / and / dʒ / are lingua-palatal oral affricates.*
/ tʃ / is voiceless; / dʒ / is voiced.

How Are / tʃ / and / dʒ / Made?

There are two elements in each sound. The / tʃ / phoneme consists of the plosive stop / t / and the voiceless fricative / ʃ /. The / dʒ / phoneme is formed by combining the plosive stop / d / with the voiced fricative / ʒ /.

First, the tongue tip presses firmly against the upper gum ridge for / t / and / d / and then moves quickly back, farther away from the upper front teeth, without touching the hard palate for / ʃ / and / ʒ /. The sides of the tongue are in close contact with the upper side teeth.

The biting edges of the upper and lower front teeth are close together; the lips are slightly protruded. The plosives are brief and explosive, but the fricatives may be sustained.

---

* Although two symbols are used in the IPA, they represent and are counted as one sound or phoneme.

/ tʃ / is produced with a strong puff of air. This is particularly evident when / tʃ / occurs before a vowel in a stressed syllable.

If you place your finger in front of yor lips as you produce / tʃ / in these words, you can feel the air as it is emitted.

EXAMPLE: choose watch achieve

When / tʃ / appears at the end of a word, the biting edges of the upper and lower front teeth remain close together; the sides of the tongue maintain contact with the upper back teeth.

EXAMPLE: catch each rich

/ dʒ / is produced with strong voicing and no emission of air. If you place your hands at your larynx and say / dʒ / in these words, you can feel the vibration of the vocal cords.

EXAMPLE: gypsy wages change

The / dʒ / is produced in final position with less force than at the beginning of a word. The biting edges of the teeth remain close together; the sides of the tongue maintain contact with the upper back teeth.

EXAMPLE: judge badge page

So in contrasting these sounds, there is no vibration at the larynx for the / tʃ / and no air released for the / dʒ / sound.

What Are the Problems or Patterns in Spelling?

/ tʃ / is represented by the letters **ch, tu,** and **tch.**

EXAMPLE: chapter feature witch

/ dʒ / is represented by the letters **ge, dge, ju, j, di,** and **du.**

EXAMPLE: age judge jury major soldier procedure

What Are the Problems in Pronunciation?

/ tʃ / may be pronounced / ts /.

EXAMPLE: *cats* instead of *catch*

may be replaced by / ʃ /.

EXAMPLE: *wash* instead of *watch*

may be followed by the schwa / ə / and pronounced / tʃə /.

EXAMPLE: *catch* (ə) / kætʃə / instead of *catch* / kætʃ /

/ ʤ / may be pronounced / dz /.

EXAMPLE: *aids* instead of *age*

may be replaced by / ʒ /.

EXAMPLE: *lesion* instead of *legion*

may be pronounced / j /.

EXAMPLE: *mayor* instead of *major*

may be pronounced / ʧ /

EXAMPLE: *batch* instead of *badge*

may be pronounced / ʤə /.

EXAMPLE: *judge* (ə) / ʤʌʤə / instead of *judge* / ʤʌʤə /

Listening/Speaking

A. Listen to your instructor and repeat: / ʧ /   / ʧ /   / ʧ /

Repeat the following syllables with / ʧ /:   / ʧi /   / ʧa /   / ʧou /

B. Listen to your instructor and repeat: / ʤ /   / ʤ /   / ʤ /

Repeat the following syllables with / ʤ /:   / ʤi /   / ʤa /   / ʤou /

C. Compare / ʧ / and / ʤ / in the *initial position*. Are these words the same or different?

1	2	1	2
chain	Jane	chess	Jess
cheer	jeer	chin	gin
char	jar	cheap	jeep
choke	joke	chest	jest

Can you *feel* and *hear* the differences between / ʧ / and / ʤ / as you repeat after your instructor?

Your instructor will say words from columns 1 and 2 for each pair. Indicate the pattern that you hear.

EXAMPLE: If you hear *cheer, jeer, cheer,* the pattern is 1 2 1.

Note: Students who speak French, Spanish, Greman, or Asian languages may need to work on distinguishing and producing / ʧ / and / ʤ / phonemes.

D. Compare the / tʃ / and the / dʒ / in *final position.*

1	2	1	2
rich	ridge	batch	badge
etch	edge	lunch	lunge
perch	purge	search	surge
match	Madge	beseech	besiege

E. Compare the / tʃ / and the / dʒ / in *medial position.*

1	2	1	2
riches	ridges	batches	badges
matches	Madge's	lunches	lunges
etches	edges	searches	surges

F. Underline the contrastive words in each sentence. As you read aloud, remember to produce the / tʃ / and / dʒ / sounds in the underlined words.

> **EXAMPLE.**   Mr. <u>Ch</u>in does not like to drink <u>g</u>in.

1. There were jeers and cheers at the convention.

2. The rich man fell off the ridge.

3. Our larch tree is not as large as your oak tree.

4. That jeep is cheap.

5. Jane wears a chain on her wrist.

6. Jess plays chess very well.

7. Madge is looking for a match.

8. He thought he'd choke when he heard that joke.

9. The bartender dropped a cherry into my sherry.

10. Joe's wife chose to leave.

G. Problems with / tʃ /

1. / ʃ / and / tʃ / may be confused. Compare the sound of / ʃ / and / tʃ /. Note that the tongue tip must touch the upper gum ridge to produce the / t / sound in / tʃ /.

a. Initial position

1	2	1	2
shoe	chew	shoes	choose
sheep	cheap	sheet	cheat
ship	chip	shin	chin
share	chair	shows	chose
shop	chop	sheer	cheer

b. Final position

1	2	1	2
wish	witch	mash	match
dish	ditch	crush	crutch
cash	catch	lash	latch
wash	watch	marsh	march

c. Medial position

1	2	1	2
wishes	witches	cashes	catches
mashes	matches	crushes	crutches
washes	watches	marshes	marches
leashes	leeches	dishes	ditches

d. Underline the contrastive words in each sentence. As you read aloud, remember to produce the / ʃ / and the / tʃ / sounds in the underlined words.

> **EXAMPLE:** Joe threw a <u>dish</u> into the <u>ditch</u>.

1) When I fell, I cut my shin and my chin.

2) He watched as she washed the windows.

3) I wouldn't choose those shoes.

4) Did you like the shows he chose?

5) Let's share this chair.

6) I'll buy a chop in this shop.

7) The ship does not sell chocolate chip cookies.

8) Which pair of shoes should I choose?

9) Sherry owns two cherry trees.

10) She's going to buy some cheese.

2. / tʃ / and / ts / may be confused.

The single phoneme / tʃ / and the consonant cluster / ts / may sound alike, but the articulatory movements are quite different.

a. Repeat after your instructor to feel and hear the differences.

1	2	1	2
itch	its	batch	bats
catch	cats	arch	arts
match	mats	witch	wits
watch	watts	each	eats

b. Underline the contrastive words in each sentence. As you read aloud, remember to produce the / tʃ / and / ts / sounds in the underlined words.

EXAMPLE: What's <u>wrong</u> with my <u>watch</u>?

1) The dog couldn't catch the cats.

2) The arts and crafts show was held under the arch.

3) The wicked witch knew how to use her wits.

4) A single match can ignite those mats.

5) Because of our schedules, each of us eats at a different time.

6) Juan keeps his batch of baseball bats in his closet.

7) Burt's birch tree was damaged by the storm.

8) I have a hunch my cat hunts for mice in the cellar.

9) If you itch, it's probably an allergy.

10) We have two wonderful mutts to whom we are much attached.

3. / dʒ / and / dz / may be confused.

The single phoneme / dʒ / and the consonant cluster / dz / may sound the same, but the articulatory movements are different.

a. Repeat after your instructor to feel and hear the differences.

1	2	1	2
wage	wades	wedge	weds
rage	raids	judge	Judd's
age	aids	hedge	heads
budge	buds	sledge	sleds

b. Underline the contrastive words in each sentence. As you read aloud, remember to produce the / ʤ / and / dz / sounds in the underlined words.

      EXAMPLE: <u>Judd's</u> father is a <u>judge</u>.

1) The agency aids people of any age.

2) Mr. Wades asked for a higher wage.

3) The police raids threw him into a rage.

4) That cat always heads for the hedge.

5) He used a sledge hammer to destroy the sleds.

4. / ʤ / and / ʒ / may be confused.

Although these words are not as close in sound, or appearance, it is helpful to practice them aloud to feel and to hear the differences between these phonemes.

1	2	1	2
age	beige	barge	barrage
large	loge	message	massage
garbage	garage	legion	lesion

Listening/Writing

A. Listen carefully for / ʧ / and / ʤ / as your instructor pronounces each word. Write these sounds when they occur in initial, medial, or final position using the symbols of the IPA. If / ʧ / or / ʤ / are not heard, write a dash in the space provided.

      EXAMPLE: catch /_____ʧ_/   jam /_ʤ_____/   rouge /____—____/

1. wage	_____	7. arranged	_____	13. aids	_____
2. wades	_____	8. efficient	_____	14. danish	_____
3. cheerful	_____	9. stitches	_____	15. damage	_____
4. polished	_____	10. special	_____	16. shorthand	_____
5. weds	_____	11. whiplash	_____	17. college	_____
6. wedge	_____	12. age	_____	18. garage	_____

B. Circle the word spoken by the instructor.

1. cheap	jeep	sheep	6. cherry	Jerry	Sherry
2. cheer	jeer	sheer	7. match	Madge	mash
3. chore		shore	8. chock	jock	shock
4. chip	gyp	ship	9. batch	badge	bash
5. chin	gin	shin	10. chose	Joe's	shows

C. Your instructor will select one of the words in parentheses and read the entire sentence aloud. Listen carefully and circle the word you hear. Practice reading each sentence aloud using either one of the words in parentheses.

1. That's a big (gyp, chip).

2. He did not want to (lunch, lunge).

3. They (besieged, beseeched) him.

4. We won't (cash, catch) any.

5. Don't sit on the (match, mats).

6. Let's (watch, wash) now.

7. He (shows, chose) flowers.

8. He has a (batch, badge) at home.

9. He hurt his (chin, shin).

10. (Jerry, Sherry) isn't here now.

D. Circle the stressed syllable as each word is read aloud. Then write the number of syllables in each word.

1. psychology ____	6. damaged ____	11. insured ____
2. confusion ____	7. casual ____	12. relationship ____
3. conscious ____	8. experienced ____	13. polished ____
4. algebra ____	9. arranged ____	14. whiplash ____
5. danish ____	10. sensational ____	15. luncheonette ____

E. *Additional review.* These exercises review the differences between / ʧ / and / ʤ / and similar sounds such as / ʃ /, / ts /, and / dz /.

1. Your instructor will say three words from columns 1 and 2 for each pair. Indicate the pattern that you hear.

      EXAMPLE: If you hear *choke, joke, choke*, write 1 2 1.

	1	2	*Pattern*
a.	rich	ridge	___ ___ ___
b.	choke	joke	___ ___ ___
c.	etch	edge	___ ___ ___
d.	lunch	lunge	___ ___ ___
e.	catch	cats	___ ___ ___
f.	batch	badge	___ ___ ___
g.	seeds	siege	___ ___ ___
h.	witch	wits	___ ___ ___
i.	leech	leash	___ ___ ___
j.	weds	wedge	___ ___ ___
k.	aids	age	___ ___ ___
l.	cherry	sherry	___ ___ ___

2. Circle the words read aloud by your instructor.

a.	rid	rids	ridge		f.	cat	cats	catch
b.	wade	wades	wage		g.	bat	bats	batch
c.	raid	raids	rage		h.	wit	wits	witch
d.	wed	weds	wedge		i.	what	what's	watch
e.	bud	buds	budge		j.	it	its	itch

Chapter 5 Homework Review

NAME: _____ **DATE:** _____

A. Fill in the missing sounds using the symbols of the IPA. Write the number of sounds in each word.

    EXAMPLE: joined / <u>ʤ</u>ɔɪnd / <u> 4 </u>

1. check / ___ ɛ ___ / _____

2. message / mɛsɪ___ / _____

3. rouge / ru___ / _____

4. collision / kəlɪ___ ən / _____

5. arranged / əreɪ___ ___ d / _____

6. gentlemen / ___ ɛntəlmən / _____

7. Russia / ___ ʌ ___ ə / _____

8. casual / kæ___ ʊəl / _____

9. punctual / pʌŋk___ ʊəl / _____

10. algebra / æ___ ___ əbrə / _____

11. garage / gərɑ___ / _____

12. polished / pɑ___ ɪ ___ t / _____

13. sugar / ___ ʊgɚ / _____

14. Asia / ___ ___ ə / _____

B. Circle the stressed syllable in each word. Write the number of syllables in each word.

1. visual _____

2. message _____

3. massage _____

4. unusually _____

5. efficient _____

6. accident _____

7. insurance _____

8. experienced _____

9. psychology _____

10. assorted _____

11. polished _____

12. garage _____

13. confusion _____

14. pleasure _____

15. occurred _____

C. Write the following words using the symbols of the IPA. Note the number of sounds in each word.

1. danish / / _____

2. cheese / / _____

3. stitches / / _____

4. legion / / _____

5. check / / _____

6. special / / _____

7. choice / / _____

8. occasion / / _____

D. Study the pronunciation given for each word. If it is correct, write C. If incorrect, write I and show the correct pronunciation using the symbols of the IPA.

EXAMPLE: wage / weɪz / _____I_____ _____/ weɪʤ /_____

		C/I	Correction
1. casual	/ kæsuəl /	_____	/ _____ /
2. joking	/ ʤoukɪŋ /	_____	/ _____ /
3. damaged	/ dæmɪdzd /	_____	/ _____ /
4. unusually	/ ənjuʒuəlɪ /	_____	/ _____ /
5. garbage	/ gɑrbɪʒ /	_____	/ _____ /
6. message	/ mɛsɪdz /	_____	/ _____ /
7. suggest	/ səʤɛst /	_____	/ _____ /
8. machine	/ mətʃin /	_____	/ _____ /
9. purchase	/ pɝˆʃɪs /	_____	/ _____ /
10. imagine	/ ɪmæʤɪn /	_____	/ _____ /

E. *Additional review: / tʃ / and / ʤ / in medial position.* Circle the stressed syllable. Practice saying each word aloud, making sure these sounds are produced accurately.

/ tʃ /

achieve	lecture	purchase	eventually
attachment	fracture	picture	question
beseeched	bachelor	pitcher	punctual

/ ʤ /

besieged	adjust	imagine	arrangement
sociology	religion	major	reject
soldiers	margin	region	majority

F. Select five words from the list in Exercise E and compose a sentence for each. Underline each selected word in the sentence and practice reading aloud using accurate pronunciation.

G. Select the appropriate word from Exercise E and write it on the line. Circle the stressed syllable of the underlined word and practice reading the sentence aloud.

EXAMPLE: His (lec)ture lasted over an hour.

1. Charles has always tried to ＿＿＿＿＿＿ good grades.

2. The ＿＿＿＿＿＿ on the wall fell on my white ＿＿＿＿＿＿.

3. The American political system favors ＿＿＿＿＿＿ rule.

4. The town was ＿＿＿＿＿＿ by enemy ＿＿＿＿＿＿.

5. Why did they ＿＿＿＿＿＿ my application for the position?

6. The x-ray showed a bad ＿＿＿＿＿＿ in the right ankle.

7. I forgot to leave a wide ＿＿＿＿＿＿ on the left side of my letter.

8. Jane ＿＿＿＿＿＿ the priest to find housing for her family.

9. John's sister is never ＿＿＿＿＿＿.

10. A ＿＿＿＿＿＿ problem for many students is writing term papers for college courses.

Reading Aloud

A. This dialogue will help you review the sounds / ʃ /, / ʒ /, / tʃ /, and / ʤ /. Remember to link the words within phrases and stress the important words, while maintaining the conversational tone of the dialogue. Work for variety in pitch and clarity of articulation.

Divide the sentences into phrase units, using single and double slashes, and underline the stressed words.

> **EXAMPLE:** Why do you <u>hang</u> around / with those <u>kid</u> <u>musicians</u> / so <u>much</u>? / /

Your instructor may serve as your model for correct and fluent oral reading. Be prepared to enact this dialogue in class.

All That Jazz

◆————

JASPER:	Good morning, Miss Santiago. Welcome to the Marketing Division of Charles and Company.
SANTIAGO:	It's a pleasure to be here, Mr. Jasper.
JASPER:	And such a charming assistant, in addition.
SANTIAGO:	*Executive* assistant, Mr. Jasper.
JASPER:	Naturally. By the way, we're very informal here. You can call me Jack.
SANTIAGO:	I'd like to be shown my workstation.
JASPER:	Let's enjoy a little celebration on your first day here. Why don't you pick up coffee and danish in the company cafeteria and we can have a cozy little chat.
SANTIAGO:	I don't drink coffee—
JASPER:	Then make it tea—
SANTIAGO:	And I don't go to cafeterias. I believe this is a good time to discuss my schedule.
JASPER:	*Your* schedule?
SANTIAGO:	You'll find me very punctual. I work from eight to five, take half an hour for lunch, the other half hour at the gym. I am both efficient and energetic.
JASPER:	Ah, but there's the workplace. Establishing relationships is a major concern. The flourishing of friendship.
SANTIAGO:	Mr. Jasper, forget the public relations bit. What I need is a desk, a chair, a computer, and a job description. I suggest you fill me in on any special projects that need researching.
JASPER:	Very well, *Miss Santiago.* (aside, to himself) And I thought this was going to lead to a sensational relationship!

Reviewing the Fricatives / s z ʃ ʒ tʃ ʤ /

A. Divide the following words from the dialogue in Section D into syllables. Indicate how many syllables in each word and circle the stressed syllable.

1. explanation _____	6. encouragement _____	11. decision _____
2. miserable _____	7. cheerful _____	12. insistence _____
3. screaming _____	8. refused _____	13. gradually _____
4. apologize _____	9. terrified _____	14. agitated _____
5. necessary _____	10. choice _____	15. section _____

B. Select the approprite word from Exercise A to complete each sentence. Practice reading aloud for accuracy and fluency.

1. It was _____ to make a _____ immediately.

2. He always read the sports _____ first.

3. The cashier at the checkout counter was always _____ .

4. He was _____ at the thought of making the wrong _____ .

5. The child _____ to _____ for _____ in class.

C. Write five sentences of your own using the vocabulary listed above.

D. This dialogue focuses on the accurate production of the fricatives and affricates / s z ʃ ʒ tʃ ʤ /. Do not omit these sounds in the middle or at the end of a word. Be careful to differentiate between / tʃ / and / ʃ / and / ʤ / and / ʒ /. Use the **'s** for possessives and contractions and the **-s** and **-es** endings for plural nouns as well as the singular of present tense verbs.

Remember to link the words within the phrase and stress the important words, while maintaining the conversational tone of the dialogue. Work for variety in pitch and clarity of articulation.

> **EXAMPLE:**   I thought she'd be excited / when I told her / I was joining the police force. //

Your instructor may serve as your model for correct and fluent oral reading. Prepare to enact the dialogue in class.

Past and Present

◆

ISABEL: Luis, get your shoes off the couch! What's the matter? You look miserable.

LUIS: Izzy, Mom's furious with me. She was right in the middle of seasoning the fish stew and rushed out of the room yelling and screaming.

ISABEL: Please, Luis, stop with the Izzy. My name's Isabel.

LUIS: Sorry, sis, it slipped out. I just can't understand Mom's reaction to my decision.

ISABEL: What decision?

LUIS: Joining the police force. What's so terrible about that?

ISABEL: She's upset and it's not your fault. In her country the police were the bad guys.

LUIS: But she's been here for ages.

ISABEL: The past lives on. The sound of a siren still terrifies her.

LUIS: I never realized. She's usually so cheerful and well-adjusted.

ISABEL: This is a shock. But you should go ahead with your plans. You've made a wise choice.

LUIS: Thanks. I need encouragement. The sergeant told me it was a plus that I could speak Spanish.

ISABEL: Which Mom insisted that you speak. Strange how parents come in handy. I'm going upstairs now. She needs some reassurance. She may even want to apologize.

LUIS: That's not necessary. Just tell her I'm checking up on the stew. She may forgive me for joining the police force, but she'd never forgive me for ruining our supper.

Target Sounds: / θ / and / ð /

Distinctive Features

/ θ / and / ð / are lingua-dental (tongue-tip, teeth) oral fricatives.
/ θ / is voiceless; / ð / is voiced.

How Are / θ / and / ð / Made?

The tongue tip is placed between the upper and lower front teeth. The upper teeth rest lightly on the tongue without pressing; these sounds may be released without interruption. Both sounds are long in duration, unlike the stop consonants, which are brief explosions.

/ θ / is produced by directing the airstream over the protruding tongue tip.

If you place your finger in front of your lips as you produce / θ / in these words, you can feel the air as it is released.

> **EXAMPLE:**   think   faith   nothing

When / θ / is produced in final position, the tongue tip remains between the upper and lower front teeth.

> **EXAMPLE:**   earth   breath   eighth

/ ð / is produced when the tongue tip is placed between the upper and lower front teeth. There is no release of air.

If you place your hand at your larynx and produce / ð / in these words, you can feel the vibration of the vocal cords.

> **EXAMPLE:**   they   father   bathe

When / ð / is produced in final position, the tongue tip remains between the upper and lower front teeth. This phoneme is not voiced as strongly at the end of the word as in the initial position.

> **EXAMPLE:**   loathe   teeth   breathe

So in contrasting these sounds, there is no vibration at the larynx for the / θ / sound and no air released for the / ð / sound.

What Are the Problems or Patterns in Spelling?

/ θ / is represented by the digraph **th.**

> **EXAMPLE:**   thought   breath   anything

/ ð / is represented by the digraph **th.**

> **EXAMPLE:**   they   breathe   brother

Note: Most non-native students and some native speakers may need to work on distinguishing and producing the voiced and voiceless **th** sounds.

What Are the Problems in Pronunciation?

/ θ / may be replaced by the voiceless stop plosive / t / if the tongue tip touches the upper gum ridge or if excessive pressure on the tongue tip prevents air from being released.

EXAMPLE: *tank* instead of *thank*

may be replaced by the voiceless fricative / f / if the upper front teeth press on the lower lip.

EXAMPLE: *fought* stead of *thought*

may be replaced by the voiceless fricative / s / if upper and lower teeth are in contact and the tongue tip rests on the upper gum ridge.

EXAMPLE: *sink* instead of *think*

/ ð / may be replaced by the voiced stop plosive / d / if the tongue tip is pressed against the upper gum ridge.

EXAMPLE: *dare* instead of *their*

may be replaced by the voiced fricative / v / if the upper front teeth touch the lower lip.

EXAMPLE: *vat* instead of *that*

may be replaced by the voiced fricative / z / if the tongue tip rests on the upper gum ridge and if the upper and lower teeth are in contact.

EXAMPLE: *breeze* instead of *breathe*

Listening/Speaking

A. Repeat the following syllables with the voiceless fricative / θ /:

/ θɑ /   / θɪ /   / θʌ /   / θɔ /

B. Repeat the following syllables with the voiced fricative / ð /:

/ ðæ /   / ði /   / ðʌ /   / ðɛ /

C. Repeat the words listed below after your instructor. Be sure that the tongue tip protrudes between the upper and lower front teeth.

1. Voiceless / θ /

   a. Initial position

thin	thick	thief
thumb	thank	theory
thousand	think	theme
thought	theater	thigh

Note: Most non-native students and some native speakers may need to work on distinguishing and producing the voiced and voiceless **th** sounds.

b. Medial position

anything	author	truthful
birthday	nothing	earthquake
arithmetic	something	bathtub
ruthless	authority	mathematics

c. Final position

bath	mouth	south
both	breath	ninth
month	north	oath
myth	earth	growth

2. Voiced / ð /

a. Initial position

than	those	their
that	these	though
this	they	then
the	them	there

b. Medial position

another	brother	feather
rhythm	rather	together
mother	either	although
weather	neither	leather

c. Final position

breathe	unclothe	smoothe
with	bathe	seethe
clothe	smooth	loathe

D. Problems with voiceless / θ /

1. / θ / and / t / may be confused.

a. Compare the voiceless fricative / θ / and the voiceless plosive / t / in the initial position. Are these words the same or different?

1	2	1	2
thank	tank	theme	team
through	true	three	tree
thought	taught	thigh	tie
thin	tin	thrust	trust
thick	tick	thongs	tongs

Can you *feel* the difference as you repeat after your instructor?

Can you *hear* the difference between / θ / and / t /?

Your instructor will say three words from columns 1 and 2 for each pair. Indicate the patterns that you hear.

    EXAMPLE: If you hear *thank, tank, thank,* the pattern is 1 2 1.

b. Observe the / θ / and / t / sounds in *final position.* Omission of the final consonants changes the pronunciation and the meaning of the word.

    EXAMPLE: claw–cloth

Words with and without final / θ /

1	2	1	2
bow	both	two	tooth
Fay	faith	tee	teeth
rue	Ruth	he	heath
owe	oath	she	sheath

Words with final / θ /

1	2	1	2	1	2
both	boat	booth	boot	death	debt
myth	mitt	fourth	fort	wrath	rat
path	pat	broth	brought	width	wit
tooth	toot	math	mat	oath	oat
tenth	tent	bath	bat	faith	fate

c. Underline the contrastive words in each sentence. As you read aloud, remember to produce the / θ / and / t / sounds in the underlined words.

    EXAMPLE: <u>Pat</u> followed me down the <u>path</u>.

1) The tin was too thin.

2) We thank you for the new fish tank.

3) I thought I taught you to be neat.

4) It's true we're through.

5) They both fell out of the boat.

6) He was assigned to the tenth tent.

7) I have no faith in fate.

8) Ruth needs root canal work on her teeth.*

---

* In some dialect areas speakers may not contrast the vowel sounds in **Ruth** and **root.**

9) Bert attended the birth of his child.

10) The theme of the team was "Through thick and thin, we'll always win."

2. / θ / and / s / may be confused.

a. Initial position

1	2	1	2
thank	sank	think	sink
theme	seem	thought	sought
thick	sick	thigh	sigh
thing	sing	thaw	saw

b. Final position

1	2	1	2
myth	miss	wraith	race
bath	bass	faith	face
path	pass	mouth	mouse
math	mass	worth	worse
growth	gross	tenth	tense

c. Underline the contrastive words in each sentence. As you read aloud, remember to produce the / θ / and / s / sounds in the underlined words.

   EXAMPLE: I <u>think</u> this boat will <u>sink</u>.

1) The thick sandwich did not appeal to the sick child.

2) It's a myth to think I'll miss you.

3) I seem to remember the theme of that movie.

4) The bass was kept alive in the bath.

5) Did you pass Tom on the path?

6) A mass of people dislike math.

7) The mouse has sharp teeth in his mouth.

8) The tenth person was tense.

9) I saw the meat was beginning to thaw.

10) I can't think of a thing to sing.

3. / θ / and / f / may be confused.

   a. Initial position

1	2	1	2
thought	fought	three	free
threat	fret	thrill	frill
thin	fin	thirst	first

   b. Final position

1	2	1	2
death	deaf	Ruth	roof
myth	miff	wreath	reef
oath	oaf	sheath	sheaf

   c. Underline the contrastive words in each sentence. As you read aloud, remember to produce the / θ / and / f / sounds in the underlined words,

     1) I thought we fought a good fight.

     2) Fred could not thread the needle.

     3) We had three free tickets to the theater.

     4) Ruth fell off the roof.*

     5) The deaf boy's death affected everyone.

     6) The fin of that fish is very thin.

     7) A wreath for the dead was placed on the coral reef.

     8) Don't fret about that threat to your family.

     9) At first I had a terrible thirst for water.

     10) Those three are finally free.

E. Problems with voiced / ð /

1. / θ / and / ð / may be confused.

   a. Compare the voiced fricative / ð / and the voiced plosive / d / in the *initial position.* Are these words the same or different?

---

* In some dialect areas speakers may not contrast the vowel sounds in **Ruth** and **root.**

1	2	1	2
they	day	those	doze
then	den	than	Dan
their	dare	they've	Dave
though	dough	they'll	dale

Can you *feel* the difference as you repeat after your instructor?

Can you *hear* the difference between / ð / and / d /?

Your instructor will say three words from columns 1 and 2 for each pair. Indicate the pattern that you hear.

> **EXAMPLE:**   If you hear *they, day, they,* the pattern is 1 2 1.

b. Observe the / ð / and / d / sounds in *final position.* Omission of the final consonants changes the pronunciation and meaning of the word.

Words with and without final / ð /

1	2	1	2
low	loathe	wry	writhe
bay	bathe	tie	tithe
see	seethe	tee	teethe
sue	soothe	lay	lathe

Words with final / ð /

1	2	1	2
breathe	breed	writhe	ride
loathe	load	soothe	sued
bathe	bade	tithe	ride
seethe	seed	lithe	lied
teethe	teed*	lathe	laid

c. Observe / ð / and / d / in *medial position*

1	2	1	2
breathing	breeding	writhing	riding
loathing	loading	seething	seeding
father	fodder	lather	ladder

d. Underline the contrastive words in each sentence. As you read aloud, remember to produce the / ð /and / d / in the underlined words.

> **EXAMPLE:**   They've already seen Dave.

---

* The golf term is "teed off."

1) We can bathe in the bay.

2) I was afraid to take their dare.

3) There are those who like to doze after dinner.

4) I loathe carrying a heavy load.

5) My father fed fodder to his cattle.

6) It didn't rain the day they came.

7) Dan is a better cook than Fran.

8) Though the dough was heavy, the pie filling was fine.

9) The police are afraid they've kidnapped Dave.

10) Try to soothe her because she's being sued.

2. / ð / and / z / may be confused.

Repeat after your instructor to feel and to hear the differences between these phonemes.

a. Final position

1	2	1	2
breathe	breeze	teethe	tease
loathe	lows	seethe	seize
bathe	bays	clothes	close
writhe	rise	soothe	sues

b. Medial position

1	2	1	2
breathing	breezing	teething	teasing
writhing	rising	clothing	closing

3. / ð / and / v / may be confused.

1	2	1	2
than	van	that	vat
thy	vie	they'll	veil
thine	vine	thou	vow

Listening/Writing

A. Listen carefully for / ð / and / θ / as your instructor pronounces each word. Write these sounds when they occur in the initial, medial, or final position using the symbols of the IPA. If / ð / or / θ / is not heard, write a dash in the space provided.

> **EXAMPLE:** they /_ð_____ /   oath /_θ_____ /   height /_____—_ /

1. think _____
2. truthful _____
3. those _____
4. bother _____
5. anything _____

6. thoroughly _____
7. breathe _____
8. death's _____
9. another _____
10. although _____

11. bath _____
12. bathe _____
13. breath _____
14. thousand _____
15. therefore _____

B. Your instructor will select one of the words in parentheses and read the entire sentence aloud. Listen carefully and circle the word you hear. Practice reading each sentence aloud using either one of the words in parentheses.

1. They needed a (bath, bat).

2. Even if he (sues, soothes) you, don't compromise.

3. I lost the (three, free) tickets.

4. Where is the (reef, wreath)?

5. His (death, debt) bothered me.

6. Who cut your (thigh, tie)?

7. Which (three, tree) did you see?

8. Her (mouth, mouse) was hurt.

9. The metal was (thin, tin).

10. "No more (breeding, breathing)" was the slogan.

C. Circle the word spoken by your instructor.

Group A				*Group B*		
1. breath	breed	breeze		8. math	mat	mass
2. teethe	teed	tease		9. Ruth	root	roof
3. writhe	ride	rise		10. loathe	load	low
4. tooth	toot	two		11. thought	taught	fought
5. sheath	sheet	she		12. three	tree	free
6. oath	oat	owe		13. death	debt	deaf
7. faith	fate	face		14. then	den	Zen

D. Circle the stressed syllable as each word is read aloud. Write the number of syllables in each word.

1. thermometer	_____		6. thousand	_____		11. authority	_____
2. nevertheless	_____		7. calendar	_____		12. thoroughly	_____
3. sympathetic	_____		8. sufferer	_____		13. throughout	_____
4. terribly	_____		9. misery	_____		14. throat	_____
5. hypochondriac	_____		10. swallowed	_____		15. throbbing	_____

E. Prepare to read these passages aloud in class. Remember to link the words within the phrase and stress important words, while maintaining the conversational tone of the passage. Work for variety in pitch and clarity of articulation.

Divide the sentences into phrase units, using single and double slashes, and underline the stressed words.

EXAMPLE: He <u>caught</u> the <u>five-thirty</u> <u>bus</u> / at the <u>Port</u> <u>Authority</u> <u>terminal</u>. / /

Your instructor will read both passages aloud.

1. In the first selection, listen carefully for the voiceless / θ /. Underline the words in which this phoneme appears.

Birthday Surprise

Arthur looked at his desk calendar. Arthur was worried. Today was Thursday. There was something special about the day. But he couldn't think what it was. Maybe Kathy would know. Kathy remembered everything. Did they have theater tickets? Or was he supposed to get a new shelf for the bathroom? Well, no sense thinking about it. Better to think about making the bus.

He caught the five-thirty bus at the Port Authority terminal and turned into Thorne Street exactly at six-thirty. The door was thrown open, and there stood his wife Kathy, with the twins, Ruth and Beth, dancing up and down.

"Happy birthday!" they cried, and threw their arms around him.

Arthur began to laugh. "So it was my birthday I forgot."

"There are thirty-three candles on your birthday cake," Ruth and Beth said. "Bet you can't blow out all thirty-three in one breath. You're getting too old!"

"But we'll give you three chances," Ruth added.

"Thank goodness for that," Arthur said, "and thank goodness for a mother who remembers everything—especially birthdays!"

2. In this selection, listen carefully for the voiced / ð /. Underline the words in which this phoneme appears.

Another Kleenex

---◆---

There are those of us who have itching eyes and a running nose. Do you feel as though you have swallowed a feather and it's stuck in your throat? Do you spend more money on Kleenex than on clothes? Do you wish your friends would go away and stop bothering you? Do you loathe your family? Your mother and father? Perhaps your sisters and brothers? Do you listen to the weather report and want to give up breathing?

If your answer is yes to all these questions, then cheer up—you're not alone. There are those of us who understand. We are the hay fever sufferers of the world. So let us gather together, listen to the pollen count every hour on the hour, and comfort each other in our misery. What was that you said? Another Kleenex? You feel as though a sneeze is coming on? Breathe deeply. That doesn't help? Take the whole box.

Chapter 5 Homework Review

A. Fill in the missing sounds using the symbols of the IPA. Write the number of sounds in each word.

EXAMPLE: breathe / bri_ð_ / __4__

1. months   / mʌn_____ / _____
2. thoroughly / ___ʌrəlɪ / _____
3. another   / ə___ʌ___ɚ / _____
4. thirst   / __ɜˆ_____ / _____
5. thousand   / __aʊ___ən__ / _____
6. although   / ɔl___oʊ / _____
7. through   / ___r___ / _____
8. rhythm   / rɪ_____ / _____
9. earthquake / ɜˆ_____weɪ__ / _____
10. birthday   / __ɜˆ_____eɪ / _____
11. throbbing / ___rɑ___ɪŋ / _____
12. anything   / ɛ__ɪ__ɪŋ / _____
13. brother   / ___rʌ___ɚ / _____
14. thought   / ___ɔ__ / _____

B. Circle the stressed syllable. Write the number of syllables in each word.

1. threat   _____
2. scribbled   _____
3. thousand   _____
4. sufferers   _____
5. thermometer _____
6. thoroughly   _____
7. throughout   _____
8. sympathetic _____
9. weather   _____
10. unannounced _____
11. authority   _____
12. examined   _____
13. hypochondriac _____
14. mathematics _____

C. Write the following words using the symbols of the IPA.

1. thought /   /
2. breath   /   /
3. death's /   /
4. smooth   /   /
5. health   /   /
6. breathe /   /
7. three   /   /
8. threat   /   /
9. tooth   /   /
10. they   /   /

D. *Additional review:* Voiced / ð / phrases

1. Repeat each phrase after your instructor using the voiced / ð / and placing your tongue between the upper and lower front teeth.

a.	to the theater	k.	in the meantime
b.	to the laundry	l.	up the hill
c.	to the store	m.	under the table
d.	by the way	n.	with the pencil
e.	with the scissors	o.	mail the letter
f.	put that there	p.	at the meeting
g.	lock the door	q.	with the knife
h.	it looks that way	r.	at the restaurant
i.	wake them up	s.	there they go
j.	turn them down	t.	at the movies

2. Compose five sentences using any of the phrases listed in Exercise D.

3. Answer each question in a complete sentence using the underlined phrase or word. Be sure to produce the voiced fricative / ð /.*

   a. Are you going <u>to the theater</u>?

   b. Are you going to <u>the store</u>?

   c. Are you going <u>to the movies</u>?

   d. Are you going <u>to the meeting</u>?

   e. Are you going <u>to the party</u>?

   f. Are you going <u>to the concert</u>?

   g. Are you going <u>to the basketball game</u>?

   h. Will you meet me <u>in the cafeteria</u>?

   i. Will you meet me <u>at the restaurant</u>?

   j. Shall I cut this <u>with the knife</u>?

   k. How's your <u>mother?</u>

   l. How's your <u>brother?</u>

   m. How's your <u>father</u>?

   n. Is <u>something</u> wrong?

   o. Is <u>everything</u> all right?

---

* The voiced **th** / ð / occurs in the frequently used article **the** and requires considerable practice.

p. Do you think you'll get <u>to the class</u> on time?

q. Can you get another ticket <u>for the play</u>?

r. Is this the way <u>to the subway</u>?

s. Would you like to go rowing <u>on the lake</u> with me?

t. Can you see <u>all the way to the top of the mountain</u>?

Reading Aloud

A. These selections focus on the accurate production of the lingua-dental fricatives: the voiceless / θ / and the voiced / ð /. Make sure that the tongue tip is placed between the upper and lower front teeth; do not omit these sounds at the end of a word.

Remember to link the words within phrases and stress important words, while maintaining the conversational tone of the word. Work for variety in pitch and clarity of articulation.

Divide the sentences into phrase units, using single and double slashes, and underline the stressed words.

> **EXAMPLE:**   <u>Doctor</u>, / <u>now</u> that you've <u>examined</u> me <u>thoroughly</u>, / <u>tell</u> me the <u>truth</u>. / /

A tape or your instructor may serve as your model for correct and fluent oral reading. Prepare to enact this dialogue in class.

The Patient and the Doctor

———◆———

PATIENT:	Doctor, now that you've examined me thoroughly, tell me the truth. I'm sure there's something terribly wrong with me!
DOCTOR:	Sorry to disappoint you, but I can't find anything wrong. You're in good health.
PATIENT:	In good health? That's impossible! I never thought I'd get to this office alive. I could hardly catch my breath.
DOCTOR:	Nevertheless, there's nothing the matter with you. I've gone over you with a fine-tooth comb.
PATIENT:	You're keeping something from me. I know it. My head is throbbing. My mouth is dry. I can hardly breathe.
DOCTOR:	Now, calm down. When I saw you two months ago, you told me you were at death's door. And all you had was a sore throat!
PATIENT:	It was a bad sore throat. I was sick for three weeks.
DOCTOR:	Three weeks?
PATIENT:	Well—two weeks.
DOCTOR:	How many weeks?
PATIENT:	Well, I was home for three days.
DOCTOR:	What a hypochondriac!
PATIENT:	Who's a hypochondriac?
DOCTOR:	You are, and that's the truth!
PATIENT:	I'm no such thing.

DOCTOR: Name another person who walks around with a thermometer sticking out of his pocket.

PATIENT: You should be more sympathetic.

DOCTOR: And you should let me worry about your health. Unless you want another opinion.

PATIENT: Of course not. You've taken care of me and my whole family—my mother, my father, my brother and sister. But my health does bother me.

DOCTOR: We both know that. And I really am sympathetic. Just try not to die a thousand deaths.

PATIENT: You're right. I'll try not to make a little thing into a big thing. Good-bye, and thank you.

The Other Day

———◆———

The other day, our math professor gave us an unannounced quiz. He told us he was thoroughly disgusted with us. "If you don't bother to do your homework, why should I bother teaching you?" he asked. "You gather together in this room and expect me to do all the work. I'm through being sympathetic! If you fail the next three quizzes, I have the authority to fail you for the course. There are another three weeks left in the semester. This is not a threat, just a statement of fact. Nevertheless, I want you to know how I feel. Now, I'm through lecturing. The rest lies with you."

I thought you should know that I did my math homework last night.

Vacation Plans

———◆———

I paid a visit to Matthew Witherspoon, our local authority on everything. I wanted his thoughts on my forthcoming trip.

"I hear you're spending a month in South America," he said, peering at me through his thick glasses. "When are you leaving?"

"In three weeks."

He thought for a moment. "Earthquakes. Unstable weather. The air's too thin. Hard to breathe up there. Get your teeth checked."

These things were coming at me thick and fast. "My teeth?"

"Lost three molars. Terrible dentists." He leaned toward me. "Don't let them know you're wealthy."

"Me? Wealthy? It took me a year to gather the money together." By this time, I was thoroughly alarmed.

He looked at me sympathetically. "Having second thoughts?" I had second thoughts and third thoughts, but I went anyway.

The weather was perfect. I had no trouble breathing. The guides helped me up the rocky paths. I bought hand-woven cloths in the markets. A little girl made me a wreath of flowers. The hotels were air-conditioned. The bathmat said "Welcome."

I paid a visit to Matthew Witherspoon when I returned. He said, "You look thin. Was the food that bad?"

"The food was fine, and the trip was thrilling." I leaned back in my chair and regarded him thoughtfully. "Tell me, how long ago were you in South America?"

He rubbed his nose with his thumb. "Hard to say. Thirty years ago, maybe more."

I nodded. "Well, things have changed in those thirty years."

"Anything's possible," he answered.

Target Sounds: / **f** / *and* / **v** /

Distinctive Features

/ f / and / v / are labio-dental oral fricatives.
/ f / is voiceless; / v / is voiced.

How Are / f / *and* / v / *Made?*

The upper front teeth rest lightly on the lower lip. These sounds are long in duration and released without interruption, unlike the plosive consonants, which are brief explosions.

/ f / is produced by directing the airstream through the narrow opening created by the light contact between the upper front teeth and the lower lip.

If you place your finger in front of your lips as you produce / f / in these words, you can feel the air as it is released.

EXAMPLE: famous   leaf   after

When / f / is produced in final position, the upper front teeth maintain contact with the lower lip. Although the released breath stream is weaker at the end of the word than in the initial position, it can be heard and felt as it is emitted.

EXAMPLE: if   rough   laugh

/ v / is produced when the upper front teeth rest lightly on the lower lip. There is no release of air.

If you place your hand at your larynx and produce / v / in these words, you can feel the vibration of the vocal cords.

EXAMPLE: very   leave   living

When / v / is produced in final position, the upper front teeth maintain contact with the lower lip. This phoneme is not voiced as strongly at the end of the word as in the initial position.

EXAMPLE: believe   olive   wave

So in contrasting these sounds, there is no vibration at the larynx for the / f / sound and no air released for the / v / sound.

What Are the Problems or Patterns in Spelling?

/ f / is represented by the digraphs **ph** and **gh** and the letters **f** and **ff.**

EXAMPLE: physics   tough   fine   office

/ v / is represented by the letters **v** and **f.**

EXAMPLE: vine   ever   relieve   of

What Are the Problems in Pronunciation?

/ f / may be produced as / p / if the lips are brought together.

EXAMPLE: *cup* instead of *cuff*

may be weak or unclear if articulatory placement is not precise or insufficient air is emitted.

EXAMPLE: *laugh* / læ / instead of / læf /

/ v / may be replaced by / b / if the lips are brought together.

EXAMPLE: *bury* instead of *very*

may be replaced by / f /.

EXAMPLE: *half* instead of *have*

may be pronounced / w / if the lips are rounded.

EXAMPLE: *west* instead of *vest*

Listening/Speaking

A. Compare the voiceless / f / and the voice / v / in the *initial position*. Are these words the same or different?

1	2	1	2	1	2
fan	van	fast	vast	fault	vault
few	view	fine	vine	feign	vain
ferry	very	feel	veal	folly	volley
fail	veil	file	vile	fairy	vary

Can you *feel* the difference as you repeat after your instructor?

Can you *hear* the difference between / f / and / v /?

Your instructor will say words from columns 1 and 2 for each pair. Indicate the pattern that you hear.

EXAMPLE: If you hear *few, view, few,* the pattern is 1 2 1.

Note: Students who speak Spanish, Russian, Chinese and other Asian languages, and German may need to work on distinguishing and producing / f /, / v /, and / b /; and / v / and / w /.

B. Observe the / f / and / v / sounds in *final position*. Omission of the final consonants changes the pronunciation and the meaning of the word.

> **EXAMPLE:**   bee—beef   grow—grove

1. Words with and without the final consonant / f /

1	2	1	2	1	2
say	safe	way	waif	she	sheaf
Lee	leaf	owe	oaf	lie	life
why	wife	low	loaf	caw	cough
rue	roof	sir	surf	bee	beef

2. Words with and without the final consonant / v /

1	2	1	2	1	2
say	save	slay	slave	grow	grove
row	rove	Lee	leave	way	wave
ray	rave	we	we've	dry	drive
doe	dove	day	Dave	lie	live

3. Contrasting / f / and / v / in *final position*

1	2	1	2	1	2
half	have	proof	prove	life	live
safe	save	grief	grieve	waif	wave
leaf	leave	shelf	shelve	surf	serve

C. Observe / f / and / v / contrasts in *medial position*.

1	2	1	2
surface	service	infest	invest
rifle	rival	safer	saver
refuse	reviews	wafer	waver

D. Underline the contrasting words in each sentence. As you read aloud, remember to produce the / f / and / v / sounds in the underlined words.

> **EXAMPLE:**   Put the <u>fan</u> in the <u>van</u>.

1. I feel the veal is too tough to eat.

2. That ferry is very old.

3. Have half an apple.

4. Can you prove that he had no proof?

5. It's his fault that the vault was robbed.

6. Can you prove that he had no proof of his identification?

7. I refuse to read your reviews of my book.

8. It isn't safe to save your money at home.

9. It is my belief that we must believe you.

10. He pointed the rifle at his rival.

E. Problems with / f /

1. / f / and / θ / may be confused.

1	2	1	2	1	2
fought	thought	first	thirst	sheaf	sheath
fret	threat	fin	thin	reef	wreath
free	three	fro	throw	whiff	with

2. Underline the contrastive words in each sentence. As you read aloud, remember to produce the / θ / and / f / sounds in the underlined words.

a. We three are free.

b. The death of the deaf boy shocked everyone.

c. Ruth fell off the roof.

d. At first, I had a terrible thirst for water.

e. Will you throw the ball to and fro?

f. I did not fret because of that threat.

g. Fred needs thread.

h. I thought they fought well.

i. Who placed that wreath on the reef?

j. The fin of that fish is very thin.

3. / v / and / w / may be confused.*

1	2	1	2
vain	wane	vary	wary
veal	we'll	vest	west
veer	we're	vine	wine

---

* The lips are rounded for the production of / w /. See the section on / w / in Chapter 7 for further work.

G. Compare the full verb form in column 1 with the contraction form in column 2. When the auxiliary verb **have** follows a noun or the pronouns **I, we,** or **you,** the shortened form **'ve** is used. Practice reading aloud.

	1	2
1.	I have lost my pen.	I've lost my pen.
2.	We have agreed to come.	We've agreed to come.
3.	You have got my notes.	You've got my notes.
4.	They have already gone.	They've already gone.
5.	I have had this work before.	I've had this work before.
6.	The books have come.	The books've come.
7.	I have been working.	I've been working.
8.	They have been away.	They've been away.
9.	Where have you been?	Where've you been.
10.	We have received many bills.	We've received many bills.

Listening/Writing

A. Listen carefully for the / f / and / v / as your instructor pronounces each word. Write the sound when it occurs in medial or final position using the symbols of the IPA. If / f / or / v / is not heard, write a dash in the space provided.

> **EXAMPLE:** five /__f____v_/   of /_____v_/   lab /_____—___/

1. few _____	7. efficient _____	13. identify _____
2. view _____	8. river _____	14. fifth _____
3. travel _____	9. service _____	15. nephew _____
4. curb _____	10. marble _____	16. expensive _____
5. thirsty _____	11. surface _____	17. elevators _____
6. believe _____	12. advertise _____	18. physician _____

B. Circle the word read aloud by your instructor.

1. grief	grieve	4. proof	prove
2. rifle	rival	5. safe	save
3. leaf	leave	6. fault	vault

7. ferry	very		9. few	view
8. refuse	reviews		10. infest	invest

C. Your instructor will select one of the words in parentheses and read the entire sentence aloud. Listen carefully and circle the word you hear. Practice reading each sentence aloud using either one of the words in parentheses.

1. Did you get a (few, view)?

2. Where's your (van, fan)?

3. He has only one (fault, vault).

4. Show us your (best, vest).

5. Look at my (rival, rifle).

6. That's an unusual (service, surface).

7. We don't need that (vote, boat).

8. I have (three, free) tickets for the game.

9. Their (thirst, first) was unbearable.

D. Circle the stressed syllable as each word is read aloud. Write the number of syllables in each word.

1. nephew	_____	7. evicted	_____
2. river	_____	8. photographed	_____
3. difficult	_____	9. efficient	_____
4. saved	_____	10. agency	_____
5. before	_____	11. afternoon	_____
6. identification	_____	12. service	_____

NAME: ______________________________ DATE: ______________

Chapter 5 Homework Review

A. Fill in the missing sounds using the symbols of the IPA. Write the number of sounds in each word.

EXAMPLE: favorite / f eɪ v ərɪt / 7

1. tough / tʌ___ / ______
2. physics / ___ɪ___ɪ___ ___ / ______
3. voiced / ___ɔɪs___ / ______
4. view / ___j___ / ______
5. survive / sɚ___aɪ___ / ______
6. private / praɪ___ɪ___ / ______
7. arrival / əraɪ___əl / ______
8. comfortable / kʌm___t___bə___ / ______
9. enough / ɪnʌ___ / ______
10. laughter / læ___ ___ɚ / ______
11. seventy-five / sɛ___ən___ɪ___aɪ___ / ______
12. cup of coffee / kʌpə___kɔ___ɪ / ______

B. Circle the stressed syllable. Write the number of syllables in each word.

1. advertise ______
2. refrigerator ______
3. approval ______
4. comfortable ______
5. office ______
6. voyage ______
7. everyone ______
8. suffered ______
9. revolt ______
10. infested ______

C. Complete the answer to each question using the contraction form. Practice reading aloud. Be sure your upper front teeth touch your lower lip for clear and accurate pronunciation of / f / and / v / sounds.

1. Where have you been these past two weeks?

   I ____________ been sick.

2. What have you been doing?

   I ____________ been looking for an apartment.

3. Have you decided to move?

   Yes, I ____________ decided to move.

4. Where have you been looking?

I _____ been looking in Queens.

5. Have you and your family been away?

Yes, we _____ been in New Jersey visiting our cousins.

6. Have you heard from John?

No, I haven't, but I _____ heard from his wife.

7. How have they been?

They _____ been fine and very busy.

8. Have they contacted their lawyer?

Yes, they _____ contacted her.

9. Have you and your friends been to Philharmonic Hall?

We _____ only been there twice this year.

10. Have you paid the doctor's bill?

No, we _____ not paid him yet.

11. Have you and your sister been shopping for Christmas?

Yes, we _____ started shopping.

12. Have your teachers given you much work this term?

Yes, they _____ given us too much work.

13. Have your sisters written to your uncle in Portugal?

Yes, they _____ written to him.

14. What have you done about getting a tutor?

I _____ done nothing. It's too late to get one.

D. Rewrite each question using the contraction form.

EXAMPLE: <u>Where have</u> you been?   <u>Where've</u> you been?

1. What have you read?

_____

2. How have you been?

_____

3. What have you done?

_____

4. Why have you gone away?

_____

5. Where have you been lately?

_____

E. Write the following words using the symbols of the IPA.

1. save　/　　　　/　　　5. we've　/　　　　/

2. safe　/　　　　/　　　6. nephew　/　　　　/

3. proof　/　　　　/　　　7. invest　/　　　　/

4. prove　/　　　　/　　　8. laughed　/　　　　/

F. *Additional review: / f / and / v / in medial position.* Circle the stressed syllable. Practice saying each word aloud, making certain that these sounds are given sufficient duration.

/ f /

confidential	affairs	refusal	comfortable
notify	platform	emphasize	sacrifices
photographers	suffered	verify	graphic

/ v /

arrival	revolution	relevant	investment
vivid	medieval	eventually	approve
vowel	average	survived	reservation

G. Select the appropriate word from Exercise F for each sentence and write it on the line. Circle the stressed syllable in the underlined word and practice reading the sentence aloud.

EXAMPLE:　*vowels:*　Some (vowels) may be difficult to pronounce.

1. _____ spend considerable money on film.

2. His nephew _____ a heart attack four months ago.

3. I'd like to confirm my airplane _____.

4. During a _____, some people make _____.

5. Can you _____ if she will _____ my application?

6. Please ⎯⎯⎯⎯⎯⎯ me when you move.

7. Some ⎯⎯⎯⎯⎯⎯ sounds are very difficult for Steven to pronounce.

8. Her ⎯⎯⎯⎯⎯⎯ designs are suitable for advertising.

9. This report is ⎯⎯⎯⎯⎯⎯.

10. Henry's ⎯⎯⎯⎯⎯⎯ proved to be profitable.

Reading Aloud

A. This dialogue focuses on the accurate production of the / f / and / v /. Make sure the upper teeth rest lightly on the lower lip. Do not omit these sounds at the end of a word. Remember to link the words within phrases and stress important words, while maintaining the conversational tone of the word. Work for variety in pitch and clarity of articulation.

Divide the sentences into phrase units, using single and double slashes, and underline the stressed words.

> **EXAMPLE:**   We have <u>$1,000</u> / for a <u>one-bedroom</u> <u>apartment</u> / on the <u>fifth</u> <u>floor</u> / of a <u>building</u> / with <u>no</u> <u>elevator</u>. / /

Your instructor may serve as your model for correct and fluent oral reading. Prepare to enact this dialogue in class.

Affordable Housing

◆

Ivan frowned at the figures on the back of the envelope. "I can afford $315, Sophia $350, and Philippe $320. We're still $15 short."

"I'll never return to Vermont," Sopha said fiercely, "except to visit."

"In that event," Philippe said, "I'll give up food and chip in the final fifteen."

"We have $1,000 for a one-bedroom apartment on the fifth floor of a building with no elevator," Ivan said.

"Sophia can have the bedroom," Philippe offered, "and my friend is giving us a sleep sofa for the living room."

"Is there a view of the Hudson River from the roof?" Sophia asked hopefully.

Ivan shook his head. "Afraid not. Just several other rooftops."

Sophia laughed. "Another unfulfilled dream. But I still intend to become a fashion designer."

"I shall become a world-famous photographer," Ivan said.

Philippe looked at his friends. "That's the future. Let's live in the present. We have a stove and refrigerator, and we're getting fabulous tips at the fancy restaurant where we work. What about telephone service, Ivan?"

"They'll install it this Friday," Ivan answered, "when we move in."

"I can't believe how fortunate we are," Sophia said, "to have finally found a place to live in New York that is affordable!"

"Provided, the landlord doesn't turn up on Friday to raise the rent another five dollars," Philippe said.

"Even if he does," Sophia said, "We'll find the funds. Think positive and everything will be fine!"

Target Sound: / h /

Distinctive Features

/ h / is a glottal oral fricative. It is voiceless.

How Is / h / *made?*

The tongue lies flat in the mouth. First, take a breath and then exhale. A strong stream of air can be heard as you release the / h / sound. The vocal bands are wide apart.*

If you place your finger in front of your lips as you produce / h / in these words, you can feel the air as it is released. There is no vibration at the throat. This sound does not appear in final position.

EXAMPLE: he   inhale   huge

What Are the Problems or Patterns in Spelling?

/ h / is represented by the letters **h** and **wh**.

EXAMPLE: house   behavior   who

is silent in some words with **ho** and **he.**

EXAMPLE: hour   honest   heir

What Are the Problems in Pronunciation?

/ h / may be omitted.

EXAMPLE: *ad* instead of *had*

may be added when it doesn't belong in the word.

EXAMPLE: *high* instead of *eye*

Listening/Speaking

A. Listen to your instructor and repeat: / h /   / h /   / h /

B. Repeat the following syllables with / h /: / hi /   / heɪ /   / hu /

---

* The space between the vocal cords is known as the glottis.

Note: Speakers from the Caribbean may need to work on distinguishing and producing the / h / sound.

C. Repeat after your instructor. Be sure you hear and feel the released breath when you produce the / h / in these words.

1. Initial position

he	who	hockey
hit	hook	hire
hate	hose	how
hat	whole	huge
help	hundred	hole

2. Medial position

inhale	unhurt	behind
ahead	unhealthy	inherit
ahead	exhale	reheat
behavior	withhold	rehearse

D. Observe the / h / in *initial position*. Omission of the / h / changes the pronunciation and the meaning of the word.

   EXAMPLE: high—I   hit—it

1. Words with and without the / h / sound

1	2	1	2	1	2
herb	Herb	as	has	ate	hate
ad	had	is	his	at	hat
and	hand	old	hold	all	hall
ale	hail	heir	hair	ear	hear
eye	high	I'd	hide	Ike	hike

Can you *feel* and *hear* the differences as you repeat after your instructor?

Your instructor will say words from columns 1 and 2 for each pair. Indicate the pattern that you hear.

   EXAMPLE: If you hear *herb, Herb, herb,* the pattern is 1 2 1.

E. Underline the contrasting words in each sentence. As you read aloud, remember to produce / h / only when indicated.

   EXAMPLE: <u>His</u> son <u>is</u> ill.

1. Herb has an herb garden.

2. That magazine had an interesting ad.

3. I am high on his list.

4. The heir to that fortune has gray hair.

5. All the students are in the hall.

6. I can't hear with my left ear.

7. There was a hedge at the edge of the garden.

8. Ike likes to hike.

9. I'd like to hide.

10. Tom can't eat because of the heat.

Listening/Writing

A. Listen carefully for the / h / as your instructor pronounces each word. Write the sound when it occurs in the initial or medial position using the symbols of the IPA. If / h / is not heard, write a dash in the space provided.

    EXAMPLE: huge / _h_____ /   odd / ____—____ /

1. hard _____	6. behind _____	11. humid _____
2. had _____	7. who _____	12. hour _____
3. hotel _____	8. heir _____	13. hospital _____
4. head _____	9. hair _____	14. humor _____
5. ad _____	10. all _____	15. hall _____

B. Circle the stressed syllable as each word is read aloud. Write the number of syllables in each word.

1. hard _____	6. helpful _____	11. inherit _____
2. exhalation _____	7. headwaiter _____	12. prohibit _____
3. how _____	8. unhappy _____	13. heard _____
4. behavior _____	9. human _____	14. anyhow _____
5. honors _____	10. hated _____	15. hundred _____

C. Your instructor will say three words from column 1 and 2 for each pair. Write the pattern that you hear.

      EXAMPLE: If you hear *hat, at, hat,* write 1 2 1.

	1	2	*Pattern*
1.	hate	eight	____ ____ ____
2.	hide	I'd	____ ____ ____
3.	hair	heir	____ ____ ____
4.	high	eye	____ ____ ____
5.	hold	old	____ ____ ____
6.	hear	ear	____ ____ ____
7.	heat	eat	____ ____ ____
8.	hire	ire	____ ____ ____
9.	his	is	____ ____ ____
10.	had	ad	____ ____ ____

Chapter 5 Homework Review

A. Fill in the missing sounds using the symbols of the IPA. Write the number of sounds in each word.

    EXAMPLE: home / __h__ oʊm /   __3__

1. ahead   / ə___ɛd /   _____   7. ear   / ___ɚ /   _____

2. hospital / ___ɑspɪtəl /   _____   8. whole   / ___oʊl /   _____

3. huge   / ___jdʒ /   _____   9. healthy   / ___ɛ___θɪ /   _____

4. humid   / ___j___mɪ___ /   _____   10. hazard   / ___ ___ ___ɚd /   _____

5. hear   / ___ɪɚ /   _____   11. husky   / ___ʌ___ ___ɪ /   _____

6. I   / ___ /   _____   12. inhale   / ɪ___ ___eɪl /   _____

B. Fill in the missing sounds using the symbols of the IPA.

1. as   / ___ ___ /   6. exhale   / ɛ___ ___ ___eɪ /

2. has   / ___ ___ ___ /   7. inherit   / ɪn___ɛ___ɪ___ /

3. is   / ___ ___ /   8. whose   / ___ ___ ___ /

4. his   / ___ ___ ___ /   9. honors   / ___nɚ___ /

5. helped / ___ɛl___ ___ /   10. hoped   / ___oʊ___ ___ /

C. *Additional review: / h / in medial position.* Circle the stressed syllable. Practice saying each word aloud, making certain that the / h / is produced clearly.

inheritance	rehire	prohibit
reheat	behavior	coherent
rehearse	behind	inhibitions
alcoholic	adhesive	withhold

D. Select five words from the list in Exercise C and compose a sentence for each. Underline each selected word in the sentence, and practice reading aloud using correct pronunciation.

E. Select the appropriate word from Exercise C for each sentence and write it on the line. Circle the stressed syllable in the underlined word, and practice reading the sentence aloud.

EXAMPLE: *ahead:*   The car (a̲head) is stalled.

1. We'll have to _____ often before our opening night.

2. Henry's _____ from his aunt was small.

3. It is illegal to _____ information from the Internal Revenue Service.

4. They did not _____ wine at the restaurant.

5. I hope they will _____ me next semester.

6. Mary gave a _____ report to the police.

7. We need more _____ tape for this bandage.

8. Helen had no _____ about speaking up to her employer.

9. Tom's _____ at work was very popular.

10. I stood _____ you in the registration line.

Reading Aloud

A. This selection focuses on the accurate production of the / h / sound. Make sure that you exhale air as you produce this sound.

Remember to link the words within phrases and stress important words, while maintaining the conversational tone of the word. Work for variety in pitch and clarity of articulation.

Divide the sentences into phrase units, using single and double slashes, and underline the stressed words.

> **EXAMPLE:** During the <u>day</u>, / <u>Helen</u> was <u>headmistress</u> at <u>Haddon Hall</u>. / /

A tape or your instructor may serve as your model for correct and fluent oral reading. Prepare to enact this dialogue in class.

Moving Ahead

Harry and Helen Hill hoped to own a small hotel. They happily enrolled in a hotel management course at night and worked very hard. During the day, Helen was the headmistress at Haddon Hall, a private high school for one hundred young women who hated school. Harry taught history and was also the hockey coach.

In the summer, Harry was hired as a headwaiter in a high-class resort hotel. Helen helped in the kitchen. They graduated with highest honors, but they didn't have enough money to buy a hotel. Helen and Harry were very unhappy and hated their long hours, but they worked hard, hoping something would happen. At the end of the school year, they heard that Haddon Hall had a huge debt and would be closing.

With the money they had saved, Helen and Harry took over Hadden Hall and now run a hotel management school for the hundred young women who used to hate school.

Reviewing the Fricatives / θ ð f v h /

A. Divide the following words from the passage in Section D into syllables. Circle the stressed syllable, and write the number of syllables in each word.

1. movies _____
2. television _____
3. authentic _____
4. theater _____
5. another _____
6. huge _____

7. breathing _____
8. fabulous _____
9. confined _____
10. conflict _____
11. failures _____
12. triumphs _____

13. magnificent _____
14. unfaithful _____
15. invalid _____
16. thrilling _____
17. invited _____
18. performance _____

B. Select an appropriate word from Exericse A to complete the sentence. Practice reading aloud for accuracy and fluency.

1. The _____ was _____ to a wheelchair.

2. The actor gave a _____ _____ in the play.

3. She left her husband because he was _____.

4. He had to drop a course because of a _____ in his schedule, but he had trouble

   finding _____ course.

5. Life is a mixture of _____ and _____.

C. Write five sentences of your own using the vocabulary listed in Exercise A.

D. This reading passage focuses on the fricatives / f v θ ð h /. Be sure to produce these sounds accurately. Remember to produce the / h / when appropriate. Do not confuse / f / with / θ /, or / v / with / ð /.

Divide the selection into phrase units, using single and double slashes, and underline the stressed words.

    EXAMPLE: The <u>critics</u> <u>rave</u> / and <u>lines</u> <u>form</u> / at the <u>box</u> <u>office</u>. / /

Your instructor may serve as your model for correct and fluent oral reading.

The Fabulous Invalid

Film, video, and television provide entertainment for all. They're easily available and inexpensive. Watching TV? Find you're ravenously hungry? Raid the fridge between commercials. Sitting in the movie house? Feast on popcorn while watching five previews before the feature film finally flashes on the screen.

I go to the movies, I watch television, and I love popcorn! However, if push comes to shove, what I love most is the theater—living, breathing theater. I know it's always on the verge of dying. That's why it's referred to as "The Fabulous Invalid." Plays fail and theaters go dark. The Invalid is gravely ill. Then, one evening, something marvelous happens. A play opens and it's a hit! The critics rave, and lines form at the box office.

How wonderful to watch as the houselights dim, the curtains part, and the play unfolds before our eyes. No one eats popcorn or drinks sodas. All eyes are riveted on the stage until the final curtain falls and applause fills the theater. Once again, the Fabulous Invalid has worked her magic.

What is so special about the theater for me? I've thought about it often. The difference, I feel, lies in the fact that while we *watch* movies, we *live* theater.

CHAPTER SIX

The Nasals

Only three sounds in the English language are produced through the nose:

/ m /   as in *my*

/ n /   as in *now*

/ ŋ /   as in *sing*

The feature of nasality is a function of the soft palate, also known as the velum. Unlike the hard palate, the soft palate is capable of movement and has a certain limited flexibility.

1. It may be elevated and extended back to the wall of the throat, closing the passage to the nose.

2. It may be lowered so that there is a passageway between the palate and the wall of the throat.

When the soft palate is raised, it prevents the airstream from exiting through the nose. Thus the air is forced out through the mouth, as are the sounds.

When the soft palate is lowered, there is no longer any obstruction, and the sounds are emitted through the nose.

The nasal sounds are all voiced, but each has different articulatory placement.

/ m /   bilabial (both lips come together)

/ n /   lingua-alveolar (tongue tip on the upper gum ridge)*

/ ŋ /   lingua-velar (back section of the tongue against the soft palate)

The nasal phonemes are not cognates. The / m / and / n / appear in initial, medial, and final positions. The / ŋ /, however, occurs only in medial and final position following a vowel sound, as in **bring** and in **nothing.** As continuants, the nasal phonemes are prolonged, providing a rich, resonant quality to the voice.

---

* The tongue tip touches the upper gum ridge for the production of / t /, / d /, / l /, and / n /.

Target Sounds: / m / and / n /

Distinctive Features

/ m / and / n / are nasal continuants. They are voiced.
/ m / is bilabial; / n / is a lingua-alveolar sound.

How Are / m / and / n / Made?

The soft palate is lowered, permitting sounds to be emitted through the nose.
/ m / is made by pressing the lips lightly together and producing a humming sound.

If you place your hand at your larynx and produce / m / in these words, you can feel the vibration of the vocal cords.

EXAMPLE: me   him   summer   stamp

When you pronounce / m / in final position, the lips remain together and the sound is prolonged.

EXAMPLE: some   calm   hymn   comb

/ n / is made by raising the tongue tip and pressing it firmly on the upper gum ridge (alveolar) behind the upper front teeth.
If you place your hand at your larynx and produce / n / in these words, you can feel the vibration of the vocal cords.

EXAMPLE: know   ten   runner   tent

When you pronounce / n / in final position, the tongue tip maintains contact with the upper gum ridge and the sound is prolonged.

EXAMPLE: line   sane   burn   sign

What Are the Problems or Patterns in Spelling?

/ m / is represented by the letters **m, mm, mn,** and **mb.**

EXAMPLE: my   summer   column   bomb

/ n / is represented by the letters **n, nn, gn, kn,** and **pn.**

EXAMPLE: new   sunny   gnat   knew   pneumonia

What Are the Problems in Pronunciation?

/ m / may be omitted or unclear if the lips are not brought together.

EXAMPLE: *see* instead of *seem*

tie instead of *time*

/ n / may be pronounced / m / if the lips are closed and the tongue is not raised against the upper gum ridge.

EXAMPLE: *comb* instead of *cone*

same instead of *sane*

may be omitted.

EXAMPLE: *say* instead of *sane*

sigh instead of *sign*

Listening/Speaking

A. Compare the / m / and / n / sounds in the *initial position*. Are these words the same or different?

1	2	1	2	1	2
me	knee	mitt	knit	might	night
mice	nice	meat	neat	male	nail
mow	know	meal	kneel	map	nap
mat	gnat	mere	near	moat	note

Can you *feel* the difference as you repeat after your instructor?

Can your *hear* the difference between / m / and / n /?

Your instructor will say three words from columns 1 and 2 for each pair. Indicate the pattern that you hear.

   EXAMPLE: If you hear *me, knee, me,* the pattern is 1 2 1.

B. Observe the / m / and / n / sounds in *final position*. Omission of the final consonants changes the pronunciation and the meaning of the word.

   EXAMPLE: sea—seam   see—seen

Note: Students who speak Spanish and Asain languages may need to work on distinguishing and producing / m / and / n /.

1. Words with and without the final consonant / m /

1	2	1	2	1	2
see	seem	tea	team	say	same
bee	beam	die	dime	day	dame
lie	lime	rye	rhyme	tie	time
crow	chrome	too	tomb	rue	room
gay	game	who	whom	grew	groom

2. Words with and without the final consonant / n /

1	2	1	2	1	2
see	seen	may	main	sue	soon
sea	scene	too	tune	do	dune
bee	bean	blow	blown	tea	teen
lie	line	toe	tone	Fay	feign
die	dine	bow	bone	ray	rain

3. Contrasting / m / and / n / in final position

1	2	1	2	1	2
am	an	gum	gun	warm	warn
same	sane	rum	run	foam	phone
some	son	bum	bun	seem	seen
beam	bean	comb	cone	Tim	tin
hem	hen	game	gain	doom	dune

C. Observe / m / and / n / sounds in medial position

1	2	1	2
simmer	sinner	mummy	money
gaming	gaining	foaming	phoning
Emmy	any	tumor	tuner

D. Underline the contrastive words in each sentence. As you read aloud, remember to produce the final / m / and / n / sounds in the underline words.

EXAMPLE: He <u>came</u> without his <u>cane</u>.

1. Some people dislike the sun.

2 May dropped her ice cream cone while looking for her comb.

3. What can you gain when you play that game.

4. It's impossible to dine for a dime.

5. His warm coat is worn.

6. Does your son need some money?

7. Tim kept his money in a tin box.

8. Wipe the gum off the gun.

9. Then we met them at the movie.

10. That scene of the sea is a fine painting.

11. Run and get some rum for our party tonight.

12. Warn Manny that it's warm outside.

E. Compare the full form of the verb in column 1 with the contraction form in column 2. When the verb **am** follows the pronoun **I,** the shortened form **'m** is used. Practice reading aloud.

1. I am late.	I'm late.
2. I am expecting you.	I'm expecting you
3. I am worried about my job.	I'm worried about my job.
4. I am busy.	I'm busy.
5. I am going to the doctor.	I'm going to the doctor.
6. I am wondering about that.	I'm wondering about that.
7. I am interested in the job.	I'm interested in the job.
8. I am disappointed.	I'm disappointed.
9. I am sorry.	I'm sorry.
10. I am not going away.	I'm not going away.

Listening/Writing

A. Listen carefully for the / m / and / n / as your instructor pronounces each word. Write these sounds when they occur in initial, medial, or final position using the symbols of the IPA. If / m / or / n / is not heard, write a dash in the space provided.

> **EXAMPLE:** mine / _m_____ _n_ /   long /_____—_____ /

1. game	_____	6. dine	_____	11. token	_____
2. gain	_____	7. dime	_____	12. anytime	_____
3. remember	_____	8. arm	_____	13. manners	_____
4. nine	_____	9. sandwich	_____	14. friend	_____
5. agent	_____	10. mind	_____	15. conversation	_____

B. Circle the word read aloud by your instructor.

1. mock	knock	6. maim	mane
2. gum	gun	7. warm	warn
3. same	sane	8. comb	cone
4. some	son	9. foam	phone
5. dime	dine	10. lame	lane

C. Your instructor will select one of the words in parentheses and read the entire sentence aloud. Listen carefully and circle the word you hear. Practice reading each sentence aloud using either one of the words in parentheses.

1. That is a wild (sea, scene).

2. I'd like to buy a (cone, comb).

3. Have you observed any (gains, games) lately?

4. (Whom, who) did you meet?

5. Does Tom need a (nap, map)?

6. Is this (nail, mail) necessary?

7. What type of (gun, gum) do you want?

8. He didn't want to (die, dine) on his birthday.

9. We need (Jan, jam) immediately.

10. Those (sane, same) persons appeared three times.

D. Circle the stressed syllable as each word is read aloud. Write the number of syllables in each word.

1. wondering	_____	6. insurance	_____	11. sandwich	_____
2. mayonnaise	_____	7. nickels	_____	12. jammed	_____
3. disconnected	_____	8. motto	_____	13. continue	_____
4. agent	_____	9. scene	_____	14. knowledge	_____
5. disappointed	_____	10. tomato	_____	15. economy	_____

F. Your instructor will say three words from columns 1 and 2 for each pair. Indicate the pattern that you hear.

EXAMPLE: If you hear *some, son, some,* write 1 2 1.

1	2	Pattern
1. mice	nice	___ ___ ___
2. male	nail	___ ___ ___
3. map	nap	___ ___ ___
4. seem	scene	___ ___ ___
5. gum	gun	___ ___ ___
6. warm	worn	___ ___ ___
7. ram	ran	___ ___ ___
8. dimes	dines	___ ___ ___
9. game	gain	___ ___ ___
10. comb	cone	___ ___ ___

Chapter 6 Homework Review

A. Fill in the missing sounds using the symbols of the IPA. Write the number of sounds in each word.

      EXAMPLE: games / geɪ <u>m</u> z /   <u> 4 </u>

1. nineteen   / ___ aɪ ___ ti ___ /   _____   9. someone / sʌ ___ ___ ʌ ___ /   _____

2. foreign   / fɑrɪ ___ /   _____   10. anytime / ɛ ___ ɪtaɪ ___ /   _____

3. insurance   / ɪ ___ ʃurə ___ ___ /   _____   11. mind / ___ aɪ ___ ___ /   _____

4. something   / sʌ ___ θɪŋ /   _____   12. finish / ʃɪ ___ ɪʃ /   _____

5. enough   / ɪ ___ ʌ ___ /   _____   13. alone / əlou ___ /   _____

6. dimes   / daɪ ___ ___ /   _____   14. next / ___ ɛk ___ t /   _____

7. rinsing   / rɪ ___ ___ ɪŋ /   _____   15. funny / fʌ ___ ɪ /   _____

8. climb   / klaɪ ___ /   _____   16. comb / kou ___ /   _____

B. Circle the stressed syllable. Write the number of syllables in each word.

1. disappointed _____   6. announce _____

2. disconnected _____   7. criminal _____

3. I'm _____   8. economics _____

4. chicken _____   9. accommodations _____

5. salad _____   10. among _____

C. Write the following words using the symbols of the IPA.

1. don't /   /   5. blame /   /

2. lent /   /   6 train /   /

3. scene /   /   7. team /   /

4. seem /   /   8. jammed /   /

D. *Additional review: / m / and / n / in medial position:* Circle the stressed syllable. Practice saying each word aloud, prolonging / m / and / n /.

/ m /

comfortable	commitments	prominent	exempt
numerous	demands	economy	themselves
plumber	immigrants	immediate	employment

/ n /

announcer's	conscious	unnecessary	accountant
incomplete	conscience	inquire	gymnastics
abnormal	government	identify	pronunciation

E. Select five words from the list above in Exercise D and compose a sentence for each. Underline each selected word in the sentence, and practice reading aloud using the correct pronunciation.

F. Select an appropriate word from Exercise D for each sentence and write it on the line. Circle the stressed syllable in the underline word, and practice reading the sentence aloud.

EXAMPLE: *incomplete:* My paper is still <u>incom(plete)</u>.

1. The _____ found the leak somewhere in the ceiling.

2. Is the _____ concerned about the economy?

3. Did you hear the _____ report on those nine fires?

4. Tom was not _____ during the operation.

5. It is important to _____ about that course before you register.

6. Mary's _____ skills were noted by the judge.

7. They found _____ in disagreement with the Internal Revenue Service.

8. That woman is a _____ attorney.

9. I was quite _____ at that meeting.

10. _____ people have made _____ to donate blood.

G. Complete the answer to each question using the appropriate contraction.

> **EXAMPLE:** Are you leaving soon?   Yes, <u>I'm</u> leaving soon.

1. Are you staying overnight? Yes, _____ staying overnight.

2. Who are you visiting? _____ visiting my sister.

3. Are you going alone? _____ going alone.

4. Which train are you taking? _____ taking a nine o'clock train.

5. What are you doing tonight? _____ working tonight.

6. Are you free for coffee? _____ not free now.

7. Are you mad? Yes, _____ mad at my friend.

8. Are you concerned about your math? No, _____ not concerned.

9. Are you graduating now? No, _____ not graduating now.

10. When are you expecting that letter? _____ expecting that letter by tomorrow.

Reading Aloud

A. These selections focus on the accurate production of / m / and / n /. Do not omit these sounds at the end of a word. Remember to link the words within phrases and stress important words, while maintaining the conversational tone of the word. Work for variety in pitch and clarity of articulation.

Divide the sentences into phrase units, using single and double slashes, and underline the stressed words.

> **EXAMPLE:** <u>Come</u> <u>on</u>, / <u>Nat</u>, / we'll <u>miss</u> the <u>train</u>. / /

A tape or your instructor may serve as your model for correct and fluent oral reading. Prepare to enact this dialogue in class.

Matt and Nat

———◆———

MATT: Come on Nat, we'll miss the train.

NAT: Okay. What a mob! We'll never make the train. It's too jammed.

MATT: Push, Nat, push. Jam your way in. Give it all you've got.

NAT: Lady, mind your manners. That was my arm you broke.

WOMAN: Young man, arm or no arm, I'm making this train. Out of my way.

MATT: Madam, you can be on my team anytime.

WOMAN: Kill or be killed, that's my motto. Now, one more push and we're in. Let's move it, men!

NAT: We made it. Or is that my arm caught in the door?

WOMAN: What's an arm among friends?

MATT: I feel like a ham sandwich.

WOMAN: Make mine chicken salad—with tomato and a big dab of mayonnaise.

NAT: Very funny.

MATT: Madam, do you mind moving to one side so I can talk to my friend?

WOMAN: Be my guest. Meet you at the next mob scene. Bye-bye, boys. Have fun. My station is next.

MATT: It's been a pleasure, madam.

NAT: Mine, too.

B. Practice reading the following passage aloud. Remember to produce the / m / and / n / sounds distinctly.

Minute by Minute

Nina, this is my last telephone call from a public phone. I've lost enough money in phone booths. I'm planning to buy a cell phone soon, but I'm uncertain about which plan to choose. Lennie told me I could get 500 minutes on weekends plus 100 minutes on weekdays for a monthly rate of $39. Do I use more minutes during the week? Maybe. I think I do. I know I make at least seven phone calls every morning—business calls. Oh, you think I need more minutes during the week—more than 100 minutes for the entire month? Another plan would include a maximum of 900 minutes for a month of weekend and weekday phone use for much more money. I'm completely confused. Mathematics was never my strong point. All I know is, by this time tomorow evening, I'll be calling you on my cell phone, but only for a few minutes. No, I can't give you my number. I'm also charged when you call me. That would use up too many of my precious minutes. Bye for now. See you tomorrow.

Exercise

List the words with the / m / and / n / sounds.

Target Sounds: / ŋ /

Distinctive Features

/ ŋ / is a lingua-velar sound and a nasal continuant. It is voiced.

How Is / ŋ / made?

The soft palate is lowered, permitting sounds to be emitted through the nose. The back section of the tongue is raised and touches the soft palate.

If you place your hand at your larynx and produce / ŋ / in these words, you can feel the vibration of the vocal cords.

EXAMPLE: thing   think   jungle   bringing

When the / ŋ / is produced in final position, the soft palate and the back section of the tongue maintain contact, and the sound is prolonged. The / ŋ / never occurs in the initial position in the English language.

What Are the Problems or Patterns in Spelling?

/ ŋ / is represented by the letters **ng, nk,** and **nc** in medial and final position.*

EXAMPLE: sing   sink   finger   thinking   zinc

What Are the Problems in Pronunciation?

/ ŋ / may be omitted and replaced by / n /.

EXAMPLE: *dancin* instead of *dancing*

   thin instead of *thing*

may be pronounced / ŋg / at the end of stem words or when **ng** letters precede the vowel of the following word.

EXAMPLE: *ring* / rɪŋg / instead of / rɪŋ /

   long ago / lɔŋgəgou / instead of / lɔŋəgou /

Listening/Speaking

A. Compare the / n / and / ŋ / sounds in the *final position.* Are these words the same or different?

---

* In some African languages, the / ŋ / is a frequently occurring sound produced in the initial position as well as in the medial and final position.

Note: Native and non-native speakers who often produce / n / instead of / ŋ / may need to work on distinguishing and producing these sounds. Educated speakers retain / ŋ / in casual speech.

1	2		1	2		1	2
lawn	long		ban	bang		clan	clang
kin	king		ton	tongue		stun	stung
sin	sing		thin	thing		ran	rang
win	wing		gone	gong		fan	fang
pan	pang		run	rung		sun	sung

Can you *feel* the difference as you repeat after your instructor?

Can your *hear* the difference between / n / and / ŋ /?

B. Observe / n / and / ŋ / in *medial position.*

1	2		1	2
sinning	singing		banning	banging
winning	winging			

C. / ŋ / and / ŋk / may be confused.

1. Final position

1	2		1	2		1	2
bang	bank		sang	sank		thing	think
rang	rank		wing	wink		bring	brink
sting	stink		ring	rink		ping	pink

2. Medial position

1	2		1	2
banging	banking		winging	winking
stinging	stinking		singing	sinking

D. Underline the contrastive words in each sentence. As you read aloud, remember to produce the / ŋ / and / n / sounds in the underlined words.

> **EXAMPLE:** A song about the <u>sun</u> was <u>sung</u> by the children.

1. We haven't mowed the lawn for a long time.

2. Did the king and his kin attend the wedding?

3. The phone rang and he ran to answer it.

4. As the boat sank, they sang their last song.

5. Is it a sin to sing rock songs in church?

6. Mary skated within the ring at the rink.

7. To stay thin, don't think of a thing to eat.

8. The statesman with the highest rank just rang me up.

9. I was already gone when the gong rang.

10. His problem could bring him to the brink of disaster.

E. / ŋ / and / ŋg / may be confused.

1. The / ŋ / sound is produced when **ng** letters occur at the end of a stem word or before a vowel in the word that follows, or when a suffix is added to the stem.

Stem Word	*Stem + Suffix*	*Final **ng** Before a Vowel*
/ ŋ /	/ ŋ /	/ ŋ /
sing	singer	Sing a song.
long	longer	Where's Long Island?
young	younger	He's a young actor.
hang	hanger	Hang up the phone

2. The / ŋg / sound is produced when ng occurs within a stem word or in a comparative superlative adjective.

Stem Word		*Adjective*	
/ ŋg /		/ ŋg /	
English	finger	stronger	strongest
language	angry	younger	youngest
linger	single	longer	longest

F. Underline the contrastive words in each sentence. As you read aloud, remember to produce the / ŋ / and / ŋg / sounds in the underlined words.

1. Although she was strong, her two sisters were stronger.

2. Tom hung up his coat before he complained of hunger.

3. Why are they swinging on a broken swing.

4. The longest belt on the rack is too long for me.

5. The singer did not linger in the hotel lobby.

6. Hang your coat on this hanger.

7. Not a single actress could sing on key.

Listening/Writing

A. Listen carefully for the / ŋ / as your instructor pronounces each word. Write the sound when it occurs in medial or final position using the symbols of the IPA. If / ŋ / is not heard, write a dash in the space provided.

> **EXAMPLE:** wrong /____ŋ____ /   win /____—____ /

1. banging _____
2. orange _____
3. ton _____
4. tongue _____

5. brink _____
6. thin _____
7. thing _____
8. think _____

9. untangle _____
10. younger _____
11. lawn _____
12. long _____

B. Circle the word read aloud by your instructor.

1. ban   bang   bank
2. ran   rang   rank
3. pin   ping   pink
4. sin   sing   sink

5. win   wing   wink
6. thin   thing   think
7. sun   sung   sunk
8. clan   clang   clank

C. Your instructor will select one of the words in parentheses and read the entire sentence aloud. Listen carefully and circle the word you hear. Practice reading each sentence aloud using either one of the words in parentheses.

1. Have you seen your (king, kin) recently?

2. They (sank, sang) only three.

3. Which boy (rang, ran)?

4. Some people like to (sin, sing).

5. Do you know what that (bang, ban) is?

6. I hate to look at that big (fan, fang).

D. Circle the stressed syllable as each word is read aloud. Write the number of syllables in each word.

1. recommended _____
2. antagonize _____
3. anxiety _____

4. angry _____
5. younger _____
6. continual _____

7. worrying _____
8. evening _____
9. unpleasant _____

Chapter 6 Homework Review

A. Fill in the missing sounds using the symbols of the IPA. Write the number of sounds in each word.

EXAMPLE: ink / ɪ_ŋ_k / ___3___

1. gone   / ___ɑ___ /   _____   9. angry   / æ___grɪ /   _____
2. gong   / ___ɑ___ /   _____   10. single   / sɪ___ ___əl /   _____
3. banging / bæ___ɪ___ /   _____   11. language / læ___gwɪʤ /   _____
4. rang   / ræ___ /   _____   12. hungry   / hʌ___ ___rɪ /   _____
5. rank   / ræ___ ___ /   _____   13. belonging / bəlɔ___ɪŋ /   _____
6. banker   / bæ___ ___ɚ /   _____   14. hung   / hʌ___ /   _____
7. crank   / ___ ___æ___ ___ /   _____   15. morning   / mɔr___ɪ___ /   _____
8. slamming / slæ___ɪ___ /   _____   16. ringing   / rɪ___ɪ___ /   _____

B. Circle the stressed syllable. Write the number of syllables in each word.

1. hired   _____   6. happening _____
2. anxious   _____   7. radiators _____
3. oranges   _____   8. worrying   _____
4. changed   _____   9. gangster   _____
5. anxiety   _____   10. younger   _____

C. Write the following words using the symbols of the IPA.

1. sin   /   /   4. thin   /   /   7. sun   /   /
2. sing /   /   5 thing   /   /   8. sung /   /
3. sink /   /   6. thinking /   /   9. sunk /   /

Reading Aloud

A. This passage focuses on the accurate production of the / ŋ / sound. Do not omit this sound at the end of a word. Remember to link the words within phrases and stress important words, while maintaining the conversational tone of the passage. Work for variety in pitch and clarity of articulation.

Divide the sentences into phrase units, using single and double slashes, and underline the stressed words.

> **EXAMPLE:**   When <u>Mr. Orange called</u> his <u>landlord</u>, / <u>Mr. Hong</u>, / the <u>secretary hung</u> up. / /

Your instructor may serve as your model for correct and fluent oral reading. Prepare to read aloud in class.

Mr. Orange

◆

Did you hear about Mr. Orange and his problems with his apartment? All sorts of terrible things were happening. The radiators were banging all night. The upstairs neighbors kept playing records and singing at the top of their lungs until five in the morning. Some kids were using the hallway as a skating rink and were slamming against the Oranges' door. When Mr. Orange called his landlord, Mr. Hong, the secretary hung up. Then Mrs. Orange began having anxiety attacks and stopped cooking and cleaning. When they started getting crank calls every evening, Mrs. Orange told her husband she was leaving and moving in with her cousin, Inga, who lived in Washington Heights.

This made Mr. Orange so angry that he hired a smart young lawyer, who was recommended by his banker, Mr. Winkler. The lawyer told Mr. Orange that they could stop worrying. The building had so many violations that Mr. Hong would be anxious to stay out of court. And do you know what? The lawyer was right. It didn't take long for the banging, the singing, and the skating to stop. As for the crank telephone calls, Mr. and Mrs. Orange changed their number.

Reviewing the Nasals: / m ŋ n /

A. Divide the following words from the passage in Exercise D into syllables. Circle the stressed syllable, and indicate the number of syllables in each word.

1. interview	_____	7. millionaire	_____	13. condominium	_____
2. investment	_____	8. neighbors	_____	14. responsibility	_____
3. advice	_____	9. business	_____	15. anonymous	_____
4. brokers	_____	10. discovered	_____	16. columns	_____
5. nieces	_____	11. plumber	_____	17. important	_____
6. mended	_____	12. insurance	_____	18. agent	_____

B. Select the appropriate word from Exercise A to complete each sentence. Practice reading aloud for accuracy and fluency.

1. He brought his torn jacket to the tailor to be _____.

2. He _____ a leak in the sink and called in the _____.

3. The teacher had an _____ piece of _____ to give to his students.

4. The real estate _____ said that buying a _____ was a sound _____.

5. Running a _____ is a major _____.

C. Write five sentences of your own using the vocabulary listed above.

D. This review passage concentrates on the three nasal sounds: / m /, / n /, and / ŋ /. Be sure to produce these sounds accurately, remembering they are emitted nasally. Do not confuse / m / with / n /, or with / ŋ / in final position.

Divide the selection into phrase units, using single and double slashes, and underline the stressed words.

> **EXAMPLE:**   He bought a million-dollar mansion with a swimming pool, / a private plane, / and five motorcyles. / /

Your instructor may serve as your model for correct and fluent oral reading.

Norman the Millionaire

———◆———

Norman Nieman was one of those middle-aged, anonymous men who worked in middle management and made no ripples in the world. That all changed when he won ten million dollars in the lottery. Suddenly, he was the Man of the Moment. He made the front page of the *New York Times*. Investment brokers hounded him day and night. Women wanted him to marry them. Nephews and nieces he hardly knew knocked on his door. The telephone never stopped ringing.

Norman decided there was only one thing to do—spend his money. He bought a million-dollar mansion with a swimming pool, a private plane, and five motorcycles. He endowed universities. He spent his money until there was not a penny left. He even owed the government money. So he sold his mansion, his plane, and four of his five motorcycles. He was welcomed back to his job in middle management. Now, every morning, he gets on his gleaming motorcycle, his one remaining luxury, and roars off to work. Norman is once again a contented man.

CHAPTER SEVEN

Lateral and Glides

Four sounds make up the lateral and glides groups of consonants:

/ l /	as in *lie*
/ r /	as in *read*
/ w /	as in *we*
/ j /	as in *you*

These phonemes are voiced and orally produced.*

The / l / is classified as a lateral. Its special feature is that the air is emitted over the sides of the tongue, which are lowered and not in contact with the upper side teeth. This phoneme occurs in initial, medial, or final position, as in **late, million,** or **feel.**

The / r /, / w /, and / j / sounds are classified as glides. Unlike stops and fricatives, these phonemes are produced while the articulators are in motion. In the production of / r / and / j / the tongue slides from its first articulatory position to that of the vowel that follows. In the production of / w /, the lips move from a rounded articulatory position to that of the vowel that follows. As you produce the first two sounds in the words **we** and **want,** you can feel the change in the movement of the lips.

All four phonemes can be sustained. There is less obstruction in the mouth than is characteristic of consonants. Because of their dual function, they are sometimes classified as semivowels. The / w / and / j / phonemes precede vowels, as in **war** and **away,** and in **youth** and **cure,** and never occur in final position.

The / l / and the / r / phonemes appear in initial and final consonant clusters.

/ l /		/ r /	
play	help	frame	farm
flight	self	grass	guard**

---

* The / l /, / w /, and / r / sounds are often troublesome for many speakers of Asian languages as well as some native speakers of English.

** The **r** in final consonant clusters may be omitted by speakers in certain sections of the United States.

253

As you produce these sounds, you will notice that the articulatory placement is different.

/ l /	lingua-alveolar (tongue tip against the upper gum ridge)
/ w /	bilabial (both lips rounded)
/ r /	lingua-palatal (tongue tip raised toward the roof of the mouth)
/ j /	lingua-palatal (midsection of the tongue against the central section of the roof of the mouth)

Unlike most of the phonemes in American English, the / r / phoneme offers problems in classification and in pronunciation. This phoneme may function as a consonant or a vowel. As a consonant, the **r** appears before vowel sounds in initial and medial position. For the production of / r / in **run** and **arrive** and for the consonant clusters in **price** and **grow,** the tongue tip curls up toward the middle of the roof of the mouth but makes no contact; the sides of the tongue maintain contact with the upper back teeth. In initial consonant clusters, the **r** combines with plosives and fricatives before a vowel sound, as in **drop, praise, free,** and **three.**

When the **r** follows a vowel sound, it functions like a vowel in several different spelling patterns that represent variations in pronunciation. This is further complicated by regional differences in the pronunciation of the **r** following a vowel sound.*

Variations in pronunciation and spelling patterns are found in

1. the diphthongs / ɪɚ ɛɚ ɔɚ ʊɚ /, as in **beer, bear, bore,** and **boor.**

2. the low back vowel and the final **r** / ɑr /, as in **car, card,** and **cart.**

3. the mid-central vowel / ɜˆ / for stressed syllables as in **bird, world, search,** and **fur.**

4. the low-central vowel / ɚ / for unstressed syllables as in **mother, actor, scholar,** and **leisure.***

Target Sound: / l /

Distinctive Features

/ l / is a lingua-alveolar oral lateral. It is voiced.

How Is / l / Made?

The tongue tip presses firmly on the upper gum (alveolar) ridge.** The airstream is emitted laterally over the sides of the tongue, which do not touch the upper back teeth.

If you place your hand at your larynx and produce / l / in these words, you feel the vibration of the vocal cords.

EXAMPLE: light   allow   call   slow

---

* In General American Dialect and in most sections of the country, except in areas in the East and South, the final **r** following a vowel is pronounced as a schwa with **r** coloring / ɚ /. Certain Eastern and Southern areas omit the final **r** and use a schwa without **r** coloring / ə /. In **ar** words, the **r** may be omitted and the vowel lengthened, as in **car** / kɑː /.

** In order to achieve / l / in final position, it may be necessary for some students to place the tongue tip against the back of the upper front teeth.

There are two variants of the / l / commonly used in English. The clear / l / occurs in the initial position and in consonant clusters before a vowel. The tongue tip is raised and pressed directly against the upper gum ridge and then released. The back section of the tongue is relatively low.

EXAMPLE: leaf   lip   laugh   black   glass

The dark / l / occurs in the final and medial position. The tongue tip may be placed on the upper gum ridge or further back behind the alveolar ridge away from the teeth. The / l / sound is prolonged as this contact is maintained. The back section of the tongue is relatively high.

EXAMPLE: bill   almost   coal   million

The dark / l / occurs in final consonant clusters.

EXAMPLE: milk   help   shelf   bald

The dark / l / occurs in unstressed syllables that end in **le** or **el.** The syllabic / l / is preceded by a short vowel sound known as the schwa / ə /.

EXAMPLE: battle   / bætəl /   tunnel   / tʌnəl /

whistle   / wɪsəl /   muzzle   / mʌzəl /

riddle   / rɪdəl /   label   / leɪbəl /

What Are the Problems or Patterns in Spelling?

/ l / is represented by the letters **l** and **ll.**

EXAMPLE: line   silk   hill

is silent.

EXAMPLE: talk   could   calm

What Are the Problems in Pronunciation?

/ l / may be omitted in final position.

EXAMPLE: *row* instead of *roll*

awe instead of *all*

may be omitted or indistinct in consonant clusters when the tongue tip lies flat in the mouth.*

---

* See Appendix B for additional practice with consonant clusters.

Note: Speakers of Asian languages may need to work on distinguishing and producing / l /, with special attention given to the final position. Speakers of French, Italian, and Spanish tend to use the clear / l / in final position. Some native speakers of English also have problems with the pronunciation of / l /.

EXAMPLE: *back* instead of *black*

head instead of *held*

/ l / may be replaced by / r /.

EXAMPLE: *rise* instead of *lies*

may be replaced by / n /.

EXAMPLE: *niece* instead of *lease*

Listening/Speaking

A. Listen to your instructor and repeat: / l /   / l /   / l /   / l /

B. Repeat the following syllables with / l / using a raised tongue position and no lip movement.

/ lɑ /   / li /   / loʊ /   / leɪ /   / lu /

C. Repeat after your instructor using the directions given below.

1. Initial position

When the clear / l / occurs at the beginning of a word and precedes a vowel sound, the tongue tip presses against the upper gum (alveolar) ridge and is then released.

leak	led	log
lit	lack	loved
lake	low	lady
light	loom	liked
local	location	lobster

2. Medial position*

alarm	only	ugly
alive	silent	alone
follow	belong	collect
hello	believe	absolutely
elevator	eleven	eyelashes

3. Final position

When / l / occurs at the end of a word, the tongue tip is placed behind or on the upper gum ridge, not against the upper front teeth.

---

* The clear / l / is also used in medial position when / l / precedes a vowel sound.

It is helpful to practice these pairs of words to feel the differences in the tongue position between the initial (clear) and the final (dark) / l / sound.

1	2	1	2
let	tell	lit	till
light	tile	lame	mail
law	all	lap	pal

For the final / l /, hold the tongue firmly on the roof of the mouth.

all	fell	candle
feel	whole	stable
cell	still	horrible
April	bowl	wonderful
while	turtle	technical

D. Problems with / l /

1. Omission of the final / l / changes the pronunciation and the meaning of the word.

   EXAMPLE: bow—bowl   why—while

   a. Repeat after your instructor, remembering to place the tongue tip on or behind the upper gum ridge.

1	2	1	2	1	2
awe	all	may	mail	toe	toll
say	sale	bay	bale	fee	feel
sea	seal	pie	pile	sew	soul
me	meal	tie	tile	ray	rail

   b. Underline the contrastive words in these sentences. As you read aloud, remember to produce the final / l / in the underlined word.

   EXAMPLE: <u>May</u> I get the <u>mail</u> for you?

   1) I won't row unless you give me a roll.

   2) All the students were in awe of the president.

   3) The shoemaker tried to sew the sole of the shoe.

   4) I can't see the small seal.

   5) Did you say the clock is on sale?

   6) We are all in awe of Mel.

   7) I feel the dentist's fee is too high.

8) The chef promised to cook a special meal for me.

9) Fay hoped she didn't fail the exam.

10) Matilda didn't say if she wanted to sail.

2. / l / and / w / may be confused.

a. Repeat after your instructor. Remember to place the tongue tip on the upper gum ridge for the production of / l /. Keep the tongue tip flat and the lips rounded for the pronunciation of / w /.

1	2	1	2
lies	wise	lied	wide
life	wife	lake	wake
late	wait	lip	whip
lot	what	leap	weep
let	wet	lane	wane

b. Underline the contrastive words in these sentences. As you read aloud, remember to produce the / l / and / w / in the underlined words.

   EXAMPLE: <u>Wait</u> for me if I'm <u>late</u>.

1) The wise old man told no lies.

2) He was so late we couldn't wait.

3) Don't let the dog wet the floor.

4) The lady with the wide hat lied.

5) I'll weep if you leap.

6) His energy began to wane as he jogged down the lane.

7) Last week, Tom complained about the leak in his kitchen.

8) Life with his wife was pleasant.

9) What do you plan to build on this lot?

10) Wake me when we arrive at the lake.

3. / l / and / n / may be confused.

Repeat after your instructor, making sure that your tongue tip is pressed on the upper gum ridge for the production of / l / and / n / sounds. Remember to nasalize the / n /.

a. Initial position

1	2	1	2	1	2
night	light	need	lead	knack	lack
know	low	niece	lease	name	lame
not	lot	neighbor	labor	knock	lock
knit	lit	noose	loose	nip	lip

Can you *feel* and *hear* the difference between / l / and / n / as you repeat after your instructor?

Your instructor will say three words from columns 1 and 2 for each pair. Indicate the pattern that you hear.

> **EXAMPLE:** If you hear *low, know, low,* the pattern is 1 2 1.

b. Final position

1	2	1	2	1	2
seen	seal	fawn	fall	Ben	bell
sin	sill	win	will	fine	file
sane	sale	been	Bill	main	mail
pin	pill	ten	tell	pan	pal
kin	kill	pain	pale	bone	bowl

c. Medial position

1	2	1	2
falling	fawning	failing	feigning
willing	winning	allot	a knot
filed	fined	told	toned

4. Underline the contrastive words in each sentence. As you read aloud, remember to produce the final / n / and / l / sounds in the underlined words.

> **EXAMPLE:** <u>Tell</u> me about the <u>ten</u> people.

a. Have you seen that small seal?

b. Sane people avoided the crowded sale.

c. He feigned surprise when he failed the exam.

d. The fawn did not fall when he was first shot.

e. My mail is in the main post office.

f. Who threw the bone into the bowl?

g. Where have you been, Bill?

h. The pale student was in pain.

i. Our team will win the game.

j. The war did not kill all of his kin.

E. Consonant Clusters

Omission of / l / in consonant clusters changes the meaning and the pronunciation of the word.

Repeat after your instructor, remembering to place your tongue tip on the upper gum ridge for the / l / blends.

1. Initial position

bl		*fl*		*cl*	
bed	bled	fame	flame	came	claim
bank	blank	fed	fled	camp	clamp
bade	blade	fat	flat	keen	clean

gl		*sl*		*pl*	
go	glow	sew	slow	pay	play
gas	glass	say	slay	pace	place
gazed	glazed	sight	slight	peasant	pleasant

2. Final position

ld		*lt*		*lk*	
ball	bald	fell	felt	mill	milk
coal	cold	hall	halt	sill	silk
mile	mild	bowl	bolt	hull	hulk

lp		*lf*	
hell	help	sell	self
gull	gulp	shell	shelf
yell	yelp	wool	wolf

3. Underline the contrasting words in each sentence. As you read aloud, remember to produce the / l / sound in the consonant clusters in the underlined words.

EXAMPLE: We didn't <u>pay</u> to see the <u>play</u>.

a. All his slacks were thrown into sacks.

b. The man with the bald head caught the ball.

c. On a mild day, I can walk at least a mile.

d. The back of the chair was painted black.

e. After the fight, they caught a quick flight to Alaska.

f. They never came to claim their baggage.

g. My sister has a slight problem with her sight.

h. She cleaned the place at a very fast pace.

i. Bill gazed at the glazed pottery.

j. On the plane, Tom developed a pain in his ears.

F. Syllabic Consonants

When **l** follows consonants **b, d, k, p, s, t,** or **z** at the end of a word, it is known as a syllabic consonant because another syllable is formed. The schwa / ə / is pronounced between the last two consonants.

EXAMPLE: bat<u>tle</u>   ta<u>ble</u>

Repeat after your instructor, giving special attention to the final / l /.

<u>ble</u> / bəl /	<u>dle</u> / dəl /	<u>kle</u> / kəl /	<u>ple</u> / pəl /
able	puddle	nickel*	sample
label*	ladle	tackle	example
terrible	medal*	miracle	staple

<u>stle</u> / səl /	<u>tle</u> / təl /	<u>zle</u> / zəl /
castle	bottle	easel*
hustle	little	dazzle
whistle	metal*	nozzle

G. Compare the full form of the verb in column 1 with the contraction form in column 2. When the auxiliary verb **will** follows the pronoun or the noun, the shortened form **'ll** is used.

EXAMPLE: I will write son.   <u>I'll</u> write soon.

1. I will go later.	I'll go later.
2. We will write tomorrow.	We'll write tomorrow.
3. You will see us soon.	You'll see us soon.
4. He will be paid tomorrow.	He'll be paid tomorrow.
5. You will be expected to come.	You'll be expected to come.
6. She will arrive at five.	She'll arrive at five.
7. They will follow your car.	They'll follow your car.

---

* Note the spelling variations in these categories of syllabic **l** words.

8. What will we do?   What'll we do?

9. That will be all.   That'll be all.

10. Where will you go?   Where'll you go?

Listening/Writing

A. Listen carefully for the / l / as your instructor pronounces each word. Write these sounds when they occur in initial, medial, or final position using the symbols of the IPA. If / l / is not heard, write a dash in the space provided.

        EXAMPLE: lily /_l_____l_/   hill /_____l_/ calm /____—____/

1. collect	_____	6. lovely	_____	11. bulbs	_____
2. eyelashes	_____	7. help	_____	12. young	_____
3. talk	_____	8. electric	_____	13. replied	_____
4. old	_____	9. marry	_____	14. July	_____
5. alert	_____	10. firmly	_____	15. false	_____

B. Circle the word spoken by your instructor.

1. awe	all	6. night	light
2. sew	sole	7. knock	lock
3. see	seal	8. ten	tell
4. wise	lies	9. win	will
5. wait	late	10. seen	seal

C. Your instructor will select one of the words in parentheses and read the entire sentence aloud. Listen carefully and circle the word you hear. Practice reading each sentence aloud using either one of the words in parentheses.

1. He has a difficult (life, wife).

2. The dog looked for his (bone, bowl).

3. We won't (need, lead) you.

4. Lulu doesn't have a (niece, lease).

5. He (pays, plays) so well.

6. Who broke the (shell, shelf)?

7. Our (neighbor, labor) is appreciated.

8. Last year they had no (say, sale).

9. What kind of (life, knife) does he have?

10. Where are those (pains, planes)?

D. Circle the stressed syllable as each word is read aloud. Write the number of syllables in each word.

1. ruin	_____	6. alert	_____	11. absolutely	_____
2. eyelashes	_____	7. sweetly	_____	12. dialogue	_____
3. peculiar	_____	8. happily	_____	13. brilliant	_____
4. nineteen	_____	9. bachelor	_____	14. complained	_____
5. allowance	_____	10. ugly	_____	15. likable	_____

E. Your instructor will say three words from columns 1 and 2 for each pair. Write the pattern that you hear.

> **EXAMPLE:** If you hear *say, sail, say,* write 1 2 1.

1	2	*Pattern*
1. row	role	_____ _____ _____
2. mow	mole	_____ _____ _____
3. toe	toll	_____ _____ _____
4. sea	seal	_____ _____ _____
5. bow	bowl	_____ _____ _____
6. pay	play	_____ _____ _____
7. gas	glass	_____ _____ _____
8. head	held	_____ _____ _____
9. bet	belt	_____ _____ _____
10. made	mailed	_____ _____ _____

F. Prepare to read this selection aloud in class. Remember to link words within phrases and stress important words, while maintaining the conversational tone of the reading passage. Work for variety in pitch and clarity in articulation.

Divide the sentences into phrase units, using single and double slashes, and underline the stressed words.

> **EXAMPLE:** His <u>left</u> <u>leg</u> was <u>mangled</u> / in the <u>elevator</u> <u>door,</u> / and <u>tragically,</u> / he will <u>always</u> <u>walk</u> with a <u>limp.</u> / /

A tape or your instructor may serve as your model for correct and fluent oral reading.

Your instructor will read the following selection aloud. Listen carefully for the / l / and underline the words in which this phoneme appears.

Alas, Poor Lionel!

———◆———

RECEPTIONIST:	Help! Help! I'm calling the police! No large dogs allowed in this office.
WOMEN:	Down, Lionel. Stop licking the young lady. He's only being friendly.
RECEPTIONIST:	Get that animal away from me.
WOMEN:	Lionel is not an animal, he's a full bred English sheepdog. Large but gentle as a lamb. He's here on legal business to see Lorna Fallon of Fallon, Fallon, Fallon, and Dewlap.
RECEPTIONIST:	Our chief litigator?
WOMEN:	Lionel is suing our building and the elevator company. His left leg was mangled in the elevator door, and tragically, he will always walk with a limp.
RECEPTIONIST:	This law office deals with people, madam.
WOMEN:	None of that lip! Lionel is the last of a long line of champions. Loads of blue ribbons. Now that's all over. He's no longer perfect. Kennels refuse to show him. Now he's only a dog. How would you like to live with that?
RECEPTIONIST:	A dog's life's not too bad. Sorry, Lionel, lie down. I didn't mean to hurt your feelings. I'll tell Miss Fallon you're here. What is your name, madam?
WOMEN:	Just say that Lionel is willing to see Miss Fallon.

Chapter 7 Homework Review

A. Fill in the missing sounds using the symbols of the IPA. Write the number of sounds in each word.

EXAMPLE: willing / wɪ_l_ɪŋ / _5_

1. belong / bə___ɔŋ / _____
2. while / waɪ___ / _____
3. I'll / aɪ___ / _____
4. animal / æ___ɪ___ə___ / _____
5. police / ___ə___is / _____
6. only / ou_____ɪ / _____
7. half / hæ___ / _____
8. lamb / ___æ___ / _____

9. alive / ə___aɪv / _____
10. listen / ___ɪsə___ / _____
11. styles / staɪ_____ / _____
12. licking / ___ɪ___ɪ___ / _____
13. likable / ___aɪ___əbə___ / _____
14. litigator / ___ɪ___ɪ___eɪ___ə / _____
15. legal / ___ɪ___ə___ / _____
16. little / ___ɪtə___ / _____

B. Circle the stressed syllable. Write the number of syllables in each word.

1. until _____
2. technological _____
3. absolutely _____
4. eleven _____
5. delighted _____
6. collect _____

7. telephoned _____
8. ruin _____
9. peculiar _____
10. old-fashioned _____
11. bottle _____
12. happily _____

C. Write the following words using the symbols of the IPA.

1. glasses / /
2. whole / /
3. hold / /
4. sweetly / /
5. false / /

6. ball / /
7 bald / /
8. planted / /
9. ugly / /
10. she'll / /

D. Write the appropriate contractions for the full form verbs using the space provided. Practice reading aloud.

 EXAMPLE: She will want to help.   <u>She'll</u> want to help.

1. I will _____ telephone you next week.

2. He will _____ lock your neighbor's door.

3. He will _____ mail your letter.

4. They will _____ believe you.

5. She will _____ collect her check this afternoon.

6. You will _____ feel better later on.

7. I will _____ tell you all about it.

8. What will _____ they do next July?

9. It will _____ rain today.

10. Who will _____ pay the bill?

E. *Additional review: / l / in medial position.* Circle the stressed syllable. Practice saying each word aloud, making certain that / l / is produced clearly.

alarm	election	elated
allow	relieved	delete
complaints	delicious	illuminate
delegate	technologies	effectively

F. Select five words from the list in Exercise E and compose a sentence for each. Underline each selected word in the sentence and practice reading aloud using the correct pronunciation.

1. _____

2. _____

3. _____

4. _____

5. _____

G. Select the appropriate word from Exercise E to complete each sentence. Circle the stressed syllable in the underlined word, and practice reading the sentence aloud.

> **EXAMPLE:** They did not a(low) us to leave early.

1. The false _____ annoyed the firemen.

2. The yellow lights did not _____ the room very well.

3. Mary worked _____ until eleven o'clock.

4. She was _____ when she was notified about her new job.

5. New _____ require special skills for employment.

6. My neighbor was a _____ to our labor union's conference.

7. We were _____ to get a quick reply to our letter.

8. Our _____ were ignored by the landlord.

9. I was advised to _____ those last words in my announcement.

10. Did you vote in the last _____?

Reading Aloud

A. This dialogue focuses on the accurate production of the / l / phoneme. Make sure the tongue tip touches the upper gum ridge, *not* the teeth, and do not omit this sound at the end of a word. Remember to link the words within phrases and stress important words, while maintaining the conversational tone of the dialogue. Work for variety in pitch and clarity of articulation.

Divide the sentences into phrase units, using single and double slashes, and underline the stressed words.

> **EXAMPLE:** <u>Last</u> <u>night</u> / you <u>used</u> up a <u>box</u> of <u>Kleenex</u>. / /

A tape or your instructor may serve as your model for correct and fluent oral reading. Prepare to enact this dialogue in class.

Lulu and Billy

———◆———

BILLY:	Lulu, you're always crying. Last night you used up a box of Kleenex.
LULU:	I can't help it, you don't love me!
BILLY:	Of course I love you.
LULU:	Then let's get married.
BILLY:	If I love you, do I have to marry you?
LULU:	Don't you want to spend your whole life with little Lulu?
BILLY:	I like my life just the way it is.
LULU:	For eleven months, I've let you ruin my life. Well, I don't care! Go ahead! Run off to London, or California, with that other love of your life.
BILLY:	London! California! Other woman! Lulu, you're losing your mind.
LULU:	I don't want to live with you any more. I want to marry you.
BILLY:	I can't. I still go to college.
LULU:	I'll go to work.
BILLY:	You're already working.
LULU:	I'm getting old.
BILLY:	You're only nineteen.
LULU:	In July, I'll be twenty! I'll be old and ugly and nobody will look at me.
BILLY:	Now, collect yourself. Look, your false eyelashes are coming loose.
LULU:	They're not false. They all belong to me.

BILLY: Lulu, why don't we talk about this in July, when you're "old and ugly."

LULU: I can't last till July. What about April?

BILLY: But that's next month!

LULU: Please, Billy.

BILLY: All right. In April.

LULU: Oh, Billy, you are absolutely wonderful!

BILLY: Now, blow your nose and put your glasses on. And one last thing—
         put your eyelashes back on. They just fell off.

Target Sound: / w /

Distinctive Features

/ w / is a bilabial oral glide. It is voiced.

How Is / w / Made?

The lips are very rounded and protruded. The tongue tip is anchored behind the lower front teeth. The back of the tongue is raised slightly. The / w / does not appear in final position.*

If you place your hand at your larynx, you can feel the vibration of the vocal cords when you produce / w / in these words. If you place your finger at your lips, you will feel little or no air.

EXAMPLE: west   away   quiet

What Are the Problems or Patterns in Spelling?

/ w / is represented by the letters **w, wh,** ** **on** and **qu.**

EXAMPLE: w̲ar   w̲here   o̲nce   q̲uarrel

♦ is silent when it precedes the letter **r.**

EXAMPLE: wrong   wrap   write

♦ is silent in the word toward / tɔrd /.

♦ is silent in some words with the letters **wh.**

EXAMPLE: who / hu /   whole / houl /

What Are the Problems in Pronunciation?

/ w / may be produced as / v /.

EXAMPLE: *vest* instead of *west*

---

* The letters **ow** in **window, swallow,** and **own,** represent the / ou / sound. The letters **ew** in **view** represent the / u / sound; in **sew** they represent the / ou /. The letters **ow** in **now** and **how** represent the / au / sound.

** In most sections of the United States, many educated speakers use the / w / instead of / hw / in **wh** words such as **what, whether,** and **why.** The / hw / sound is a combination of the voiceless fricative / h / and the voiced semivowel glide / w /. It is phonemic and can be used to distinguish **whale** and **wail, whine** and **wine, what** and **watt.** This distinction is not made by most newscasters today.

Note: Speakers of German, Russian, and Asian languages may need to work on distinguishing and producing the / w / sound.

Listening/Speaking

A. Listen to your instructor and repeat: / wə /   / wə /   / wə /

B. Repeat the following syllables with / w /, making certain to round the lips:

/ wi /   / weɪ /   / woʊ /   / wɔ /

C. Repeat after your instructor. Be sure that the tongue tip is flat and the lips are rounded.

1. Initial position

wet	once	waste	which*
won't	works	wise	whether
would	wondering	warning	what
wind	wandering	wash	when
weak	weapons	wax	why

2. Medial position

away	bewilder	coward
aware	request	acquire
award	awhile	between
awake	vowel	require
always	anyone	beware

D. Problems with / w /

1. / w / and / l / may be confused.

   a. Repeat after your instructor. Make sure that the tongue tip is flat behind the lower teeth for the production of / w /. The tongue tip is raised and pressed against the upper gum ridge when the / l / is pronounced. The sides of the tongue are lowered.

1	2	1	2	1	2
weight	late	wide	lied	week	leak
wed	led	wife	life	wake	lake
wit	lit	weep	leap	wine	line
weave	leave	wet	let	wise	lies

   Can you *feel* and *hear* the differences between the / w / and the / l / as you repeat after your instructor?

   Your instructor will say three words from columns 1 and 2 for each pair. Indicate the pattern that you hear.

   EXAMPLE: If you hear *wait, late, wait*, the pattern is 1 2 1.

---

* Some instructors in certain dialect areas may prefer the / hw / phoneme for words with **wh** spelling.

b. Underline the contrastive words in each sentence. As you read aloud, remember to produce the / w / and / l / sounds in the underlined words.

EXAMPLE: Howard prefers to work under a <u>white</u> <u>light</u>.

1. It is never too late to reduce your weight.

2. He was led to believe he would wed Wanda on Wednesday.

3. Last week, there was a leak in my kitchen.

4. I waited in a long line to buy some wine.

5. It is wise not to tell lies.

6. Don't wake me until we get to the lake.

7. Lay these papers aside on your way to the office.

8. John was lax when he had to wax the floor.

9. I can't leave until I weave this scarf.

10. His queer story is still not clear to me.

2. / w / and / v / may be confused.

a. Repeat after your instructor. For the / w / sound, the lips are rounded; for the / v / sound, the upper teeth press lightly on the lower lip.

1	2	1	2
west	vest	worse	verse
wail	veil	wise	vise
wine	vine	we	V
went	vent	why	vie

b. Underline the contrastive words in each sentence. As you read aloud, remember to produce the / w / and / v / sounds in the underlined words.

EXAMPLE: Mr. <u>Vine</u> drinks only <u>wine</u>.

1) Be wary if your hours never vary.

2) Victor bought an attractive vest when he was out west.

3) Before we went shopping, the plumber installed the vent.

4) Why do you always vie with me?

5) We used a "V for victory" symbol in our graphic design.

6) The woman with the black veil did not wail at the funeral.

7) His verse is worse than his prose.

8) The vicar wanted a wicker chair.

9) We'll have some veal tonight.

10) The carpenter thought it wise to use a vise.

E. Consonant Clusters

1. Omission of / w / in consonant clusters changes the meaning and pronunciation of the word. Repeat after your instructor, remembering to round your lips for the / w / sound.

   EXAMPLE: cake—quake

1	2	1	2
skis	squeeze	keen	queen
scare	square	kick	quick
skid	squid	tin	twin
scholar	squalor	court	quart

2. Underline the contrasting words in each sentence. As you read aloud, remember to produce the / w / in the underlined words.

   EXAMPLE: The poor <u>scholar</u> lived in <u>squalor</u>.

   a. I had a scare while walking in Washington Square Park.

   b. Don't let the binding on your skis squeeze your boot.

   c. My twin sister created a sculpture out of tin.

   d. The horse gave his trainer a quick kick.

   e. Kit decided to quit her job.

   f. The man in the brown coat likes to quote Shakespeare.

   g. It's quite easy to fly that kite.

   h. The court reporter ordered a quart of milk.

Listening/Writing

A. Listen carefully for the / w / sounds as your instructor pronounces each word. Write this sound when it occurs in the initial or medial position using the symbols of the IPA. If / w / is not heard, write a dash in the space provided.

EXAMPLE: wait /_w_____ /   away /_____w____ /   wrap /_____—_____ /

1. verse   _____
2. worse   _____
3. quarrel   _____
4. only   _____
5. one   _____

6. quality   _____
7. wreck   _____
8. award   _____
9. twice   _____
10. vineyards _____

11. require   _____
12. awakened   _____
13. reply   _____
14. toward   _____
15. wrong   _____

B. Circle the word spoken by your teacher.

1. lies   wise
2. leak   weak
3. lake   wake
4. line   wine
5. laid   wade

6 veil   wail
7. verse   worse
8. vest   west
9. lied   wide
10. leave   weave

C. Circle the stressed syllable as these words are read aloud. How many syllables in each word?

1. suggestion   _____
2. value   _____
3. differences   _____
4. preferably   _____
5. considerably   _____

6. possibility   _____
7. sufficient   _____
8. extremely   _____
9. quality   _____
10. coincidence   _____

D. Your instructor will select one of the words in parentheses and read the entire sentence aloud. Listen carefully and circle the word you hear. Practice reading each sentence aloud using either one of the words in parentheses.

1. He did not want to leave the (west, vest).

2. That (wail, veil) frightened the child.

3. We can't (weave, leave) this.

4. We don't need another (week, leak).

5. He went to the (wake, lake) this morning.

6. We'll need more (line, wine) on our boat.

7. Isn't this (clear, queer)?

8. Who dislikes the (lies, wise)?

E. Your instructor will say three words from columns 1 and 2 for each pair. Write the pattern that you hear.

      EXAMPLE: If you hear *late, weight, late,* write 1 2 1.

	1	2	*Pattern*
1.	let	wet	____ ____ ____
2.	leave	weave	____ ____ ____
3.	lake	wake	____ ____ ____
4.	clear	queer	____ ____ ____
5.	wake	quake	____ ____ ____
6.	verse	worse	____ ____ ____
7.	vent	went	____ ____ ____
8.	vest	west	____ ____ ____
9.	vicar	wicker	____ ____ ____
10.	leak	week	____ ____ ____

Chapter 7 Homework Review

A. Fill in the missing sounds using the symbols of the IPA. Write the number of sounds in each word.

    EXAMPLE: away / ə__w__eɪ / __3__

1. while / ____aɪ____ / _____
2. wines / ____aɪ____ ____ / _____
3. values / væ____juɪ____ / _____
4. twice / t____aɪ____ / _____
5. five / ____aɪ____ / _____

6. vowels / ____aʊ____ə____z / _____
7. require / re____ ____aɪɚ / _____
8. one / ____ʌ____ / _____
9. winter / ____ɪntɚ / _____
10. awake / ə____ ____ ____ / _____

B. Circle the stressed syllable. Write the number of syllables in each word.

1. investigate _____
2. favorite _____
3. unusual _____
4. wedding _____
5. travelled _____

6. wonderful _____
7. coward _____
8. qualified _____
9. question _____
10. visiting _____

C. Write the following words using the symbols of the IPA.

1. sweet /   /
2. west /   /
3. vest /   /
4. quick /   /

5. when /   /
6. whose /   /
7. once /   /
8. quiet /   /

D. *Additional review: / w / in medial position.* Circle the stressed syllable. Practice saying each word aloud, making certain / w / is produced clearly.

delinquency	reward	languages
requirements	subways	inquiry
cowardly	acquaintance	meanwhile
colloquial	bequest	midweek

E. Select five words from the list in Exercise D and compose a sentence for each. Underline each selected word in the sentence and practice reading aloud using the correct pronunciation.

1. _____

2. _____

3. _____

4. _____

5. _____

F. Select the appropriate word from Exercise D to complete each sentence. Circle the stressed syllable in the underlined word, and practice reading the sentence aloud.

   EXAMPLE: William acted (co)wardly.

1. Juvenile _____ is a major problem in this city.

2. The _____ are a necessity in large cities.

3. Wanda is an _____ of mine.

4. The victim's family offered a _____ for information.

5. Harry speaks three _____ .

6. The college responded promptly to my _____ .

7. _____ expressions are informal.

8. Tom's aunt left him a large _____ when she died.

9. Howard's job interview was held _____ .

10. They fulfilled all the _____ for graduation.

Reading Aloud

A. This dialogue focuses on the accurate production of the / w /. Make sure the lips are rounded and the tongue tip is flat behind the lower teeth. Remember to link words within phrases and stress important words, while maintaining the conversational tone of the dialogue. Work for variety in pitch and clarity of articulation.

Divide the sentences into phrase units, using single and double slashes, and underline the stressed words.

> **EXAMPLE:** Why, / I'm even <u>willing</u> / to go to <u>Washington</u> / for the <u>wine-tasting</u> fair. / /

Your instructor may serve as your model for correct and fluent oral reading. Prepare to enact this dialogue in class.

Wilma and Wine

—————◆—————

WILMA:	I'm quitting. I won't work in your shop one more week.
HOWIE:	My shop! It's been our wine shop for twenty years.
WILMA:	There, you said that word. Wine, wine, wine, always wine! Awake or asleep, I hear it. French wine, Italian wine, red wine, white wine—
HOWIE:	But Wilma, it's our business and we're successful. We've raised wonderful twin boys—
WILMA:	Then let Willie and Wallie take over the business.
HOWIE:	They're still in high school. They can't even buy wine.
WILMA:	I want to drink something else for a change.
HOWIE:	Like what?
WILMA:	Beer. I wish for a bottle of beer.
HOWIE:	Beer! My wife—the best nose in the business, who knows wine like no one else. I'm cut to the quick, wounded to the core.
WILMA:	Wake up, Howie. Beer is drunk world wide. Remember that bottle of wine you opened on our wedding night?
HOWIE:	It was a rare vintage.
WILMA:	It was full of cobwebs. I didn't like wine then, and I like it less now. You know, many people like to drink water.
HOWIE:	That awful clear stuff?
WILMA:	I've been so weary of pretending. Why, I even pretended I'm willing to go to Washington for that wine-tasting fair.
HOWIE:	What a woman! I can't wait to see the new winery near Walla Walla. I hear it's a winner.
WILMA:	Howie, you haven't been listening to a word I've said!
HOWIE:	I will in time, when the shock wears off.

Target Sound: / **r** /

Distinctive Features

/ r / is a tongue tip-palatal oral glide. It is voiced.

How Is / **r** / Made?

The tongue tip is raised, tensed, and curled back toward the central section of the hard palate without touching the roof of the mouth.* The sides of the tongue maintain contact with the upper side teeth. The lips are apart and not rounded. As the tongue descends for the articulatory position of the following vowel, the / r / is produced in initial and medial positions and in consonant clusters when the **r** precedes a vowel.

If you place your hand at your larynx and say the / r / in these words, you can feel the vibration of the vocal cords.

EXAMPLE: rode   sorrow   crime

What Are the Problems or Patterns in Spelling?

/ r / is represented by the letters **r, rr,** and **wr.**

EXAMPLE: rate   errand   wrap

What Are the Problems in Pronunciation?

/ r / may be omitted or indistinct in consonant clusters if the tongue lies flat behind the lower teeth.**

EXAMPLE: *two* instead of *true*

   fame instead of *frame*

may be pronounced / w / if the tongue tip is flat and the lips are rounded.

EXAMPLE: *wise* instead of *rise*

   wait instead of *rate*

---

* This position of the tongue is used when the consonant **r** precedes a vowel. An alternative position is to elevate the midsection of the tongue.

** See Appendix B for further practice on consonant clusters.

Note: In some languages, the / r / is trilled. You can feel the tongue tip flapping or tapping rapidly against the upper gum ridge when you produce a very fast / d / in "veddy" instead of "very." Spanish, Greek and Russian-speaking students, who use various trilled **r**s, may need to work on distinguishing and producing the consonant / r / in English.

   Students who speak French use the back section of the tongue to produce a gutteral sounding uvular **r.**

Listening/Speaking

A. Listen to your instructor and repeat: / r /   / r /   / r /   / r /   / r /

B. Repeat the following syllables with the / r / sound: / rɑ /   / ri /   / ræ /   / ru /

C. Repeat after your instructor. Be sure that the tongue tip is raised and curled back without touching the hard palate

1. Initial position

raw	ray	reach	wrap
rock	rye	rate	race
read	road	write	riot
wrong	role	wreck	run
rid	rude	ranch	rib

2. Medial position

sorry	weary	arrange	garage
arrow	fairy	arrive	carry
operator	curious	bury	directions
restaurant	already	secretary	paroled

3. Final position

Repeat after your instructor, feeling the tongue tip as it curls back slightly toward the palate when the **r** follows the vowel in **ar** spelling patterns.*

car	card	star	start
bar	barn	char	chart
far	farm	par	part

D. Problems with / r /

1. / r / and / w / may be confused.

   a. Repeat after your instructor. Be sure that your tongue is curled back and does not touch the palate when you produce / r /. The tongue tip should be flat and lips rounded when you pronounce the / w / in these words.

---

* As you pronounce "ar," you can get a sense of the tongue movement for the pronunciation of **r** when it functions like a vowel. Speakers in parts of the South and East are known for the omission of the final **r** and the lengthening of the vowel / ɑ /, as in **car** / kɑ: / and in **card** / kɑ:d /. In most other sections of the country, the tongue tip is curled back slightly to produce / kɑr / and / kɑrd /.

1) Initial Position

1	2	1	2	1	2
ray	way	rot	what	rest	west
run	one	rate	where	write	white
read	wed	rate	weight	rye	why
rent	went	ride	wide	reed	weed

Can you *feel* and *hear* the difference between / r / and / w /?

Your instructor will say three words from columns 1 and 2 for each pair. Indicate the pattern that you hear.

EXAMPLE: If you hear *ray, way, ray* the pattern is 1 2 1.

b. Underline the contrastive words in each sentence. As you read aloud, remember to produce / r / and / w / sounds in the underlined words.

EXAMPLE: My friend was <u>wed</u> in a <u>red</u> hat.

1) The wise man did not rise early.

2) Let's go West for a rest.

3) I paid the rent and went away.

4) One day he'll run away.

5) Don't write on white paper.

6) Marie was wooed by the rude man.

7) I can't wait to know the rate.

8) He was wed in a red suit.

2. / r / and / l / may be confused.

a. Repeat after your instructor. Be sure that the tongue tip touches the upper gum ridge only when you pronounce the / l / sound.

1) Initial Position

1	2	1	2	1	2
right	light	wrong	long	wrap	lap
rate	late	rid	lid	read	lead
road	load	rock	lock	ray	lay

2) Medial position

1	2	1	2
arrive	alive	parrot	palate
array	allay	berry	belly
correct	collect	hearing	healing
pirate	pilot		

3) Final position

Repeat after your instructor. Be sure to place the tongue tip against the upper gum ridge for the / l / sound. For the final **r** following a vowel, the tongue tip is raised and curled back slightly, not touching the hard palate.

1	2	1	2
core	call	store	stall
bore	ball	ear	eel
shore	shawl	more	mall
war	wall	four	fall

b. Underline the contrastive words in each sentence. As you read aloud, remember to produce / r / and / l / sounds in the underlined words.

EXAMPLE: Don't put that <u>load</u> of garbage on the <u>road</u>.

1. Wrap the package on your lap.

2. Don't make a right turn on a red light.

3. I didn't think I'd arrive there alive.

4. It's too late to ask for the telephone rate.

5. I'll rake the leaves near the lake.

6. Did you read that Mary will lead the committee?

7. Collect the papers and I'll correct them.

8. You were wrong to take the long route to the beach.

9. Robert lied about the cost of his ride

E. Consonant Clusters

1. Omission of / r / in consonant clusters changes the meaning and pronunciation of the word.

   Repeat after your instructor, making certain that the tongue tip is curled back slightly for the / r / sound. The tip is rather close to the upper gum ridge but does not touch the roof of the mouth.

	br		*pr*		*fr*
bed	bread	pay	pray	fame	frame
bide	bride	pie	pry	fight	fright
bake	break	pose	prose	fee	free

	dr		*gr*		*cr*
dip	drip	gas	grass	come	crumb
dive	drive	go	grow	cook	crook
die	dry	gain	grain	cash	crash

	tr		*str*		*scr*
tip	trip	stay	stray	scheme	scream
two	true	steam	stream	skew	screw
tie	try	stole	stroll	skipped	script

	spr		*shr*		*thr*
spy	spry	shank	shrank	threw	threat
spade	sprayed	shine	shrine	through	three
sped	spread	shed	shred	thruway	thrifty

2. Underline the contrastive words in each sentence. As you read aloud, remember to produce the /r/ consonant clusters in the underlined words.

>   **EXAMPLE:**   They <u>skipped</u> a few pages in the <u>script</u>.

a. We pray the play will be a success.

b. The picture frames were destroyed by the flames.

c. The crew had no clue about the murder.

d. Watch for broken glass on the grass.

e. She was glad to be present at such a pleasant event.

f. How much should we tip on our trip?

g. They stole our bags when we went for a stroll.

h. He lost his cash after the crash.

i. Try to tie your tie neatly.

j. She bought a drip-dry blouse on her trip.

F. Compare the full form of the verb with the contraction form. When the verb **are** follows the pronouns **you, they,** or **we,** the shortened form **'re** is used.

1. We are going now.   We're going now.

2. You are late.   You're late.

3. They are here.   They're here.

4. We are early.   We're early.

5. You are wrong.   You're wrong.

6. They are right.   They're right.

7. You are not listening.   You're not listening.

8. We are staying here.   We're staying here.

9. They are not leaving.   They're not leaving.

10. We are coming later.   We're coming later.

Listening/Writing

A. Listen carefully for / r / as your instructor pronounces each word. Write this sound when it occurs in initial and medial positions and in consonant clusters using the symbols of the IPA. If / r / is not heard, write a dash in the space provided.

> **EXAMPLE:** secretary / _r_____ _r_ /   twin / ___—___ /

1. robber _____

2. frightened _____

3. librarian _____

4. healing _____

5. prison _____

6. freight _____

7. alive _____

8. arrive _____

9. operator _____

10. family _____

11. traveled _____

12. truth _____

13. crook _____

14. finally _____

15. shrimp _____

B. Circle the word read aloud by your instructor.

1. way   ray   lay

2. wade   raid   laid

3. white   right   light

4. wed   red   lead

5. went   rent   lent

6. wide   ride   lied

7. weight   rate   late   9. what   rot   lot

8. week   reek   leak   10. weep   reap   leap

C. Your instructor will select one of the words in parentheses and read the entire sentence aloud. Listen carefully and circle the word you hear. Practice reading each sentence aloud using either one of the words in parentheses.

1. We didn't expect to (pay, pray).

2. His (weight, rate) is too high.

3. Don't let the cat (stay, stray).

4. They needed the (tip, trip).

5. Bob chose the (wrong, long) way to solve the problem.

6. He was a poor (reader, leader).

7. Is the story about the (pirate, pilot) true?

8. The (store, stall) was cleaned yesterday.

9. Did you like the (flute, fruit)?

10. Look at that (glass, grass).

11. The doctor says that Rita is (healing, hearing) well.

12. Tom has a wonderful (wife, life).

D. Circle the stressed syllable as each word is read aloud. Write the number of syllables in each word.

1. report ＿＿＿	6. responsible ＿＿＿	11. operator ＿＿＿
2. librarian ＿＿＿	7. sentenced ＿＿＿	12. married ＿＿＿
3. secretary ＿＿＿	8. threatened ＿＿＿	13. crashed ＿＿＿
4. rescued ＿＿＿	9. preparing ＿＿＿	14. directions ＿＿＿
5. earrings ＿＿＿	10. indicted ＿＿＿	15. restaurant ＿＿＿

E. Your instructor will say three words from columns 1 and 2 for each pair. Write the pattern that you hear.

> **EXAMPLE:** If you hear *raise, ways, raise,* write 1 2 1.

1	2	*Pattern*
1. rise	wise	____ ____ ____
2. rose	woes	____ ____ ____
3. reap	weep	____ ____ ____
4. rest	west	____ ____ ____
5. rip	lip	____ ____ ____
6. rate	late	____ ____ ____
7. pray	play	____ ____ ____
8. frame	flame	____ ____ ____
9. grass	glass	____ ____ ____
10. stream	steam	____ ____ ____

Chapter 7 Homework Review

A. Fill in the missing sounds using the symbols of the IPA. Write the number of sounds in each word.

EXAMPLE: errand / ___ə___ɛ_____ɚ / ___5___

1. agree   / ə___ ___i /   ___   8. remember   / ___əmɛm___ɚ /   ___

2. right   / ___aɪ___ /   ___   9. responsible   / ___ə___ ___ɑn___ə___ə___ /   ___

3. problems / ___ ___ɑ___ ___əm___ / ___   10. remained   / ___ə___eɪ___ ___ /   ___

4. quarrels / kwɑ___ə___ ___ /   ___   11. carried   / ___æ___ɪ___ /   ___

5. screens / s___ ___in___ /   ___   12. background / ___æk___ ___ɑʊn___ /   ___

6. reason   / ___i___ə___ /   ___   13. sport   / ___ ___ɔ___ ___ /   ___

7. pride   / ___ ___aɪ___ /   ___   14. territory   / tɛ___ɪ___ɔ___ɪ /   ___

B. Circle the stressed syllable. Write the number of syllables in each word.

1. responsible   _____   6. career   _____   11. respectable   _____

2. international   _____   7. Brazil   _____   12. recognized   _____

3. trophy   _____   8. Germany   _____   13. reached   _____

4. backgrounds   _____   9. greatest _____   14. surpassed   _____

5. varied   _____   10. surpass _____   15. Olympics   _____

C. Write the following words using the symbols of thr IPA.

1. cash   /   /   5. freight /   /

2. clash   /   /   6. await   /   /

3. crashed /   /   7. prison   /   /

4. grass   /   /   8. truth   /   /

D. Write the contractions for the full form verbs to complete each sentence.

1. We are _____ moving tomorrow.

2. They are _____ writing letters to protest unemployment.

3. You are _____ very late.

4. They are _____ undecided about their courses.

5. We are _____ definitely convinced.

6. I wonder what you are _____ doing this weekend.

7. After graduation we are _____ taking a trip to France.

8. They are _____ planning to get new glasses.

9. I believe they are _____ frightened.

10. We are _____ determined to pass these courses.

E. *Additional Review: / r / in medial position.* Circle the stressed syllable. Practice saying each word aloud, making certain the / r / is produced clearly.

guarantee	career	contributed
parade	Congress	integrated
irresponsible	parole	security
voluntary	military	comparison

F. Select five words from the list in Exercise E and compose a sentence for each. Underline each selected word in the sentence and practice reading aloud using the correct pronunciation.

1. _____

2. _____

3. _____

4. _____

5. _____

G. Select the appropriate word from Exercise E to complete each sentence. Circle the stressed syllable in the underlined word, and practice reading the sentence aloud.

> **EXAMPLE:** *parade:* Harry marched in the St. Patrick's Day Para(de).

1. Your contributions to the Red Cross are _____.

2. Henry is planning for a _____ in data processing.

3. It is _____ to be late continually.

4. Do you know who represents your state in _____?

5. Compared to fifty years ago, society today is more _____.

6. This equipment has a _____ for three months.

7. Can you make a _____ between these two authors?

8. The prisoner was granted a _____.

9. Harry's family _____ several books to the library.

10. Every resident in the United States must have a social _____ number.

Reading Aloud

A. This dialogue concentrates on the accurate production of the consonant / r /. Make sure the tongue tip is curled back without touching the palate, and pronounce this sound in the initial and medial positions and in consonant clusters. Remember to link the words within the phrase and stress the important words, maintaining the conversational tone of the dialogue. Work for variety of pitch and clarity of articulation.

> **EXAMPLE:** Don't <u>forget</u> <u>Ronaldo,</u> / once more their <u>star</u> <u>player,</u> / who was <u>responsible</u> / for their <u>day</u> of <u>glory</u>. / /

Your instructor may serve as your model for correct and fluent oral reading. Prepare to enact this dialogue in class.

The World Cup

◆

GERALDO: You're wrong, my friend. The Super Bowl is not the greatest.

RICKY: We're agreeing on the Olympics, then.

GERALDO: Try once more.

RICKY: The World Series?

GERALDO: You're not on target. No, the answer is soccer, the greatest international sport in the world. On June 30th, 2002, a billion or more people remained rooted to their TV screens.

RICKY: You're correct. I'll never forget the roar of the crowd when Brazil trounced Germany and carried that golden trophy back to their country.

GERALDO: Don't forget Ronaldo, once more their star player, who was responsible for their day of glory. Honor and pride of country, that's what soccer represents.

RICKY: Brazil's greatest hero is Pelé. No one can surpass him.

GERALDO: Quien sabe? Who knows what the future will bring?

RICKY: Strange that soccer's not really recognized here.

GERALDO: We're starting to change. Remember, the United States reached the quarter finals, a very respectable showing. Do you realize 200 countries compete for four years to play in the finals?

RICKY: I live in Maspeth, Queens, part of New York City. Metropolitan Oval is the oldest soccer playing field for youngsters in the U.S. They come from so many varied backgrounds—Latin and South America, Europe, the Far East. Soccer is truly international in our neighborhood. Parents root for their kid's team. Everybody gets along. No racial problems, no personal quarrels, just concentration on reaching the goal.

GERALDO: That's where careers start. On home territory. In 2006, I'm rooting for the United States to make a truly impressive showing.

Target Sound: / j /

Distinctive Features

/ j / is a lingua-palatal oral glide. It is voiced.

How Is / j / Made?

The midsection of the tongue is elevated toward the central part of the hard palate. The sides of the tongue touch the upper back teeth. The shape of the lips is dependent on the vowel following the / j / sound.

If you place your hand at your larynx and say the / j / in these words, you can feel the vibration of the vocal cords.

EXAMPLE: you   cure   million   huge

/ j / always precedes a vowel and never occurs in final position in English.

What Are the Problems or Patterns in Spelling?

/ j / is represented by the letters **ew, eu, u, ue, io, ea,** and **ia.**

EXAMPLE: f<u>ew</u>   f<u>eu</u>d   c<u>u</u>be   arg<u>ue</u>   on<u>io</u>n

million   b<u>ea</u>uty   Californ<u>ia</u>   h<u>u</u>man

is represented by the letters **y** and **u.**

EXAMPLE: youth   yes   mayor   use

What Are the Problems in Pronunciation?

/ j / may be pronounced / ʤ /.

EXAMPLE: *jello* instead of *yellow*

may be omitted.

EXAMPLE: *food* instead of *feud*

booty instead of *beauty*

Note: Some educated speakers of American English use the British pronunciation of / ju / in **Tuesday, news,** and **student.** American broadcasters using General American Dialect pronounce these words / tuzdɪ /, / nuz /, and / studənts /.

Students who speak Spanish and Scandinavian languages may need to work on distinguishing and producing the / j / and / ʤ /.

Listening/Speaking

A. Listen to your instructor and repeat: / j /   / j /   / j /

B. Repeat the following syllables with the / j / sound: / jə /   / ju /   / jɑ /   / jeɪ /

C. Repeat after your instructor, making sure the midsection of the tongue is elevated.

1. Initial position

you	yoga	youth	union
use	your	young	united
yard	yelled	yellow	unique
yawn	yogurt	yesterday	yielded

2. Medial position

few	argue	human	cute
cure	beauty	refuse	value
music	furious	interview	genius
onion	million	California	continue

D. Problems with / j /

1. Omission of / j / in the initial position changes the meaning and the pronunciation of the word.

1	2	1	2
awning	yawning	ale	Yale
ear	year	am	yam
oak	yoke	or	your

2. / j / and / ʤ / may be confused.

   Repeat after your instructor. As you produce / j /, raise the midsection of your tongue, not the front section. Place your tongue tip on the upper gum ridge to produce / d / in the / ʤ / sound.

   a. Initial Position

1	2	1	2	1	2
yet	jet	year	jeer	yam	jam
yes	Jess	yolk	joke	you'll	jewel
use	juice	Yale	jail	yip	gyp
yak	Jack	yellow	jello	yacht	jot

   Can you *feel* and *hear* the differences as you repeat after your instructor?

   Your instructor will say three words from columns 1 and 2 for each pair. Indicate the pattern that you hear.

> **EXAMPLE:** If you hear *yet, jet, yet,* the pattern is 1 2 1.

   b. Medial position

      mayor   major

3. Underline the contrastive words in each sentence. As you read aloud, remember to produce / j / sound in the underlined words.

> **EXAMPLE:** <u>Jot</u> down the name of that <u>yacht</u>.

  1. Who likes yellow jello?

  2. I ate the jam but not the yam.

  3. Jack had a yak sent from Tibet.

  4. On your next birthday, you'll receive a jewel.

  5. There was reason to jeer at the end of the year.

  6. Jess always says yes.

  7. The student from Yale is now in jail.

  8. Mr. Yoke laughed at my joke.

  9. That jet is not due in yet.

 10. The mayor of our city makes major decisions.

Listening/Writing

A. Listen carefully for / j / as your instructor pronounces each word. Write this sound when it occurs in the initial or medial position using the symbols of the IPA. If / j / is not heard, write a dash in the space provided.

> **EXAMPLE:** human / ____j____ /   hour / ____—____ /

1. yellow _____	5. yam _____	9. year _____
2. jello _____	6. peculiar _____	10. huge _____
3. few _____	7. continued _____	11. who _____
4. jam _____	8. jeer _____	12. mayor _____

B. Circle the word read aloud by the instructor.

1. use	juice	4. Yale	jail		
2. yacht	jot	5. year	jeer		
3. yet	jet	6. yard	jarred		

C. Your instructor will select one of the words in parentheses and read the entire sentence aloud. Listen carefully and circle the word you hear. Practice reading each sentence aloud using either one of the words in parentheses.

1. Tom went to (jail, Yale).

2. Those (years, jeers) were memorable.

3. Let's get some (yams, jams).

4. I visited the (mayor, major).

5. The (food, feud) bothered him.

D. Circle the stressed syllables as each word is read aloud. Write the number of syllables in each word. Practice aloud.

1. beautiful _____	6. yearned _____	11. lawyer _____
2. brilliant _____	7. Europe _____	12. genius _____
3. continued _____	8. curious _____	13. million _____
4. interviews _____	9. California _____	14. yielded _____
5. refused _____	10. battalion _____	15. abuses _____

E. Your instructor will say three words from columns 1 and 2 for each pair. Write the pattern that you hear.

    EXAMPLE: If you hear *joke, yolk, joke,* write 1 2 1.

1	2	*Pattern*
1. juice	use	_____ _____ _____
2. jeer	year	_____ _____ _____
3. jot	yacht	_____ _____ _____
4. jam	yam	_____ _____ _____

	1	2	*Pattern*
5.	oak	yolk	____ ____ ____
6.	am	yam	____ ____ ____
7.	food	feud	____ ____ ____
8.	awning	yawning	____ ____ ____
9.	jet	yet	____ ____ ____
10.	major	mayor	____ ____ ____

Chapter 7 Homework Review

A. Fill in the missing sounds using the symbols of the IPA. Write the number of sounds in each word.

 EXAMPLE: huge / h__j__uʤ / __4__

 1. union / ___ə___ə___ / _____ 6. jeer / ___ɪɚ / _____

 2. human / h___u___ən / _____ 7. young / ___ʌŋ / _____

 3. community / ___ɔ_____u___ɪt___ / _____ 8. refuse / rəf___u___ / _____

 4. argue / ɑrg___u / _____ 9. interviewed / ɪntɚv___ud / _____

 5. year / ___ɪɚ / _____ 10. brilliant / brɪl___ənt / _____

B. Write the following words using the symbols of the IPA.

 1. yard / / 5. music / /

 2. unit / / 6. few / /

 3. major / / 7. yelled / /

 4. mayor / / 8. beauty / /

C. Circle the stressed syllable. Write the number of syllables in each word.

 1. yesterday _____ 5. youngster _____ 9. yielded _____

 2. approval _____ 6. interviews _____ 10. rescue _____

 3. performances _____ 7. genius _____ 11. abuse _____

 4. unique _____ 8. million _____ 12. amuse _____

D. *Additional Review: / j / in medial position.* Circle the stressed syllable. Practice saying each word aloud, making certain the / j / is produced clearly.

beyond	backyard	furious
lawyer	contribution	preview
senior	companion	museum
opinion	distribute	curator

E. Select five words from the list in Exercise D and compose a sentence for each. Underline each selected word in the sentence and practice reading aloud using the correct pronunciation.

1. _____

2. _____

3. _____

4. _____

5. _____

F. Select the appropriate word from Exercise D to complete each sentence. Circle the stressed syllable in the underlined word, and practice reading the sentence aloud.

    EXAMPLE: Harry wanted to re(view) his work before the exam.

1. Her _____ advised her on the proper court procedures.

2. That family is advertising for a _____ for their elderly father.

3. Many _____ citizens are very active.

4. The _____ of that _____ is very knowledgeable about art.

5. The beautiful model refused to express her _____.

6. The court building is _____ the second light on Main Street.

7. I've put extra locks on the windows facing the _____.

8. It's time to _____ those handouts.

9. We were invited to see a _____ of that movie.

10. William gave a small _____ to the memorial fund for his uncle.

Reading Aloud

A. This passage focuses on the accurate production of / j /. Remember to link the words within the phrase and stress important words, while maintaining the conversational tone. Work for variety in pitch and clarity of articulation.

Divide the sentences into phrase units, using single and double slashes, and underline the stressed words.

> **EXAMPLE:**   We already have an <u>interview</u> / with an <u>independent</u> <u>filmmaker</u> / in <u>California</u>. / /

Your instructor may serve as your model for correct and fluent oral reading. Prepare to read aloud in class.

Úri's Future

My parents came to the United States from the Soviet Union. Over the years, they continued to say a college education was my key to a brilliant future. I'm a senior in high school now, so they're at me again.

"Apply to a big university, like Yale or Syracuse or Williams," my father says.

"Don't be ridiculous," I fume. "I'm no genius. I don't even want to go to a community college. Not now. Net yet."

"Úri," my mother cries, "You can become a millionaire lawyer."

"Don't regulate my life," I say. "My companion Miyoka and I intend to make documentaries about human suffering in the world. We already have an interview with an independent film maker in California."

My father's not doing his usual yelling. I wait.

Finally, he turns to me. "Úri, you're young and confused, but—" he says, shaking his head slowly, "I, too, had beautiful dreams. So, go, cure the ills of the universe, and maybe one year—who knows—you'll win an Oscar."

That was my cue to say thanks, and I did. Parents! You never know.

Reviewing the Lateral and Glides / l w r j /

A. Divide the following words from the passage in Exercise D. Circle the stressed syllable, and indicate the number of syllables in each word.

1. yellow _____
2. area _____
3. tourists _____
4. color _____
5. truce _____
6. quiet _____

7. clouds _____
8. breathes _____
9. winter _____
10. welcomes _____
11. orange _____
12. residents _____

13. approximately _____
14. leisurely _____
15. populations _____
16. restaurants _____
17. galleries _____
18. orchestra _____

B. Select the appropriate word or words from Exercise A to complete each sentence. Practice reading aloud for accuracy and fluency.

1. Two of her favorite colors are _____ and _____.

2. In the summer, the city of New York _____ all the _____, who fill the

     theaters, the _____, and the art _____.

3. Many New York City _____ leave the _____, preferring the _____

     of the country.

4. This test should take _____ fifty minutes.

5. The two countries at war declared a _____ just before the long, cold _____

     began.

C. Write five sentences of your own using the vocabulary listed in Exercise A.

1. _____

2. _____

3. _____

4. _____

5. _____

D. These selections focus on the production of / l /, / w /, / r /, and / j /. Be sure to produce these sounds accurately. Do not confuse / j / with / ʤ / or / dz /. Remember to produce / l / in final position and in consonant clusters. Be sure to link the words within the phrase and stress important words, while maintaining the conversational tone of the passages. Work for variety in pitch and clarity of articulation.

Divide the sentences into phrase units,using single and double slashes, and underline the stressed words.

EXAMPLE: <u>Suddenly</u>, / an <u>alarm</u> <u>clock</u> seems to <u>go</u> <u>off</u>, / and the <u>sleepy</u> <u>town</u> <u>springs</u> to life. / /

A tape or your instructor may serve as your model for correct and fluent oral reading. Prepare to read aloud in class.

The Town of Lenox

◆

Lenox is a relatively small village in Massachusetts, population approximately 6,500. Winter comes early and summer late. Life moves along in a leisurely fashion until May arrives. Suddenly, an alarm clock seems to go off, and the sleepy town springs to life. Storefronts glitter with fresh paint; gardens are planted and bushes pruned. Hotels check their reservation lists as the phones ring furiously. Soon the tourists will arrive and the town must be ready. Tanglewood is here, the summer home of the Boston Symphony Orchestra. So is Jacob's Pillow, the great dance company. Theater companies abound. Every season new restaurants open, as well as new spas and fitness centers. Tourists stream in and out of the shops, loaded down with purchases. Money flows freely and the town is delighted to rake it in.

And then, with barely any warning, the summer is over. Only a trickle of tourists remain. The autumn foliage burns rust and orange, and the leaves flutter to the ground. People lean on their rakes and scan the sky for the first signs of snow. Time to settle down. Time to go slow. A long, cold winter lies ahead.

The Wedding Reception

◆

WARREN: Ruth, we're going to be late. Why are we always late?

RUTH: I'm ready—just have to put on my earrings and my lipstick.

WARREN: It's our son's wedding reception. For once, we should be prompt. After all, we *are* the parents of the bridegroom.

RUTH: I'll be right there.

WARREN: Where are the directions to the reception?

RUTH: On the table in the living room.

WARREN: Where are my glasses? You know, I'm nervous.

RUTH: Well, here I am. How do I look?

WARREN: Terrific. Now, where are my glasses?

RUTH: Your glasses are on top of your head, resting on your bald spot.

WARREN: I really need a new pair of glasses.

RUTH: The ones you're wearing are just fine.

WARREN: I can hardly believe Billy and Lulu are really married. It seems only yesterday I bought Billy that set of electric trains.

RUTH: They looked so young. It's going to be lonely not having Billy around.

WARREN: Lonely! They'll be living next door.

RUTH: Next door is not here!

WARREN: Ruth, do you think they did the right thing—getting married so young?

RUTH: We can't worry about it now. It's too late.

WARREN :   You're right. The only thing we can do now is get to that reception on time. We're on our way!

syllable

vowels

Vowels

consonants

lateral and glides

diphthongs

Texas Tale

◆

One year the boll weevils got into the cotton crop and destroyed most of it. The Colonel did not provide enough food for the [farm] hands, so they stole anything they could get their hands on.

One day, the Sheriff came to the farm and arrested two white hands from another farm. They were all charged with stealing and were tried on the same day at the same hour. They were brought to court and John was so scared he trembled all over. He decided to listen the the white men's answers first and then imitate them.

The first hand was accused of stealing a horse.

"Guilty or not?" asked the Judge.

"Not guilty," answered the man. "I've owned that horse since it was a colt."

The case was dismissed.

The Judge called the second white man to the stand. He was accused of stealing a cow.

"Guilty or not guilty?" asked the Judge.

"Not guilty," the man replied. "I've raised that cow since it was a calf."

The case was dismissed.

Then John was called to the stand. He was accused of stealing a wagon.

"Guilty or not guilty?" asked the Judge.

"Not guilty," John answered. "I've owned that wagon since it was a wheelbarrow."

There are two classes of sounds: consonants and vowels. Although most speakers know intuitively which sound is a vowel and which a consonant, there are major differences in their production. Consonants may be voiced or voiceless; all vowels and diphthongs are voiced. Consonants are always produced by complete or partial blocking of the oral or nasal passage. The production of / f / in **fine** requires that the upper front teeth and lower lip touch each other, partially closing the oral cavity. Vowels, however, are formed with very little or no obstruction in the mouth. For the production of / i / in **each** or / ɔ / in **all,** the oral cavity is relatively open and there in no contact between the articulators.

Vowels carry the tune or melody of the voice. A vowel, unlike most consonants, can be sung. The vowel forms the nucleus, or the core, of the syllable.

EXAMPLE: love   com-plete   fan-tas-tic

A word always contains at least one vowel sound. No vowel, no word. A syllable contains only one vowel sound. The number of syllables in a word depends on the number of vowel sounds within the word. **Sym-pa-thy** contains three vowel sounds and has three syllables. **Psy-cho-lo-gy,** a word with four vowel sounds, has four syllables.

A vowel or a diphthong* can also stand as a word.

EXAMPLE: the article a / ə /   the pronoun I / aɪ /   the noun eye / aɪ /

A vowel or a diphthong can stand alone as a syllable.

EXAMPLE: alone / ə loʊn /   about / ə baʊt /   ideal / aɪ dil /

While consonants convey intelligibility, vowels may reveal personal feelings and aspects of one's personality. Emotional states such as fatigue, anger, or happiness are reflected in changes in the pitch, loudness, and duration of vowel sounds.

Description of Vowel	*Activity of Articulators*
Front, back, central	These terms describe the section of the tongue raised during the production of the vowel.
High, mid, low	These terms refer to the height of the tongue during the production of the vowel.
Rounded, unrounded	These terms refer to the shape of the lips during the production of the vowel.
Tense (tight), lax (relaxed)	These terms describe the degree of tension of the tongue and lips during the production of the vowel.
Long, short	These terms describe the length of time the vowel is held or the duration of the vowel.

---

*A diphthong is a combination of two vowel sounds forming a single vowel sound.

EXAMPLE: / eɪ / in **day**   / oʊ / in **go, okay, window**

Vowels are divided into several categories according to the way they are made. The formation of a vowel sound is dependent on the activity of the articulator, that is, the lips and the tongue. Figure 3 shows the various tongue positions involved in the production of vowel sounds. Figure 4 shows the position of the tongue for the production of various vowels.

More specific characteristics of vowels are described below.

1. They are front, back, or central.

   The front vowels are made with the front section of the tongue elevated.

   > **EXAMPLE:**   / i / seat   / ɪ / sit   / eɪ / safe   / ɛ / set   / æ / sat

   The back vowels are made with the back section of the tongue raised.

   > **EXAMPLE:**   / u / pool   / ʊ / pull   / oʊ / pole   / ɔ / pall   / ɑ / pond

   The central vowels are formed with the midsection of the tongue raised.

   > **EXAMPLE:**   / ʌ / luck   / ə / aloud   / ɜˆ / bird   / ɚ / father

2. They are high, mid, or low in the mouth.

   The high vowels are produced by raising either the front or back section of the tongue high in the mouth, close to but not touching the palate.

   > **EXAMPLE:**   / i / seat   / ɪ / sit   / u / pool   / ʊ / pull

   The mid vowels are made with the tongue elevated midway between the roof and the floor of the mouth.

   > **EXAMPLE:**   / eɪ / date   / ɜˆ / bird   / oʊ / boat   / ɛ / met
   >
   > / ɚ / never   / ɔ / bought   / ə / sofa

   The low vowels are made with the tongue quite flat on the floor of the mouth.

   > **EXAMPLE:**   / æ / cat   / ʌ / cut   / ɑ / cot

3. They are rounded or unrounded. The lips tend to be rounded for the back vowels. The lips are unrounded in the production of the front and central vowels.

   > **EXAMPLE:**   *Rounded vowels:*   / u / pool   / oʊ / pole
   >
   > *Unrounded vowels:*   / i / seat   / æ / sat   / ʌ / luck

4. They are tense or lax. The tension of the tongue and lip muscles may vary from a tense, constricted state to a relaxed, loose state.

   > **EXAMPLE:**   *tense*   / i / seat   / u / pool   / eɪ / same   / oʊ / pole   / ɜˆ / bird
   >
   > *lax*   / ɪ / sit   / ʊ / pull   / ɛ / set   / ɔ / all   / ʌ / bud

5. They are short or long in duration. Some phonetic differences depend on the prolongation of the vowel sound.*

> **EXAMPLE:** / i / in <u>beat</u> is longer in duration than / ɪ / in <u>bit</u>
>
> / eɪ / in <u>mate</u> is longer in duration than / ɛ / in <u>met</u>
>
> / u / in <u>pool</u> is longer in duration than / ʊ / in <u>pull</u>

The duration of the vowel sound is also dependent on the consonant that follows. If the consonant is voiced, the vowel duration is increased.

> **EXAMPLE:** / i / in <u>bead</u> is longer in duration that / i / in <u>beat</u>
>
> / ɪ / in <u>hid</u> is longer in duration that / ɪ / in <u>hit</u>

Note that the / ɪ / is relatively short in duration, and yet before the voiced consonant it is prolonged.

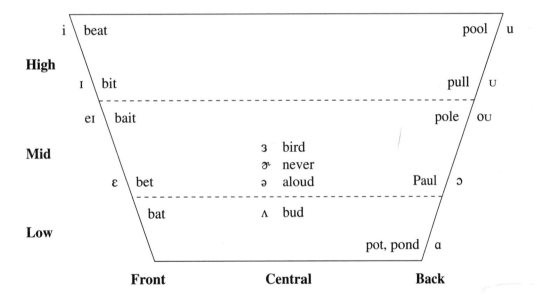

FIGURE 3. Schematic representation of tongue positions for the production of vowels.

---

* These differences in vowel duration should be noted because the foreshortening of a vowel can alter the meaning of a word. For example, if the / i / in feet is not prolonged sufficiently, the word may sound like fit / fɪt /.

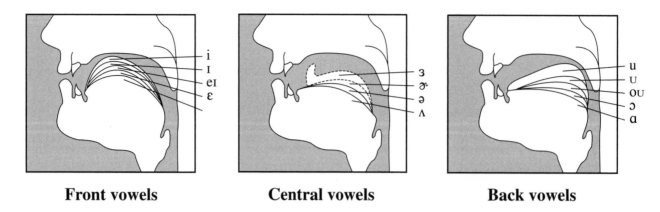

Front vowels   **Central vowels**   **Back vowels**

FIGURE 4. Position of the front, central, and back sections of the tongue for the production of vowels.

CHAPTER EIGHT

Front Vowels

Figure 5 shows a schematic representation of the positions of the tongue in the front section of the mouth for the production of the five front vowels. The tongue tip is placed behind the lower front teeth. The front section of the tongue is elevated to its high position for the / i / and / ɪ / sounds. It descends to midheight for / eɪ / and / ɛ / and becomes quite flat for the / æ / sound. Thus these vowels may be described as high, mid, or low front vowels.

/ i / is the highest of the front vowels. It is a closed, unrounded sound. The tongue is very high and tense; the lips are spread and tense. It is long in duration. When the vowel is not given full value, it may sound more nearly like / ɪ /.

EXAMPLE: / i / f<u>ee</u>t h<u>ea</u>t mach<u>i</u>ne

/ ɪ / is also a high front vowel. Made with the tongue a little lower than the / i /, it is one of the most frequently heard English vowel sounds. The lips and tongue are relaxed; the sound is very short.

EXAMPLE: / ɪ / typ<u>i</u>cal pr<u>e</u>tt<u>y</u> h<u>i</u>t

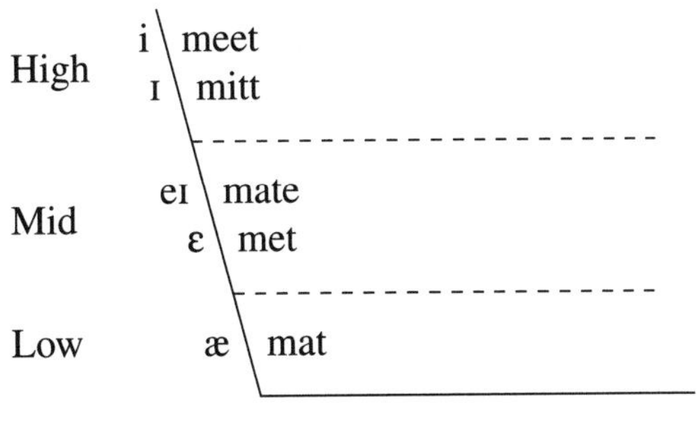

High

    i   meet

    ɪ   mitt

Mid

    eɪ   mate

    ɛ   met

Low

    æ   mat

FIGURE 5. Tongue positions for the front vowels.

/ i / and / ɪ / are often confused by non-native speakers, who substitute one for the other.

EXAMPLE: I see the <u>shee</u>p (meaning <u>shi</u>p)

I see the <u>shi</u>p (meaning <u>shee</u>p)

/ eɪ / is a mid high diphthong.* It consists of two vowel sounds, the first is longer and stronger, the second is weak. The lips are stretched and tense, and the tongue moves to the higher position to complete the diphthong. / eɪ / is a very long sound.

If the second half of the diphthong is too short in duration, or not produced, the vowel sound / ɛ / in **get** is produced.

EXAMPLE: / eɪ /   g<u>a</u>te   br<u>ea</u>k   f<u>ai</u>l

/ ɛ / is a short vowel, made with the tongue fairly low (not flat) and lax in the mouth. The lips are relaxed and unrounded. If the tongue is placed flat, the vowel sound / æ / in **sat** is produced.

EXAMPLE: / ɛ /   s<u>e</u>t   g<u>ue</u>st   br<u>ea</u>d

/ æ / is the lowest of the front vowels. It is made with the tongue flat on the floor of the mouth. The lips are open and somewhat tense. If the tongue is raised, / ɛ / in **bet** is produced.

EXAMPLE: / æ /   b<u>a</u>t   s<u>a</u>lmon   ch<u>a</u>nce

Target Sounds: / i / and / ɪ /

Distinctive Features

/ i / and / ɪ / are high, front, unrounded vowels. Like all vowels, they are voiced.

How Are / i / and / ɪ / Made?

The front section of the tongue is high in the mouth, and the tip of the tongue is locked behind the lower front teeth.

/ i / is a long vowel. The front section of the tongue, which is tense, is very high in the mouth. The lips are stretched and tense.

EXAMPLE: m<u>ee</u>t   l<u>ea</u>ve   bel<u>ie</u>ve

/ ɪ / is a very short vowel. It is made with the front section of the tongue slightly lower in the mouth than / i /. The lips and tongue are in a lax, non-tense position.

EXAMPLE: h<u>i</u>t   pock<u>e</u>t**   wait<u>e</u>d**   marr<u>ie</u>d†

---

* In American English, / eɪ / is diphthongized, and this variation is used throughout the text.

** In unstressed syllables, the / ɪ / and the schwa / ə / are often interchangeable.

† When the unstressed syllable contains the letters **y** or **ied**, / ɪ / is used.

Note: Front vowels are not rounded in English. This is not true in other languages. In French, for example, / y / as in *tu* / ty / (you) is in the tongue position for / i /, but the lips are rounded.

What Are the Problems or Patterns in Spelling?

/ i / may be represented by the several configurations.

EXAMPLE: compl<u>e</u>te   dec<u>ei</u>ve   rel<u>ie</u>ve   f<u>ee</u>t   m<u>ea</u>t

/ ɪ / may be represented by several configurations.

EXAMPLE: b<u>i</u>g   happ<u>i</u>ly*   read<u>y</u>*   bur<u>ie</u>d*   eleph<u>a</u>nt**

What Are the Problems in Pronunciation?

/ i / may be shortened and pronounced / ɪ /.

EXAMPLE: *h<u>i</u>t* instead of *h<u>ea</u>t*

/ ɪ / may be prolonged resulting in the vowel / i /.

EXAMPLE: *f<u>ee</u>l* instead of *f<u>i</u>ll*

may often be used interchangeably with the schwa / ə / in unstressed syllables.[†]

EXAMPLE: r<u>e</u>ply   dec<u>ei</u>ve   cour<u>a</u>ge   danger<u>ou</u>s

The / i / Sound

A. Variations in spelling

Repeat these words after your instructor. Observe the different spellings for the / i / sound.

we	equal	machine
ski	people	believe
key	Caesar	previous
heat	amoeba	complete
meet	receive	mosquito

---

  * When the unstressed syllable contains the letters **y** or **ied,** / ɪ / is used.

 ** In unstressed syllables, the / ɪ / and the schwa / ə / are often interchangeable.

 † In some unstressed syllables only the schwa / ə / may be used.

    EXAMPLE: <u>a</u>bility   sof<u>a</u>   hist<u>o</u>ry

Note: Non-native speakers from most language backgrounds may need to work on distinguishing and producing / i / and / ɪ /.

B. Vowel length

1. The vowel / i / is longer when it occurs before a voiced consonant.

1	2	1	2	1	2
seat	seed	relief	relieve	wheat	weed
leaf	leave	piece	peas	neat	need
receipt	recede	leak	league	heat	he'd

2. The vowel is longer when it is the last sound in the word.

me	see	tea	ski
tree	she	foresee	key

C. The / i / in sentence practice.

Stretch or lengthen the / i / sound as you read each sentence aloud.

1. Please leave your keys with me before you go.

2. Sleet and freezing rain were predicted for the entire Eastern seaboard.

3. I must complete my term theme by next week.

4. The queen's speech to her people was well received by the media.

5. He ordered roast beef, green beans, cheesecake and tea for dinner.

6. Many people are allergic to bee stings and need immediate medical attention.

7. Jiminy Peak in not an easy ski slope.

8. It was a relief when the police chief arrived.

9. Eve told Lee she would be free for dinner that evening.

10. The wheels of the car squealed as it screeched to a halt.

The / ɪ / Sound

A. Variations in spelling

Repeat these words after your instructor.

1. Observe the spelling differences in *stressed* syllables.

if	pretty	ability
it	physics	syllabus
fix	typical	syndrome
quit	realistic	women
quick	dismal	physician

2. Observe the spelling differences in *unstressed* syllables.*

wanted	different	college
lettuce	problem	department
nation	dangerous	village
tension	fortunate	infant
quizzes	quickly	psychological

B. The / ɪ / in sentence practice.

Divide each sentence into phrase units and link the words within each phrase. Pronounce the / ɪ / sound clearly in stressed syllables as you read each sentence.

1. Sylvia was a typical marketing student at City College.

2. Realistic and determined, she wanted to quit.

3. Her boyfriend, Izzy, and her cousin Phyllis convinced her to visit Finland for six months.

4. If she went with a group called Women for Freedom, her trip would cost about six hundred dollars.

5. This created a big problem because she would have to quit her job in her cousin's laundry business.

6. If she did quit, it would be difficult to find a job when she returned.

7. Her cousin Tim said he would permit her to return to his business if she left.

8. Still, Sylvia wished to leave New York and live in Europe.

9. Her sister promised to assist Cousin Tim in his business and then give up the job when Sylvia came back.

10. So off she went on her trip to Finland.

Listening/Speaking

A. Contrast / i / and / ɪ /.

Can you *feel* the difference as you repeat after your instructor?

Can you *hear* the difference between the long / i / and the short / ɪ /?**

Your instructor will say three words from columns 1 and 2 for each pair. Indicate the pattern that you hear.

---

* / ɪ / and / ə / are interchangeable in many suffixes.

** The / i / is longer in duration than the / ɪ /.

EXAMPLE: beat is longer than bit

EXAMPLE: If you hear *steal, still, steal*, the pattern is 1 2 1.

1	2	1	2
steal	still	heap	hip
neat	knit	leak	lick
peak	pick	read	rid
seat	sit	green	grin
seal	sill	leave	live
peach	pitch	ream	rim
meet	mitt	sheep	ship
bean	been	eel	ill
each	itch	peel	pill

B. Underline the contrastive words in each sentence. As you read aloud, remember to produce the / i / and / ɪ / sounds in the underlined words.

EXAMPLE: Don't <u>sit</u> in that <u>seat</u>.

1. Jean made a gin and and tonic.

2. Read this letter and get rid of it.

3. How far can you pitch your peach pit?

4. Didn't you buy it to eat?

5. List at least three references.

6. These shoes don't fit your feet.

7. The baseball team accepted Tim.

8. Please leave if you don't live here.

9. The eel was too ill to eat.

10. Does each mosquito bite itch?

Listening/Writing

A. Listen carefully for / i / and / ɪ / as your instructor pronounces each word. Write these sounds when they occur in the initial, medial, or final position using the symbols of the IPA. If / i / or / ɪ / is not heard, write a dash in the space provided.

EXAMPLE: ability /<u>ɪ   ɪ   ɪ</u>/ disagree /<u>ɪ   i</u>/ gulped /<u>   —   </u>/

1. believe _____

3. women _____

5. seasick _____

2. captain _____

4. stuffed _____

6. stealing _____

7. fly _____   12. beach _____   17. sneak _____

8. nineteen _____   13. quit _____   18. win _____

9. quietly _____   14. deal _____   19. repeat _____

10. ignored _____   15. recommend _____   20. dangerous _____

11. silly _____   16. illegal _____   21. liquor _____

B. Circle the word read aloud by the instructor.

1. sleep   slip   sleet

2. fill   filled   feel

3. reach   reached   rich

4. seek   sick   seeks

5. it   eat   eats

6. wheel   will   wills

7. sheep   ship   ships

8. heat   hit   hits

9. knit   neat   knee

10. did   deed   deeds

C. Your instructor will select one of the words in parentheses and read the entire sentence aloud. Listen carefully and circle the word you hear. Practice reading each sentence aloud using either one of the words in parentheses.

1. Who (bit, beat) that horse?

2. When did Mr. Smith (leave, live)?

3. Don't (slip, sleep) in the movie theater.

4. Don't (heat, hit) this too quickly.

5. Did he find his (sheep, ship)?

6. (Feel, fill) this bottle.

7. He made a big (fist, feast).

8. His (wit, wheat) was appreciated by the other farmers.

9. I can't study because of the (din, dean).

10. That (peach, pitch) was impressive.

D. Circle the stressed syllable as each word is read aloud. Write the number of syllables in each word. Practice aloud.

1. stewardess	_____	6. ignored	_____	11. argue	_____
2. official	_____	7. towels	_____	12. gazed	_____
3. reasonable	_____	8. immediately	_____	13. scenery	_____
4. improving	_____	9. liquor	_____	14. certainly	_____
5. examination	_____	10. mosquito	_____	15. business	_____

E. Your instructor will say three words from columns 1 and 2 for each pair. Write the pattern that you hear.

EXAMPLE: If you hear *fill, feel, fill,* write 1 2 1.

1	2	*Pattern*
1. ill	eel	_____ _____ _____
2. pill	peel	_____ _____ _____
3. still	steal	_____ _____ _____
4. mill	meal	_____ _____ _____
5. itch	each	_____ _____ _____
6. kill	keel	_____ _____ _____
7. will	we'll	_____ _____ _____
8. did	deed	_____ _____ _____
9. Tim	team	_____ _____ _____
10. knit	neat	_____ _____ _____

Chapter 8 Homework Review

A. Fill in the missing sounds using the symbols of the IPA. Write the number of sounds in each word.

EXAMPLE: typical / t_ɪ_p_ɪ_kəl /   _7_

1. ceiling / s__lɪŋ / _____
2. pills / p__lz / _____
3. lifted / l__ft__ __ / _____
4. needed / n__ __ __ __ / _____
5. this / ð__ __ / _____
6. these / ð__ __ / _____
7. scenery / s__nərɪ / _____
8. repeat / r__p__t / _____

9. belief / b__l__f / _____
10. listen / l__sən / _____
11. pleased / pl__ __ __ / _____
12. business / b__zn__z / _____
13. illegal / __l__gəl / _____
14. tonic / tɑn__ __ / _____
15. agreed / əgr__ __ / _____
16. seasick / s__s__ __ / _____

B. Circle the stressed syllable. Write the number of syllables in each word.

1. worried _____
2. situation _____
3. nineteen _____
4. towels _____
5. difficult _____

6. stewardess _____
7. baggage _____
8. officer _____
9. accused _____
10. heavy _____

11. official _____
12. reasonable _____
13. customs _____
14. physician _____
15. examination _____

C. The pronunciation of each word is given in column 2. If correct, write C. If incorrect, write I and make the corrections in column 4 using the symbols of the IPA.

EXAMPLE: will / wil /   _/ ɪ /_   ____ / wɪl / ____

1	2	3	4
Word	Pronunciation	C/I	Correction
1. sheet	/ ʃit /	_____	_____
2. rid	/ rid /	_____	_____
3. read	/ rid /	_____	_____

319

1	2	3	4
Word	Pronunciation	C/I	Correction
4. heat	/ hɪt /	_____	_____
5. hit	/ hɪt /	_____	_____
6. his	/ hɪz /	_____	_____
7. he's	/ hɪz /	_____	_____
8. sit	/ sɪt /	_____	_____
9. sister	/ sɪstɚ /	_____	_____
10. beach	/ bitʃ /	_____	_____

D. Write the following words using the symbols of the IPA. Practice aloud, producing / i / and / ɪ / accurately.

1. live   /   /   6. grin   /   /

2. feel   /   /   7. lifted   /   /

3. leave   /   /   8. still   /   /

4. seasick /   /   9. visit   /   /

5. steal   /   /   10. green   /   /

E. Fill in the appropriate IPA symbol in the space provided. Practice reading these sentences aloud, producing / i / and / ɪ / accurately.

> **EXAMPLE:**   Have you s<u>ee</u>n / i / th<u>e</u>se / i / ant<u>i</u>ques / i /?

1. You can sl<u>i</u>p /   / if you walk in your sl<u>ee</u>p /   /.

2. Don't s<u>i</u>t /   / in that s<u>ea</u>t /   /.

3. The p<u>y</u>ram<u>i</u>ds /   / in <u>E</u>gypt /   / are un<u>i</u>que /   /.

4. The h<u>ea</u>t /   / in the c<u>i</u>ty /   / affected T<u>i</u>m /   / and his t<u>ea</u>m /   /.

5. W<u>e</u>'ll /   / v<u>i</u>sit /   / W<u>i</u>ll /   / tomorrow.

6. L<u>i</u>ly /   / d<u>i</u>d /   / a good d<u>ee</u>d /   / today.

7. B<u>i</u>ll /   / sat qu<u>ie</u>tly /   / throughout the d<u>i</u>scussion /   /.

8. The sh<u>ee</u>p /   / were loaded on the sh<u>i</u>p /   /.

9. T<u>i</u>llie /   / want<u>e</u>d /   / to get r<u>i</u>d /   / of the letter she couldn't r<u>ea</u>d /   /.

10. <u>E</u>ve /   / did not b<u>ea</u>t /   / the dog who b<u>i</u>t /   / her foot.

Reading Aloud

A. These selections focus on the production of / i / and / ɪ /. Make sure that you differentiate between the two vowel sounds, giving full value to the / i /. Remember to link the words within the phrase and stress important words, while maintaining the conversational tone of the passage. Work for variety in pitch and clarity of articulation.

Divide the sentences into phrase units, single and double slashes, and underline the stressed words.

> **EXAMPLE:** Bill was worried / about the nineteen bottles of liquor / he had stuffed / into his baggage. / /

Your instructor may serve as your model for correct and fluent oral reading. Prepare to read aloud in class.

Bill and the Customs Officer

Bill was beginning to feel sick. He didn't believe he'd get seasick, but the trip from Finland to Sweden was really difficult. Even the captain of the ship agreed that the Baltic Sea was very rough. Besides being seasick, Bill had other worries. He was worried about the nineteen bottles of liquor he had stuffed into his baggage. "It's not that I'm stealing," he remarked to his sister, Eve. "I should be able to bring into the country what I wish."

"You're silly," she told him. "It's still illegal." Bill was feeling too seasick to argue with her.

When they reached England, the customs officer pulled Bill's luggage closer for examination. "This is certainly heavy, sir." Bill remained quiet. Eve gazed at the ceiling and ignored the situation. "Hmm," said the officer as he lifted one towel and then another. "Heavy towels, sir. Are you planning a liquor business?"

"Well, no," gulped Bill. "I have a sick sister in Italy who needs this. Her doctor recommends whiskey for her heart."

The customs official quietly closed Bill's suitcase. "Please follow me into the office, sir."

Exercises

1. Select the words containing the / i / and / ɪ / sounds. Write the appropriate phonetic symbol above each word.

2. Write ten words from this passage with the / i / sound.

_____ _____ _____ _____ _____

_____ _____ _____ _____ _____

3. Write ten words from this passage with the / ɪ / sound.

_____   _____   _____   _____   _____

_____   _____   _____   _____   _____

Plane Trip

◆———

EVE: Bill, will you please sit in your seat? You're stepping on my feet.

BILL: Let me look out the window and see the ground for the last time. Why did I agree to this deal?

EVE: Dr. Green says you're really improving. You're fit to fly.

BILL: Dr. Green? That shrink!* I can't stand his grin. Eve, we can still leave. I want to live.

EVE: Get ready to fasten your seat belt.

BILL: What for? In three hours, we'll be dead. Give me a bus. Give me a train. A ship. Not this. Feel my pulse. I think I'm going to be ill.

EVE: Do you want to take a pill?

BILL: Yes, I think I will. No, I won't.

EVE: See! You're going to win this battle.

BILL: Where's the stewardess? I need a drink—a gin and tonic.

EVE: No.

BILL: Lots of gin. Little tonic.

EVE: I repeat—no.

BILL: A double whiskey, neat!

EVE: Bill, you don't need pills. You don't need whiskey.

BILL: I need something.

EVE: A little belief in yourself. Just think. Today Palm Beach, Florida. Next year a trip to Sweden, Finland, Italy—.

BILL: Italy! Remember my poor sister who needed liquor for her heart?

EVE: And you, trying to sneak in all that whiskey?

BILL: Oh, was I seasick!

EVE: All because we took a ship.

BILL: Ships aren't that safe anyway. Remember the *Titanic* and the *Andrea Doria?*

EVE: Dr. Green would be so pleased if he could listen to you now. He told me you'd be reasonable.

BILL: Oh, he did, did he? Did he also tell you these are going to be the longest three hours of my life? Eve, you're sure we'll make it to Palm Beach?

EVE: Of course we will. Now just relax and enjoy the scenery.

———

* "Shrink" is an informal term for *psychiatrist.*

Target Sounds: / eɪ / *and* / ɛ /

Distinctive Features

/ eɪ / and / ɛ / are mid-high, front, and unrounded vowels.* Like all vowels, they are voiced.

How Are / eɪ / *and* / ɛ / *Made?*

The front section of the tongue is midhigh in the mouth, and the tip of the tongue is locked behind the lower front teeth.

/ eɪ / is a diphthong, a combination of two vowel sounds considered as a single unit. The first element in the diphthong is the stronger and longer, gliding into the second element, which is weaker, and not as easily perceived by the non-native speaker. It is a very long vowel, made with the lips stretched and tense.

EXAMPLE: t<u>a</u>ke   m<u>ai</u>n   r<u>a</u>ce

/ ɛ / is a very short vowel made with the tongue lax and a little lower in the mouth than for / eɪ /. It is not a diphthong, and the lips are slightly apart and lax.

EXAMPLE: h<u>ea</u>d   m<u>e</u>t   s<u>e</u>nt

What Are the Problems or Patterns in Spelling?

/ eɪ / may be represented by the letters **ai, a, ay, ea,** and **eigh.**

EXAMPLE: p<u>ai</u>d   st<u>a</u>tion   s<u>ay</u>   st<u>ea</u>k   <u>eigh</u>t

/ ɛ / may be represented by the letters, **ai, ie, ea, e,** and **a.**

EXAMPLE: s<u>ai</u>d   fr<u>ie</u>nd   h<u>ea</u>d   t<u>e</u>ll   m<u>a</u>ny

What Are the Problems in Pronunciation?

/ eɪ / may be shortened and pronounced / ɛ /.**

EXAMPLE: *<u>e</u>dge* instead of *<u>a</u>ge*

/ ɛ / may be produced / æ /.

EXAMPLE: *b<u>a</u>d* instead of *b<u>e</u>d*

---

* In American English, eɪ, a variation of / e /, is diphthongized. It is indicated as / eɪ / throughout the text.

** When the second element of the diphthong is not given full value, is too short, or is not produced at all, the vowel / ɛ / may result. The problem is particularly evident when the diphthong is followed by / l /.

    EXAMPLE: **fell** instead of **fail**

Note: Speakers from the Caribbean may need to work on distinguishing and producing the diphthong / eɪ /. Speakers of Asian languages may need additional practice in distinguishing and producing the vowel / ɛ /.

/ ɛ / may be pronounced / ɪ /.

EXAMPLE: *tin* instead of *ten*

The / eɪ / Sound

A. Variations in spelling

Repeat these words after your instructor. Observe the spelling representations for the / eɪ / sound.

aid	nation	crazy
sale	weight	arrange
agent	steak	remain
sane	okay	obey
same	quaint	vacation

B. The vowel / eɪ / is longer when it occurs before a voice consonant.

1	2	1	2	1	2
great	grade	race	raise	place	plays
safe	save	eight	aid	fate	fade
wait	wade	trace	trays	mate	made

1	2	1	2	1	2
weight	weigh	grain	gray	same	say
they'd	they	delayed	delay	obeyed	obey

C. The / eɪ / in sentence practice.

Stretch or lengthen the / eɪ / sound as you read each sentence aloud.

1. Jason Haste worked for the United Nations for eight years.

2. His girlfriend, Jane, was a real estate agent.

3. They decided it was insane to remain in New York.

4. Therefore, they arranged to buy a farm in Maine.

5. After eight years, they became bored and wanted another place to live.

6. They waited until they could get a good sale.

7. A travel agent paid eighty-eight thousand dollars for their place.

8. Then, Jane and Jason decided to take a long vacation in Spain.

9. They came back to New York last May to face major problems.

10. Jane and Jason are now selling danish, bagels, and coffee on Jay Street.

The / ɛ / Sound

A. Variations in spelling

Repeat these words after your instructor.

Ed	test	instead
says	friend	breakfast
any	against	stretch
said	ready	elevator

B. The vowel / ɛ / is longer when it occurs before a voiced consonant.

1	2	1	2
bet	bed	let	led
debt	dead	set	said
etch	edge	wet	wed

C. The / ɛ / in sentence practice.

Practice pronouncing / ɛ / as you read these sentences aloud. Remember to keep the lips slightly apart and the front section of the tongue raised—not as high as for / ɪ / and not as flat as for / æ /.

1. Ed met Ted for breakfast at the same restaurant every day.

2. The Senate met in special session at the request of the President.

3. His friend said he would be ready in ten minutes.

4. The bank would not lend him the money to pay his gambling debts.

5. She fell asleep the moment her head hit the bed.

6. I intend to mend my fence when the weather gets better.

7. He sent the rent to the landlord by the tenth of the month.

8. His guest left early to catch the express train.

9. His address met with great success.

10. I guess I should eat less and exercise more.

Listening/Speaking

A. Contrast / eɪ / and / ɛ /.

Can you *feel* the difference as you repeat after your instructor?

Can you *hear* the difference between the long / eɪ / and the short / ɛ /?

Your instructor will say three words from columns 1 and 2 for each pair. Indicate the pattern that you hear.

EXAMPLE: If you hear *pain, pen, pain,* the pattern is 1 2 1.

1	2		1	2		1	2
pain	pen		paste	pest		aid	Ed
rain	wren		trade	tread		tail	tell
age	edge		blade	bled		main	men
raid	red		saint	sent		taste	test
wait	wet		late	let		waste	west

B. Underline the contrastive words in each sentence. As you read aloud, remember to produce the /eɪ/ and / ɛ / in the underlined words.

> **EXAMPLE:**   Let me <u>tell</u> you another <u>tale</u>.

1. Although he fell, he did not fail to ring the alarm.

2. In this sale, they will sell only pens and pins.

3. She didn't let her children stay out late at night.

4. Have you met the first mate on the ship?

5. My date has a large debt to pay.

6. Ed came to the aid of his best friend.

7. You'll get wet if you wait out there.

8. The children sent St. Ann their best wishes.

9. The letter came later.

10. Which store sells nylon sails for sailboats?

C. Contrast / ɛ / and / ɪ /

Can you *feel* the difference as you repeat after your instructor?

Can you *hear* the difference between the / ɛ / and the / ɪ /?

Your instructor will say three words from columns 1 and 2 for each pair. Indicate the pattern that you hear.

> **EXAMPLE:**   If you hear *pen, pin, pen,* the pattern is 1 2 1.

1	2		1	2		1	2
pen	pin		red	rid		head	hid
bet	bit		met	mitt		hem	him
let	lit		pet	pit		bed	bid
set	sit		dead	did		mess	miss

D. Underline the contrastive words in each sentence. As you read aloud, remember to produce the / ε / and / ɪ / in the underlined words.

> **EXAMPLE:** <u>Did</u> you say he was <u>dead</u>?

1. Sid said he'd come.

2. Get rid of the red medicine.

3. Your sprained wrist needs a rest.

4. Her pet swallowed the peach pit.

5. How long has Ben been in this country?

6. I bet that dog bit her.

7. You can buy pens and pins at Macy's.

8. The suspect hid his head in his hands.

9. Six mice of the male sex were used in the study.

10. He was all set to sit there for a while.

Listening/Writing

A. Listen carefully for / e / and / ε / as your instructor pronounces each word. Write these sounds when they occur in the initial, medial, or final position using the symbols of the IPA. If / eɪ / or / ε / is not heard, write a dash in the space provided.

> **EXAMPLE:** dictate /_____eɪ___/   helped /__ε_____/   feeling /_____—___/

1. sprained	_____	7. candidate	_____	13. tennis	_____
2. stay	_____	8. hesitate	_____	14. stranger	_____
3. blame	_____	9. against	_____	15. wrenched	_____
4. aches	_____	10. raced	_____	16. memory	_____
5. rest	_____	11. credit	_____	17. scheduled	_____
6. friends	_____	12. agency	_____	18. estate	_____

B. Circle the word read aloud by the instructor.

1. bade	bed	bid		6. hale	hell	hill
2. sale	sell	sill		7. wail	well	will
3. fail	fell	fill		8. late	let	lit
4. fate	fete	fit		9. pain	pen	pin
5. wait	wet	wit		10. bait	bet	bit

C. Your instructor will select one of the words in parentheses and read the entire sentence aloud. Listen carefully and circle the word you hear. Practice reading each sentence aloud using either one of the words in parentheses.

1. The (rain, wren) settled on the grass.

2. Who could have (led, laid) the dog there?

3. I won't forget my first (debt, date).

4. We're going to (wed, wade) next Monday.

5. I made a (bit, bet) in that business deal.

6. Two more (pens, pins) are needed.

7. Don't (tread, trade) there.

8. He still has a lot of (pens, pains).

9. His (chain, chin) was broken.

10. Do you like this (test, taste)?

D. Your instructor will say three words from columns 1 and 2 for each pair. Write the pattern that you hear.

    EXAMPLE: If you hear *bait, bet, bait,* write 1 2 1.

1	2	Pattern
1. late	let	____ ____ ____
2. bane	Ben	____ ____ ____
3. raid	red	____ ____ ____
4 waist	west	____ ____ ____

	1	2	*Pattern*
5.	fail	fell	_____ _____ _____
6.	sale	sell	_____ _____ _____
7.	bail	bell	_____ _____ _____
8.	fade	fed	_____ _____ _____
9.	mace	mess	_____ _____ _____
10.	raced	rest	_____ _____ _____

E. Circle the stressed syllable as each word is read aloud. Write the number of syllables in each word. Practice aloud.

1. ashamed _____	7. major _____	13. refrigerator _____
2. nations _____	8. estate _____	14. expedition _____
3. complain _____	9. elevator _____	15. event _____
4. chased _____	10. restaurant _____	16. elegant _____
5. expensive _____	11. defense _____	17. patient _____
6. danish _____	12. September _____	18. engineer _____

NAME: _____ **DATE:** _____

Chapter 8 Homework Review

A. Fill in the missing sounds using the symbols of the IPA. Write the number of sounds in each word.

    EXAMPLE: occasion / ək_eɪ_ʒən /   __6__

1. agent	/ ___ʤɪnt /	____	8. shelves	/ʃ___ ___ ___z /	____
2. death	/ ___ ___θ /	____	9. painted	/ p___ ___təd /	____
3. mention	/ ___ ___ ___ʃən /	____	10. vacation	/ v___k___ʃən /	____
4. scheduled	/ ___ ___ ___ ___ʤuld /	____	11. main	/m___n /	____
5. eighty-eight	/ ___tɪ___t /	____	12. avocation	/ ævoʊk___ʃən /	____
6. letter	/ l___tɚ /	____	13. later	/ l___tɚ /	____
7. wait	/ w___t /	____	14. chased	/ tʃ___ ___ ___ /	____

B. Circle the stressed syllable. Write the number of syllables in each word.

1. remain ____	6. patient ____	11. complain ____
2. weather ____	7. anyone ____	12. affair ____
3. credit ____	8. explain ____	13. mistake ____
4. bagels ____	9. ashamed ____	14. eleven ____
5. arranged ____	10. telephone ____	15. wages ____

C. The pronunciation of each word is given in column 2. If correct, write C. If incorrect, write I and make the corrections in column 4 using the symbols of the IPA.

    EXAMPLE: mail /mɛl /   __I__   _____ / eɪ /

1	2	3	4
Word	Pronunciation	C/I	Correction
1. prayed	/ preɪd /	____	_____
2. pain	/ pɛn /	____	_____
3. men	/ mɛn /	____	_____
4. fail	/ fɛl /	____	_____

331

	1	2	3	4
	Word	Pronunciation	C/I	Correction
5.	fell	/ feɪl /	_____	_____
6.	train	/ trɛn /	_____	_____
7.	head	/ hɛd /	_____	_____
8.	hid	/ hɪd /	_____	_____
9.	break	/ brɛk /	_____	_____
10.	set	/ sæt /	_____	_____

D. Write the following words using the symbols of the IPA. Practice reading aloud, producing / eɪ / and / ɛ / accurately.

1. said   /   /   6. wet   /   /

2. sell   /   /   7. wait   /   /

3. sale   /   /   8. raced   /   /

4. taste   /   /   9. says   /   /

5. debt   /   /   10. break   /   /

E. Fill in the appropriate IPA symbol in the space provided. Practice reading these sentences aloud, producing / eɪ / and / ɛ / correctly.

    EXAMPLE: He f<u>ai</u>led / eɪ / his cr<u>e</u>dit / ɛ / r<u>a</u>ting / eɪ /.

1. <u>E</u>d /   / s<u>ay</u>s /   / he won't forg<u>e</u>t /   /.

2. The <u>e</u>ngineer /   / m<u>a</u>de /   / v<u>e</u>ry /   / high w<u>a</u>ges /   /.

3. Have you m<u>e</u>t /   / your travel <u>a</u>gent /   / y<u>e</u>t /   /?

4. R<u>ay</u>'s /   / pr<u>ay</u>ers /   / for T<u>e</u>d /   / were too l<u>a</u>te /   /.

5. S<u>e</u>lma /   / was ash<u>a</u>med /   / to n<u>a</u>me /   / her fri<u>e</u>nds /   /.

6. Is he the b<u>e</u>st /   / candid<u>a</u>te /   / for pr<u>e</u>sident /   /?

7. T<u>e</u>nnis /   / g<u>a</u>mes /   / were sch<u>e</u>duled /   / for S<u>e</u>ptember /   /, Nov<u>e</u>mber /   /, and F<u>e</u>bruary /   /.

8. It was a mist<u>a</u>ke /   / to eat that st<u>ea</u>k /   / for br<u>ea</u>kfast /   /.

9. We bl<u>a</u>med /   / the m<u>ay</u>or /   / for <u>e</u>verything /   /.

10. El<u>e</u>ven /   / m<u>e</u>n /   / and <u>ei</u>ght /   / l<u>a</u>dies /   / w<u>e</u>nt /   / to Sp<u>ai</u>n /   /.

Reading Aloud

A. This selection focuses on the production of / eɪ / and / ɛ /. Make sure you differentiate the two vowel sounds, giving full value to the diphthong / eɪ /. Remember to link words within the phrase and stress important words, while maintaining the conversational tone of the passage. Work for variety in pitch and clarity of articulation.

Divide the sentences into phrase units, using single and double slashes and underline the stressed words.

> **EXAMPLE:**   I promised <u>Jane</u> / a <u>gold</u> <u>chain</u> / for her <u>birthday</u>. / /

A tape or your instructor may serve as model for correct and fluent oral reading. Be prepared to enact this dialogue in class.

Mel and Mabel

◆

MABEL: Mel, here's what I've been waiting for—Macy's great sale, Now, let me get out my list.

MEL: You go. I hate shopping.

MABEL: Men—always complaining. Look, the cell phone's listed and the bedspread.

MEL: I'm definitely staying home.

MABEL: And what a break! The ten shelves we needed for the den, ready to be painted—on sale!

MEL: I distinctly remember you said seven.

MABEL: Three extra, just in case.

MEL: The weather man predicts rain. Heavy rain. Maybe a storm.

MABEL: Men's sweaters are on special. Turtlenecks in a great shade of red.

MEL: I have too many sweaters already, and they're all red.

MABEL: I promised Jane a gold chain for her birthday.

MEL: It's February. Her birthday's in May.

MABEL: But they may not be on sale in May.

MEL: What's so terrible about paying full price for a change?

MABEL: How can you even suggest such a thing!

MEL: Mabel, you're spending too much money, sale or no sale.

MABEL: Not to worry. Everything's on credit cards. Ready? Let's go.

Target Sound: / æ /

Distinctive Features

/ æ / is a low, front, unrounded vowel. Like all vowel sounds, it is voiced.

How Is / æ / Made?

The front of the tongue is low on the floor of the mouth with the tongue tip behind the lower teeth. The jaw is dropped and the mouth is open quite wide.

EXAMPLE: s<u>a</u>t   <u>a</u>ccent   pl<u>a</u>nt

What Are the Problems or Patterns in Spelling?

/ æ / is usually represented by the letter **a.**

EXAMPLE: add   master   rat

When the letter **e** follows a consonant, the short vowel / æ / becomes / eɪ /.

EXAMPLE:	cap	cape	rag	rage	lab	label
	cab	cable	pal	pale	bath	bathe

What Are the Problems in Pronunciation?

/ æ / is pronounced / ɛ /, if the tongue is raised and tensed.

EXAMPLE: *bet* instead of *bat*

/ æ / may be pronounced / ɑ / if the back section of the tongue is raised.*

EXAMPLE: *hot* instead of *hat*

The / æ / Sound

A. Variations in spelling are minimal. Repeat these words after your instructor.

man	aunt	salmon
map	lack	magic
added	ask	math
quack	half	banana

---

* The / ɑ / is a low back vowel. The tongue lies flat, the jaw is dropped, and the mouth is oval shaped. This phoneme resembles the / ɑ / in Spanish.

Note: Students speaking French, Spanish, Russian, and Asian languages may need to work on distinguishing and to producing the / æ / phoneme.

B. Vowel length

1. The vowel /æ / appears primarily in stressed syllables.

manage	accident	character
angry	practical	attractive
attacked	atmosphere	mathematics

2. The vowel / æ / is longer when it occurs before a voiced consonant.

mat	mad	half	have	lack	lag
cap	cab	match	Madge	sat	sat
rack	rag	stack	stag	hat	had

C. Practice pronouncing / æ / as you read these sentences aloud.

1. Sam, a bank manager, asked Nancy to a Saturday night dance.
2. "I can't," said Nancy, who worked in a glass factory. "Not on Saturday night."
3. "I have to help my aunt pack. She's going to Japan."
4. Sam gave her one more chance. He asked her to a basketball game, hoping she would accept another date.
5. "I can't stand basketball," said Nancy.
6. Sam was so angry he asked his math tutor, Jan, to go to the dance.
7. Jan accepted the invitation to the dance and to the basketball game.
8. They planned to get married in January.
9. Nancy and her aunt were happy for Sam and Jan.
10. They sent them a dozen glasses from the glass factory.
11. Sam realized he was no longer angry.
12. He and Jan were happy with the gift and asked Nancy and her aunt to dinner.

Listening/Speaking

A. Contrast / æ / and / ɛ /.

Can you *feel* the difference as you repeat after your instructor?

Can you *hear* the difference between the / æ / and the / ɛ /?

Your instructor will say three words from columns 1 and 2 for each pair. Indicate the pattern that you hear.

> **EXAMPLE:** If you hear *sad, said, sad,* the pattern is 1 2 1.

1	2	1	2	1	2
sad	said	had	head	bad	bed
mat	met	man	men	band	bend
pat	pet	tan	ten	bland	blend
ban	Ben	sand	send	pack	peck

B. Underline the contrastive words in each sentence. As you read aloud, remember to produce the / æ / and / ɛ / sounds in the underlined words.

> **EXAMPLE:**   The hotel <u>bed</u> was not too <u>bad</u>.

1. He kept the bottle capped.

2. She said she was sad.

3. Don't put my pen near the hot pan.

4. His dad was dead when he arrived.

5. She owns ten pairs of tan shoes.

6. His bad leg made him lag behind.

7. He was a man among men.

8. Jake was in a jam because he lost the gem.

9. All the students except Tim would not accept their grades.

10. He was so adept he could adapt to any situation.

C. Contrast / æ / and / eɪ /.

Can you *feel* the difference as you repeat after your instructor?

Can you *hear* the difference between the / æ / and the / eɪ /?

Your instructor will say three words from columns 1 and 2 for each pair. Indicate the pattern that you hear.

> **EXAMPLE:**   If you hear *man, main, man*, the pattern is 1 2 1.

1	2	1	2	1	2
mad	made	Sam	same	pad	paid
pan	pain	man	main	rat	rate
bat	bait	past	paste	dam	dame
fat	fate	mass	mace	tack	take
ban	bane	Sal	sale	mat	mate
fad	fade	add	aid	back	bake

D. Underline the contrastive words in each sentence. As you read aloud, remember to produce the / æ / and / eɪ / sounds in the underlined words.

> **EXAMPLE:** Can you <u>take</u> that <u>tack</u> out of the wall?

1. The blue jean fad may fade soon.

2. He paid too much for that pad.

3. Blake wore a black hat.

4. He threw a pan against the window pane.

5. Does that man live on Main Street?

6. The aide in the office can't add correctly.

7. I see Sam the same hour every day.

8. Mary made me so mad.

9. Add all your expenses to see how much aid you need.

E. Contrast / æ / and / ɑ /.*

Can you *feel* the difference as you repeat after your instructor?

Can you *hear* the difference between the / æ / and the / ɑ /?

Your instructor will say three words from columns 1 and 2 for each pair. Indicate the pattern that you hear.

> **EXAMPLE:** If you hear *sack, sock, sack,* the pattern is 1 2 1.

1	2	1	2	1	2
tap	top	rack	rock	packet	pocket
rat	rot	sack	sock	Jackie	jockey
pad	pod	chap	chop	adapt	adopt
lack	lock	add	odd	cad	cod
mad	mod	gnat	not	hat	hot
black	block	maps	mops	racquet	rocket

F. Underline the contrastive words in each sentence. As you read aloud, remember to produce the / æ / and the / ɑ / sounds in the underlined words.

> **EXAMPLE:** A <u>black</u> Cadillac raced down the <u>block</u>.

---

* The / ɑ / is a low back vowel. The tongue lies flat.

1. Hank, don't honk your horn.

2. Jackie wants to become a jockey.

3. A packet of nails fell out of Harry's pocket.

4. Sam threw his sock into a sack.

5. That cad said he hated my baked cod fish.

6. The adopted children adapted well to school.

7. Nat had a knot in his shoelace.

8. The cat fell off the cot.

9. I lacked a key for my locked car.

10. Who threw that rock on my car rack?

Listening/Writing

A. Listening carefully for the / æ / sound as our instructor reads each word. Write this sound when it occurs in the initial or medial position using the symbol of the IPA.

If / æ / is not heard, write a dash in the space provided.

EXAMPLE: happy /____æ____/ answer /____æ____/ except /____—____/

1. platform _____	8. pest _____	15. luck _____
2. train _____	9. past _____	16. factory _____
3. class _____	10. odd _____	17. economics _____
4. habit _____	11. adapt _____	18. attractive _____
5. adept _____	12. head _____	19. baked _____
6. not _____	13. had _____	20. mat _____
7. met _____	14. black _____	21. pocket _____

B. Circle the word read aloud by the instructor.

1. cap	cop	cape	3. add Ed aid
2. tap	top	tape	4. past pest paste

5. sack	sock	soak		8. rap	rape	rope
6. mad	mod	mode		9. black	block	bloke
7. Nat	not	note		10. rack	rock	rake

C. Your instructor will select one of the words in parentheses and read the entire sentence aloud. Listen carefully and circle the word you hear. Practice reading each sentence aloud using either one of the words in parentheses.

1. Don't leave your (bat, bait) on the bench.

2. Let's buy a (rack, rake) now.

3. How did the (pane, pan) get broken?

4. A (cap, cape) was found in the taxi.

5. The (man, men) had jumped first.

6. Those (tan, ten) shirts are very popular.

7. The (pens, pans, pins) were lost in the fire.

8. Who saw the (dame, dam)?

9. We don't (lock, lack) anything.

10. They cannot (adopt, adapt).

11. Her (pocket, packet) was torn.

12. Mary tripped on a (rack, rock).

D. Circle the stressed syllable as each word is read aloud. Write the number of syllables in each word. Practice aloud.

1. adopt _____		6. binoculars _____		11. answer _____
2. practical _____		7. angry _____		12. stamped _____
3. Japan _____		8. attached _____		13. basketball _____
4. manager _____		9. engaged _____		14. adapted _____
5. happier _____		10. gamblers _____		15. accept _____

E. Your instructor will say three words from columns 1 and 2 for each pair. Write the pattern that you hear.

> **EXAMPLE:**   If you hear *had, head, had,* write 1 2 1.

	1	2	*Pattern*
1.	tan	ten	_____ _____ _____
2.	bat	bet	_____ _____ _____
3.	pack	peck	_____ _____ _____
4.	blast	blessed	_____ _____ _____
5.	add	Ed	_____ _____ _____
6.	add	odd	_____ _____ _____
7.	lack	lock	_____ _____ _____
8.	knack	knock	_____ _____ _____
9.	packet	pocket	_____ _____ _____
10.	adapt	adopt	_____ _____ _____

Chapter 8 Homework Review

A. Fill in the missing sounds using the symbols of the IPA. Write the number of sounds in each word.

    EXAMPLE: accident / _æ_dsɪdənt / __8__

1. answer / ___n___ɚ /   _____   8. happier / h___pɪɚ /   _____

2. manager / m___ ___ədʒɚ /   _____   9. engaged / ɛn___ ___dʒd /   _____

3. adapt / əd___ ___ ___ /   _____   10. dancing / ___ ___ ___sɪŋ /   _____

4. practical / ___ ___ ___ ___tɪkəl / _____   11. binoculars / bɪ___ɑ___jələɚz / _____

5. angry /___ŋgrɪ /   _____   12. packet / ___ ___ ___ət /   _____

6. chance / tʃ___ ___ ___ /   _____   13. pocket / ___ ___ ___ət /   _____

7. bank / ___ ___ŋ___ /   _____   14. invitation / ɪ___ ___ ___t___ʃən / _____

B. Circle the stressed syllables. Write the number of syllables in each word.

1. women _____	6. horses _____	11. accident _____
2. jammed _____	7. through _____	12. atmosphere _____
3. planned _____	8. can't _____	13. hijackers _____
4. married _____	9. character _____	14. factory _____
5. relief _____	10. advertised _____	15. managed _____

C. The pronunciation of each word is given in column 2. If correct, write C. If incorrect, write I and make the corrections in column 4 using the symbols of the IPA.

    EXAMPLE: hand / hɛnd   __I__   __æ__

1	2	3	4
Word	Pronunciation	C/I	Correction
1. planned	/ plænd /	_____	_____
2. add	/ ɛd /	_____	_____
3. chance	/ tʃæns /	_____	_____
4. cap	/ kɑp /	_____	_____

341

1	2	3	4
Word	Pronunciation	C/I	Correction
5. public	/ pɑblɪk /	_____	_____
6. track	/ trɛk /	_____	_____
7. stack	/ stɑk /	_____	_____
8. lack	/ lɑk /	_____	_____
9. stand	/ stænd /	_____	_____
10. many	/ mɪnɪ /	_____	_____

D. Write the following words using the symbols of the IPA. Practice aloud producing the / æ / correctly when it appears in the word.

1. accept /   /   6. bat   /   /

2. stack   /   /   7. bet   /   /

3. fast   /   /   8. add   /   /

4. nag   /   /   9. aid   /   /

5. bait   /   /   10. planned /   /

E. Fill in the appropriate IPA symbol in the space provided. Practice reading the sentences aloud, producing the sounds correctly.

    EXAMPLE: We planned / æ / to take / eɪ / a late / eɪ / plane / eɪ /.

1. I managed /   / to get to work before the bell /   / rang /   /.

2. This is your last /   / chance /   / to see that /   / opera /   /.

3. In Japan /   / men /   / and women /   / bathe /   / together /   / in pubic baths /   /.

4. Factory /   / jobs are often advertised /   / in the papers /   /.

5. My aunt /   / is very agile /   / for her age /   /.

6. How many /   / hostages were captured /   / by the hijacker /   /?

7. Ann /   / did not accept /   / any help.

8. The cop lost his cap /   / last /   / week.

9. We planned /   / to go to the bank /   / next Saturday /   /.

10. Ed's /   / accident /   / in Alaska /   / was very bad /   /.

Reading Aloud

A. This dialogue focuses on the production of / æ /. Be sure to produce this vowel sound correctly, as well as the vowel sounds with which it is confused: / e / and / a /. Remember to link words within the phrase and stress important words, while maintaining the conversational tone of the passage. Work for variety in pitch and clarity of articulation.

Divide the sentences into phrase units, using single and double slashes, and underline the stressed words.

> **EXAMPLE:** <u>Say</u>, / is that the <u>gal</u> / who <u>lives</u> in the <u>tan house</u> / on your <u>block</u>? / /

Your instructor may serve as your model for correct and fluent oral reading. Be prepared to enact this dialogue in class.

At the Race Track

◆

SAMMY:	Manny, I've had it! This is the last time you're going to drag me to the track.
MANNY:	What's the matter, Sammy? Did you lose a lot of money?
SAMMY:	Every horse I bet on ran last.
Manny:	I've got just the jockey for you.
SAMMY:	Who cares about the jockey? I just want a fast horse.
MANNY:	Wait till you see this jockey. She's amazing. Her name's Jackie.
SAMMY:	Jackie the jockey. Say, is that the gal who lives in the tan house on your block?
MANNY:	That's the one. She's riding Handy-Andy. The horses are at the gate. Handy-Andy's on the outside. Take a look through my binoculars.
SAMMY:	Not bad. Not bad at all.
MANNY:	Good-looking horse.
SAMMY:	Is Jackie married, engaged, or otherwise attached?
MANNY:	Just mad about horses. You won't stand a chance, Sammy.
SAMMY:	You bet on Hand-Andy. I'll take my chances with Jackie the jockey.
MANNY:	Good luck! I'm happier at the track.
SAMMY:	You'll be stuck with a stack of stubs from the track, while I may be out dancing with Jackie the jockey.
MANNY:	I guess we're both gamblers. Who knows? Maybe Handy-Andy will be a winner for me and Jackie the jockey will be a winner for you.

Reviewing the Front Vowels / i ɪ eɪ ɛ æ /

A. Practice pronouncing the following words.

/ i /	/ ɪ /	/ eɪ /	/ ɛ /	/ æ /
beat	bit	bait	bet	bat
bean	been	bane	Ben	ban
meet	mitt	mate	met	mat
seat	sit	sate	set	sat
bead	bid	bade	bed	bad
lead	lid	laid	led	lad

Can you *feel* the difference as you repeat after your instructor?

Can you *hear* the difference as you produce each of the front vowel sounds?

B. Review passages

These selections focus on the correct production of the front vowels: / i /, / ɪ /, / eɪ /, / ɛ /, and / æ /. Be sure to produce these sounds accurately. Remember to link words within phrases and stress important words, while maintaining the conversational tone of the passage. Work for variety in pitch and clarity of articulation.

Divide the sentences into phrase units, using single and double slashes, and underline the stressed words.

> **EXAMPLE:**   If he <u>missed</u> the <u>train</u>, / he would be <u>late</u> / for his <u>ten</u> <u>o'clock</u> <u>class</u>. //

A tape or your instructor may serve as your model for correct and fluent oral reading. Prepare to read aloud in class.

Making the Train

◆

He raced down the steps, hoping he would make the train. If he missed the train, he would be late for his ten o'clock class. His teacher had a habit of keeping the classroom door locked after the bell sounded. Last week, he just sneaked in past the teacher as the bell rang.

Another step and he was on the subway platform. In came the train, jammed as usual, and he managed to squeeze past the closing door, almost leaving his left leg on the platform. He breathed a sigh of relief, and then suddenly hit his hand against his head. He need not have rushed after all. The class he was worried about met the next day.

Exercise

Select words with each vowel sound from the above passage and write them in the appropriate column.

/ i /	/ ɪ /	/ eɪ /	/ ɛ /	/ æ /
_____	_____	_____	_____	_____
_____	_____	_____	_____	_____
_____	_____	_____	_____	_____
_____	_____	_____	_____	_____
_____	_____	_____	_____	_____
_____	_____	_____	_____	_____
_____	_____	_____	_____	_____

Phil and Ann

———◆———

PHIL: Come in, Ann. I thought I heard the bell.

ANN: Phil, I feel terrible.

PHIL: Have a seat.

ANN: I can't sit.

PHIL: What's the matter with your head?

ANN: I can only lift it to the left.

PHIL: Is your back bent?

ANN: No, but my ankle's sprained.

PHIL: Here, take my hand. I'll help you in your seat.

ANN: Please! Stay away! I've wrenched my wrist. I have to rest it.

PHIL: You're in great shape. Did you slip in your sleep, or hit your head against the bed?

ANN: You laugh and I'll leave!

PHIL: Okay, I can see you have a sad tale to tell.

ANN: And you're to blame.

PHIL: Me?

ANN: Yes, you. You said I should take tennis lessons. Well, I did.

PHIL: But that's absolutely fantastic!

ANN: Fantastic? I'm one mass of aches and pains.

PHIL: Naturally. You're using a different set of muscles.

ANN: I like the old set better. Besides, I can't even hit that ball over the net.

PHIL: Give yourself a chance. Keep your eye on the ball and be fast on your feet.

ANN: I'm too fat to be fit.

PHIL: Stop fishing for compliments. You're not fat. But I'll tell you what you *do* need.

ANN: Be quick. I can't sit in this seat much longer.

PHIL: You need practice. And that's what you're going to get. Right now!

ANN: If you mean what I think you mean, the answer is no!

PHIL: The name of the game is—practice. Pack your racquet and your sneakers, and I'll pick you up in ten minutes.

ANN: What about my aches and pains?

PHIL: We'll take them too.

ANN: I came looking for sympathy and all I'm getting is practice. Well, maybe you're right. Let's go.

Exercise

Select words with each vowel sound from the above passage and write them in the appropriate column.

/ i /	/ ɪ /	/ eɪ /	/ ɛ /	/ æ /
_____	_____	_____	_____	_____
_____	_____	_____	_____	_____
_____	_____	_____	_____	_____
_____	_____	_____	_____	_____
_____	_____	_____	_____	_____
_____	_____	_____	_____	_____
_____	_____	_____	_____	_____

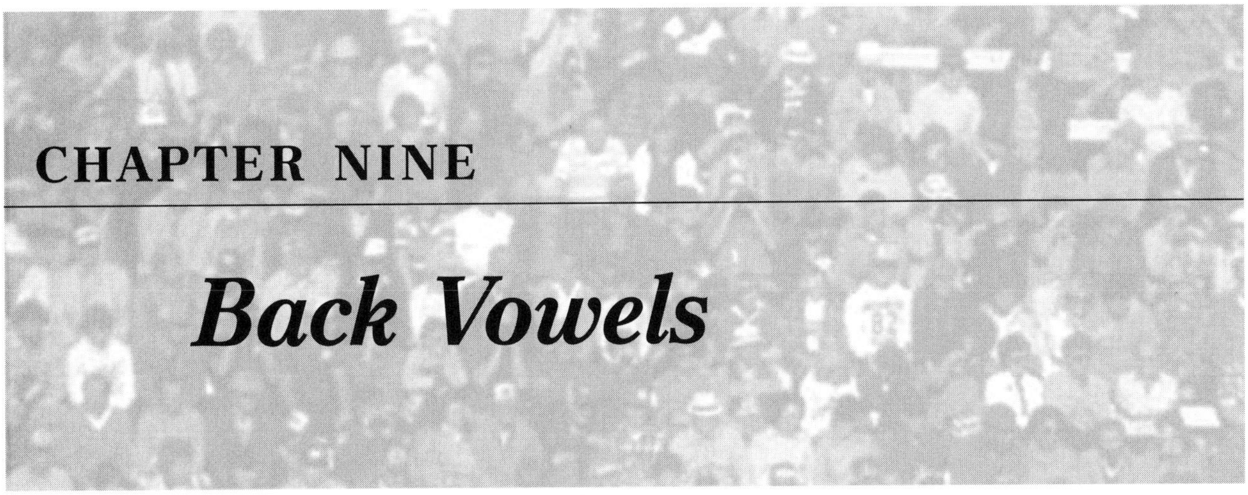

CHAPTER NINE

Back Vowels

This diagram is a schematic representation of the positions of the tongue in the back section of the mouth for the production of the five back vowels. The tongue tip is placed behind the lower front teeth. The back section of the tongue is elevated to its high position for the / u / and / ʊ / sounds. It descends to midheight for / oʊ / and / ɔ / and becomes quite flat for the / ɑ / sound. Thus these vowels may be described as high, mid, or low back vowels.

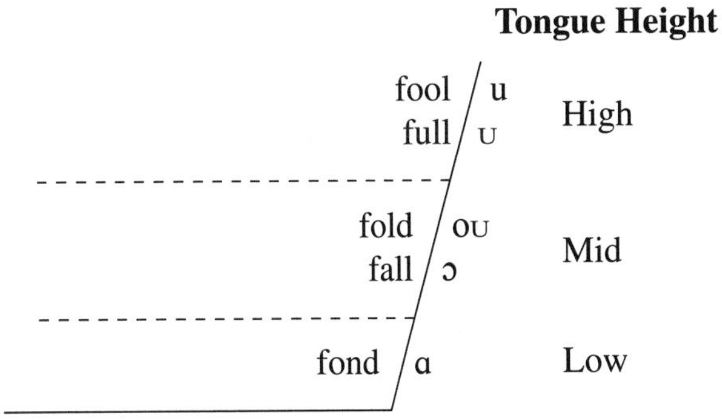

Tongue Height

```
fool / u
full / ʊ      High
- - - - - - - - - - - -
fold / oʊ
fall / ɔ      Mid
- - - - - - - - - - - -
fond / ɑ      Low
```

FIGURE 6. Tongue positions for the back vowels.

/ u / is the highest of the back vowels. The back of the tongue is high in the mouth, and tense. The lips are rounded and tense. The sound is long in duration. When this vowel sound is not given full value, it will resemble / ʊ /.

EXAMPLE: / u /   bl<u>ue</u>   sh<u>oe</u>   br<u>oo</u>m

/ ʊ / is also a high back vowel. It is made with the tongue a little lower in the mouth. The lips and tongue are relaxed; the sound is very short.

EXAMPLE: / ʊ /   c<u>oo</u>k   c<u>ou</u>ld   p<u>u</u>sh

/ u / and / ʊ / are often confused by non-native speakers, who substitute one for the other.

EXAMPLE: Why don't you clean off that *suit?* (meaning *soot*),

Why don't you clean off that *soot?* (meaning *suit*).

/ oʊ / is a mid back diphthong.* It consists of two vowel sounds, the first of which is longer and stronger, the second weaker. The lips are rounded and tense, and the tongue moves to the higher / ʊ / position to complete the diphthong. / oʊ / is a very long sound.

EXAMPLE: b<u>oa</u>t   ch<u>o</u>se   kn<u>ow</u>

/ ɔ / is a mid back vowel.** There is a slight degree of tension of the tongue. The lips are slightly tense.

EXAMPLE: c<u>au</u>ght   br<u>oa</u>d   f<u>ou</u>ght

/ oʊ / and / ɔ / are often confused by native and non-native speakers, who substitute one for the other.

EXAMPLE: Do you know how much he *owed* me? (meaning *awed*)

Do you know how much he *awed* me? (meaning *owed*)

/ ɑ / is the lowest of the back vowels. The tongue is flat on the floor of the mouth, the jaw is dropped and the mouth is opened wide in an oval position. The vowel / ɑ / is long in duration.

EXAMPLE: <u>a</u>rmy   st<u>o</u>p   h<u>ea</u>rt

/ ɑ / and / ʌ /, a low central vowel, are often confused by non-native speakers, who substitute one for the other.

EXAMPLE: I don't like the *collar* of that shirt. (meaning *color*)

I don't like the *color* of that shirt. (meaning *collar*)

Target Sounds: / u / and / ʊ /

Distinctive Features

/ u / and / ʊ / are high back vowels. They are voiced.

How Are / u / and / ʊ / Made?

The back section of the tongue is high in the mouth, and the tip of the tongue is locked behind the lower front teeth.

---

* / oʊ / is diphthongized in American English, and this variation is used throughout the text.

** / ɔ / is often described as a low back vowel.

Note: The high back vowels are all produced with rounded lips. This is not true in some other languages such as Chinese and Japanese. The Chinese word for **four** is / su /. The tongue position is that of / u /, but the lips are spread. This word in Mandarin contrasts with / su /, **speed.** Here the lips are rounded for the high back vowel.

The pronunciation of the back vowels / oʊ /, / ɔ /, and / ɑ / varies in different dialectal areas in the United States. Non-native speakers often confuse these three vowel sounds as well as the central vowel / ʌ /.

/ u / is a long vowel. The back section of the tongue, which is tense, is very high in the mouth. The lips are completely rounded and tense.

EXAMPLE: ch<u>oo</u>se   n<u>ew</u>s   cr<u>ui</u>se

/ ʊ / is a very short vowel. The lips are slightly open and relaxed.

EXAMPLE: l<u>oo</u>k   f<u>u</u>ll   sh<u>ou</u>ld

What Are the Problems or Patterns in Spelling?

/ u / may be represented by the letters **o, oo, ui,** and **ue.**

EXAMPLE: wh<u>o</u>   tw<u>o</u>   f<u>oo</u>d   fr<u>ui</u>t   bl<u>ue</u>

/ ʊ / may be represented by the letters **oo, ou,** and **u.***

EXAMPLE: g<u>oo</u>d   sh<u>oo</u>k   w<u>ou</u>ld   p<u>u</u>sh

What Are the Problems in Pronunciation

/ u / may be shortened and pronounced / ʊ /.

EXAMPLE: *f<u>u</u>ll* instead of *f<u>oo</u>l*

/ ʊ / may be prolonged resulting in the vowel / u /.

EXAMPLE: *p<u>oo</u>l* instead of *p<u>u</u>ll*

The / u / *Sound*

A. Variations in spelling

Repeat these words after your instructor. Observe the different spellings for the / u / sound.

who	cruel	nuisance
you	broom	prove
sue	brute	root
chew	food	wound
clue	fruit	jury
rheumatism	shoe	through

---

* Note that the **oo** spelling has two pronunciations.

    EXAMPLE: f<u>oo</u>d is pronounced / fud /;   g<u>oo</u>d is pronounced / gʊd /

In addition to distirnguishing between the phonemes / u / and / ʊ /, the non-native student must learn the pronunciation patterns for specific words such as **these.**

B. Vowel length

1. The vowel / u / is longer when it occurs before a voiced consonant.

1	2	1	2
brute	brood	loose	lose
lute	lewd	suit	sued
root	rude	hoot	who'd
noose	news	proof	prove

2. The vowel is longer when it is the last sound in the word.

brew	to	flew	through
sue	true	you	shoe

C. Divide each sentence into phrase units and link the words within the phrase. Be sure to lengthen the / u / as you read aloud.

1. Lulu Loon accused her husband, Hubert Loon, of hitting her with a broom.

2. Lulu sued Herbert for cruel and inhuman treatment.

3. Stuart Boon was in no mood to serve on the jury when the case came to court.

4. He needed root canal work on his tooth, and he couldn't chew solid food. All he could do was drink fruit juice and soup.

5. Nevertheless, since he knew it was his duty to be a juror, he did not choose to refuse to serve.

6. When Stuart saw Lulu, he knew Hubert would lose his case.

7. Stuart thought Lulu was cute, and he was sure she was smiling at him.

8. Stuart had no use for Hubert because he was such a brute.

9. He was so furious with Hubert, he forgot about his sore tooth.

10. But he was even more furious with the judge, who threw the case out of court.

11. "There is no proof that Hubert is a brute," said the judge.

The / ʊ / Sound

A. Variations in spelling

Repeat these words after your instructor.

bush	cushion	full
book	bullet	wooden
pull	crooked	should
would	wool	stood

B. The / ʊ / in sentence practice.

Divide each sentence into phrase units and link the words within the phrase. Stress the important words as you read aloud.

1. The elevator was full of people when Jennie pushed herself in.

2. "You stepped on my foot," complained Mrs. Cooke.

3. "I'm sorry," said Jennie Loo, as she pulled three full shopping bags in with her.

4. Her package of books and a box of cookies crashed to the floor.

5. As she stopped to put them in her shopping bag, she dropped her books on Mrs. Cooke's foot.

6. "Would you be good enough to get your books off my feet?" yelled Mrs. Cooke.

7. "I should have my own elevator," mumbled Jennie Loo. "Could you please move over to make more room for me?"

8. When Jennie left the elevator, she took only her books.

9. She left her books and cookies in her three full shopping bags.

10. "No more pushing and pulling for me," she said.

Listening/Speaking

A. Contrast / u / and / ʊ /.

Can you *feel* the difference as you repeat after your instructor?

Can you *hear* the difference between the long / u / and the short / ʊ /?

Your instructor will say three words from columns 1 and 2 for each pair. Indicate the patterns you hear.

> **EXAMPLE:** If you hear *pool, pull, pool,* the pattern is 1 2 1.

1	2	1	2
pool	pull	cooed	could
fool	full	shooed	should
stewed	stood	wooed	would
Luke	look	who'd	hood

B. Underline the contrastive words in each sentence. As you read aloud, remember to produce the / u / and / ʊ / sounds in the underlined words.

> **EXAMPLE:**   The <u>good</u> little baby <u>cooed</u> all afternoon.

1. Dr. Luke, take a look at my sore foot.

2. Don't pull me into the pool.

3. A fool is full of his own importance.

4. Who'd have thought of looking under the car's hood?

5. He stood at the stove as the meat was stewed.

6. I was so pleased I could have cooed with pleasure.

7. He would have wooed her with words, but she preferred deeds.

8. She should have shooed the children away.

9. The soot in the city does not suit me.

10. Tom's suit is covered with soot.

Listening/Writing

A. Listen carefully for / u / and / ʊ / as your instructor pronounces each word. Write these sounds when they occur in the initial, medial, or final position using the symbols of the IPA. If / u / or / ʊ / is not heard, write a dash in the space provided.

> **EXAMPLE:**   cookies /____ʊ____/   kitchen /_____—_____/   human /____u____/

1. noon _____	6. wooden _____	11. rushing _____
2. flood _____	7. look _____	12. cookies _____
3. food _____	8. spoon _____	13. fruit _____
4. foot _____	9. pushing _____	14. fury _____
5. woman _____	10. nuisance _____	15. should _____

16. soup _____   18. suits _____   20. mood _____

17. shouted _____   19. good _____   21. stood _____

B. Circle the word read aloud by the instructor.

1. pool   pull   pulled   5. fool   full   fools

2. stood   stowed   stewed   6. shoes   should   shooed

3. wood   wooed   wound   7. hoot   hood   who'd

4. code   could   cooed

C. Circle the stressed syllable as each word is read aloud. Write the number of syllables in each word. Practice aloud.

1. misunderstood _____   6. human _____   11. refuse _____

2. numerous _____   7. furious _____   12. bullet _____

3. conclusion _____   8. brute _____   13. apron _____

4. pushed _____   9. mumbled _____   14. fire _____

5. nuisances _____   10. restaurant _____   15. grinned _____

D. Your instructor will say three words from columns 1 and 2 for each pair. Write the pattern that you hear.

EXAMPLE: If you hear *pool, pull, pool,* write 1 2 1.

1	2	*Pattern*
1. pool	pull	_____ _____ _____
2. fool	full	_____ _____ _____
3. cooed	could	_____ _____ _____
4. shooed	should	_____ _____ _____
5. who'd	hood	_____ _____ _____
6. wooed	would	_____ _____ _____
7. stewed	stood	_____ _____ _____

Chapter 9 Homework Review

A. Fill in the missing sounds using the symbols of the IPA. Write the number of sounds in each word.

     EXAMPLE: nuisances / n_u_sɪnsɪz / ___8___

1. soup   / s___p /   _____
2. threw   / θr___ /   _____
3. fury   / fj___rɪ /   _____
4. cookies   / k_____z /   _____
5. hooks   / h_____s /   _____
6. wooden   / w___dɔn /   _____
7. human   / hj_____ən /   _____

8. mood   / m___d /   _____
9. through   / θr___ /   _____
10. you   / j___ /   _____
11. woman   / w_____ən /   _____
12. women   / w_____ən /   _____
13. pushed   / p___ʃ___ /   _____
14. cruel   / _____əl /   _____

B. Circle the stressed syllable. Write the number of syllables in each word.

1. kitchen   _____
2. advanced   _____
3. dishwasher   _____
4. muttering   _____
5. sighed   _____

6. mumbled   _____
7. nuisances   _____
8. shouted   _____
9. crashed   _____
10. occupied   _____

11. stepped   _____
12. fired   _____
13. pulled   _____
14. ducked   _____
15. fury   _____

C. The pronunciation of each word is given in column 2. If correct, write C. If incorrect, write I and make the corrections in column 4 using the symbols of the IPA.

     EXAMPLE: prove / pruv /   _I_   _/ prʊv /_

1	2	3	4
Word	*Pronunciation*	*C/I*	*Correction*
1. foot	/ fʊt /	_____	_____
2. fruit	/ frʊt /	_____	_____
3. cookies	/ kʊkɪz /	_____	_____
4. books	/ bʊks /	_____	_____

1	2	3	4
Word	Pronunciation	C/I	Correction
5. should	/ ʃʊld /	_____	_____
6. stood	/ stud /	_____	_____
7. stool	/ stʊl /	_____	_____
8. food	/ fʊd /	_____	_____
9. good	/ gʊd /	_____	_____
10. would	/ wʊd /	_____	_____

D. Write the following words using the symbols of the IPA. Practice aloud, producing / u / and / ʊ / accurately.

1. noon /   /   6. grinned /   /

2. full /   /   7. spoon /   /

3. fool /   /   8. fruit /   /

4. cook /   /   9. pulled /   /

5. food /   /   10. foot /   /

E. Fill in the appropriate IPA symbol in the space provided. Practice reading these sentences aloud, producing / u / and / ʊ / accurately.

EXAMPLE: The st<u>u</u>dent / u / left his n<u>ew</u> / u / b<u>oo</u>k / ʊ / in the classr<u>oo</u>m / u /.

1. P<u>u</u>t /   / your coat on the h<u>oo</u>k /   /.

2. She st<u>oo</u>d /   / on a st<u>oo</u>l /   / to p<u>u</u>ll /   / down the c<u>oo</u>kie /   / jar.

3. We all like g<u>oo</u>d /   / f<u>oo</u>d /   /.

4. He p<u>u</u>lled /   / off his wet b<u>oo</u>ts /   /.

5. He thr<u>ew</u> /   / the b<u>u</u>shel /   / of fr<u>ui</u>t /   / into the w<u>oo</u>den /   / crate.

6. Who ch<u>ew</u>ed /   / up the sleeve of my n<u>ew</u> /   / s<u>ui</u>t /   /?

7. She thr<u>ew</u> /   / the c<u>oo</u>k's /   / b<u>oo</u>k /   / at him.

8. The b<u>u</u>llet /   / tore thr<u>ough</u> /   / his s<u>ui</u>t /   /.

9. I w<u>ou</u>ld /   / if I c<u>ou</u>ld /   /, but I sh<u>ou</u>ldn't /   /, so I won't.

10. N<u>u</u>merous /   / people misunderst<u>oo</u>d /   / my concl<u>u</u>sion /   /.

Reading Aloud

A. This selection focuses on the production of / u / and / ʊ /. Make sure that you differentiate the vowel sounds, giving full value to the / u /. Remember to link the words within the phrase and stress important words, while maintaining the conversational tone of the passage. Work for variety in pitch and clarity of articulation.

Divide the sentences into phrase units, using single and double slashes and underline the stressed words.

EXAMPLE: With a <u>splash</u>, / the <u>spoon</u> <u>crashed</u> / into the <u>sink</u>. / /

Your instructor may serve as your model for correct and fluent oral reading. Prepare to read aloud in class.

The Cook

It was noon, and the restaurant was full, every table occupied. In the kitchen, the cook was screaming at the help. "Move, will you! Get the food into the dining room! Look out," she shouted at a passing waiter. "You stepped on my foot!"

"Then get your big foot out of my way!" the waiter yelled back. In a fury, the cook threw a wooden spoon, dripping with hot soup, at the man.

He grinned, ducked, and pushed through the swinging door. The spoon landed on a tray of fruit and cookies, sending cookies and fruit all over the floor.

"Fools! Nuisances!" cried the cook, stamping her foot, and jumping up and down. "If I could, I'd fire all of you!"

"Who cares?" said the dishwasher.

"Suits me," added the kitchen boy.

The cook, a tall woman, pulled down her apron, pushed up her sleeves, and advanced upon them with another large wooden spoon.

"Look out, Luke," the kitchen boy called.

With a splash, the spoon crashed into the sink. The dishwasher took the spoon, bowed, and returned it to the cook. "Feel good now?" he asked. "Is your bad mood over?"

The cook moved back to her stove. Waiters pushed in and out of the room, but the cook just kept stirring a big pot of soup, muttering to herself, "Fools! You should all be fired." The dishwasher shook his head and grinned at the kitchen boy. "Give her another hour and she'll calm down. The lunch rush will be over, and she'll be human again." The kitchen boy, who was new on the job, looked at the cook and sighed.

"I hope you're right," he said. "I wouldn't want that bowl of soup down my back."

Target Sounds: / oʊ / and / ɔ /

Distinctive Features

/ oʊ / and / ɔ / are mid back vowels. They are voiced.

How Are / oʊ / and / ɔ / Made?

The back section of the tongue is midhigh in the mouth, and the tip of the tongue is locked behind the lower front teeth.

/ oʊ / is a diphthong, a combination of two vowel sounds considered as a single unit. The first element in the diphthong is the stronger and longer, gliding into the second element, which is weaker and not as easily perceived by the non-native speaker. It is a very long vowel, made with the lips completely rounded, and tense.

EXAMPLE: c<u>oa</u>l c<u>o</u>ld t<u>oe</u> kn<u>ow</u>

/ ɔ / is shorter than / oʊ /, made with the tongue slightly lower in the mouth. There is much less rounding of the lips, but they do remain somewhat tense. The jaw is dropped.

EXAMPLE: <u>a</u>ll b<u>o</u>ss <u>ou</u>ght t<u>au</u>ght

What Are the Problems or Patterns in Spelling?

/ oʊ / may be represented by the letters **ough, oa, ew, ou,** and **o.**

EXAMPLE: thor<u>ough</u> b<u>oa</u>t s<u>ew</u> sh<u>ou</u>lder g<u>o</u>

/ ɔ / may be represented by the letters **augh, aw, oa, a,** and **au.***

EXAMPLE: c<u>au</u>ght s<u>aw</u> br<u>oa</u>d t<u>a</u>lk h<u>au</u>l

*What Are the Problems in Pronunciation?***

/ oʊ / may be shortened so that the resulting sound may resemble the schwa / ə /. This is particularly evident in a stressed syllable.

EXAMPLE: *home* / həm / instead of / hoʊm /

/ ɔ / may be pronounced / oʊ / if the lips are rounded.

EXAMPLE: *boat* instead of *bought*

---

* Spelling variations contribute to the problems in pronunciation.

   EXAMPLE: r<u>oa</u>d is pronounced / roʊd /   br<u>oa</u>d is pronounced / brɔd /

The **oa** spelling has two pronunciations. In addition to distinguishing between the phonemes / oʊ / and / ɔ /, the non-native student must learn the pronunciation patterns of different words for lack of consistent rules.

** Instructors may note regional differences in pronunciation and teach accordingly.

The / oʊ / Sound

A. Variations in spelling

Repeat these words after your instructor. Observe the spelling representations for the / oʊ / sound.

go	beau	toast
bow	only	moment
sew	goal	shoulder
owe	joke	throne
toe	throw	although

B. Vowel length

1. The diphthong / oʊ / is longer when it occurs before a voiced consonant.

1	2	1	2	1	2
rope	robe	colt	cold	oat	ode
bolt	bold	wrote	rode	moat	mode
note	node	tote	toad	coat	code

2. The diphthong / oʊ / is longer when it is the last sound in the word.

sew	below
snow	hello
undergo	bestow

C. The / oʊ / in sentence practice.

Remember to stretch or lengthen the / oʊ / sound as you read each sentence aloud.

1. Joe phoned Joan before eight o'clock.

2. Joan woke, opened one eye, and groaned, "It's so early, Joe."

3. "The radio says snow," said Joe.

4. "So what!" moaned Joan.

5. Holding the phone, she put her toes on the floor. "Oh, it's so cold."

6. "I'm not going in for my sociology exam. I have a cold, a sore throat, and a stuffy nose!" she told Joe.

7. "I thought we'd go skiing after the sociology test," Joe replied.

8. "My toes are frozen," said Joan, blowing her nose.

9. "Okay I'll ask Rhonda to go. She showed me her notes yesterday."

10. Joan thought for a moment. "I'll throw on my old coat and see you in ten minutes."

The / ɔ / Sound

A. Variations in spelling

Repeat these words after your instructor.

law	ought	author
all	broad	shore
awe	office	cough
salt	almost	brought
walk	caught	toward

B. Vowel length

1. The vowel / ɔ / is longer when it occurs before a voiced consonant.

1	2	1	2
ought	awed	sought	sawed
caught	cawed	taught	toward
thought	thawed	nought	gnawed

2. The vowel / ɔ / is longer when it is the last sound in the word.

thaw	saw	law
claw	jaw	draw

C. The / ɔ / in sentence practice.

Divide each sentence into phrase units and link the words within phrases. Remember to drop the jaw for the / ɔ / sound as you read aloud.

1. Paul Small was very tall, which caused his boss, Mr. Long, to become very cross.

2. Paul Small was almost seven feet tall, and Mr. Long was barely five feet four.

3. How can you give an order to such a tall man and not feel awkward?

4. All the other employees talked about business in Mr. Long's law office, but Mr. Long would only talk to Paul on the telephone.

5. One day, Paul Small walked into a furniture store and bought a chair, which was delivered to his office.

6. While Mr. Long was out, Paul hauled the chair into his boss's office and waited.

7. Mr. Long walked into his office, saw Paul, and looked cross.

8. He sat down at his desk, looked across at Paul, and smiled. He was taller than Paul.

9. "Do you mind if I leave my new chair in your office when we talk?" Paul asked. "It has such short legs, and I have such long ones. I can really stretch out in this chair."

10. "Of course," his boss answered. "You just leave that chair in my office, and we can talk over business matters together."

11. The long and short of the story is that Mr. Long was never cross with Paul again, and he became an important partner in the law firm.

Listening/Speaking

A. Contrast / ou / and / ɔ /.

Can you *feel* the difference as you repeat after your instructor?

Can you *hear* the difference between the / ou / and / ɔ /?

Your instructor will say three words from columns 1 and 2 for each pair. Indicate the pattern that you hear.

EXAMPLE: If you hear *boat, bought, boat,* the pattern is 1 2 1.

1	2	1	2
owe	awe	oat	ought
boat	bought	row	raw
coal	call	stole	stall
goes	gauze	woke	walk
low	law	choke	chalk
pole	Paul	tool	tall

B. Underline the contrastive words in each sentence. As you read aloud, remember to produce the / ou / and / ɔ / in the underlined words.

EXAMPLE: I <u>woke</u> too late to take my early morning <u>walk</u>.

1. Yesterday we bought a boat.

2. I caught my coat on a nail.

3. You can choke on all that chalk dust.

4. They had to haul the child out of the hole.

5. We should call for more coal.

6. The bald man bowled well.

7. Moe called to say he had a cold.

8. I saw you sew that button on his coat.

9. Who stole the horses from the stall?

10. He'll row until his hands are raw.

Listening/Writing

A. Listen carefully for / ou / and / ɔ / as your instructor pronounces each word. Write these sounds when they occur in the initial, medial, or final position using the symbols of the IPA. If / ou / or / ɔ / are not heard, write a dash in the space provided.

> **EXAMPLE:** order /_____ɔ_____/   odor /_____ou_____/   chew /_____—_____/

1. called	_____	7. ocean	_____	13. row	_____
2. cold	_____	8. storm	_____	14. raw	_____
3. boat	_____	9. board	_____	15. blue	_____
4. bought	_____	10. boss	_____	16. morning	_____
5. horse	_____	11. coast	_____	17. chose	_____
6. hose	_____	12. hauled	_____	18. fought	_____

B. Circle the word read aloud by your instructor.

1. ball	bowl	bull		6. odor	order	odors
2. flaw	flow	flew		7. boat	bought	but
3. raw	row	rue		8. woke	walk	walks
4. coat	caught	cut		9. sews	saws	sues
5. coal	call	cool		10. boast	bossed	boost

C. Your instructor will select one of the words in parentheses and read the entire sentence aloud. Listen carefully and circle the word you hear. Practice reading each sentence aloud using either one of the words in parentheses.

1. Who threw the (bowl, ball)?

2. Watch how well she (sews, saws).

3. Did you get the (coal, call)?

4. He walked into the (hole, hall).

5. Did you note that animal's (pose, paws)?

6. The salesman is (bold, bald).

7. They all observed the (flow, flaw).

8. We bought some (coke, caulk).

9. Everyone (awed, owed) him.

10. We dislike that (odor, order).

D. Circle the stressed syllable as each word is read aloud. Write the number of syllables in each word. Practice aloud.

1. open	_____	6. chartering	_____	11. although	_____
2. moaned	_____	7. business	_____	12. strong	_____
3. radio	_____	8. interested	_____	13. frozen	_____
4. sociology	_____	9. awkward	_____	14. horses	_____
5. ocean	_____	10. moment	_____	15. tomorrow	_____

E. Your instructor will say three words from columns 1 and 2 for each pair. Write the pattern that you hear.

EXAMPLE: If you hear *owe, awe, owe,* write 1 2 1.

1	2	Pattern
1. bowl	ball	_____ _____ _____
2. soul	Saul	_____ _____ _____
3. owed	awed	_____ _____ _____
4. tote	taught	_____ _____ _____
5. loan	lawn	_____ _____ _____
6. coat	caught	_____ _____ _____
7. boat	bought	_____ _____ _____
8. mole	mall	_____ _____ _____
9. coast	cost	_____ _____ _____
10. boast	bossed	_____ _____ _____

Chapter 9 Homework Review

A. Fill in the missing sounds using the symbols of the IPA. Write the number of sounds in each word.

EXAMPLE: hoped / houpt / __4__

1. strong   / str___ŋ /   _____   8. morning   / m___rnɪŋ /   _____

2. moment   / m_____ɪ___t /   _____   9. though   / ð___ /   _____

3. awfully   / ___fəlɪ /   _____   10. story   / _____rɪ /   _____

4. although   / _____ðou /   _____   11. chose   / tʃ_____ /   _____

5. tomorrow / təmɑ_____ /   _____   12. choose   / tʃ_____ /   _____

6. toward   / t___r___ /   _____   13. odors   / ___dɚz /   _____

7. office   / _____ɪs /   _____   14. orders   / ___rdɚz /   _____

B. Circle the stressed syllable. Write the number of syllables in each word.

1. dangerous _____   6. awkward _____   11. cajole _____

2. diploma _____   7. probably _____   12. groaned _____

3. awfully _____   8. moment _____   13. suppose _____

4. commotion _____   9. chauffeur _____   14. important _____

5. auction _____   10. hopelessly _____   15. who's _____

C. The pronunciation of each word is given in column 2. If correct, write C. If incorrect, write I and make the corrections in column 4 using the symbols of the IPA.

EXAMPLE: haul / houl / ___I___ ___/ ɔ /___

1	2	3	4
Word	Pronunciation	C/I	Correction
1. storm	/ stɔrm /	_____	_____
2. guard	/ gwɑrd /	_____	_____
3. owns	/ ounz /	_____	_____

1	2	3	4
Word	*Pronunciation*	*C/I*	*Correction*
4. bought	/ boʊt /	_____	_____
5. store	/ stoʊr /	_____	_____
6. morning	/ moʊnɪŋ /	_____	_____
7. cold	/ kɔld /	_____	_____
8. called	/ kɔlɪd /	_____	_____
9. thought	/ toʊt /	_____	_____
10. boss	/ bɔs /	_____	_____

D. Write the following words using the symbols of the IPA. Practice reading aloud, producing / oʊ / and / ɔ / accurately.

1. woke /   /
2. walk /   /
3. ought /   /
4. court /   /
5. coast /   /

6. taught /   /
7. dawn /   /
8. cross /   /
9. bossed /   /
10. boast /   /

E. *Additional review.* In the following two exercises, stress the vowel sound and the word endings.

1. The diphthong / oʊ /. Read the words vertically and then horizontally.

go	goat	goal	gold	ghost
bow	boat	bowl	bowled	boast
row	wrote	roll	rolled	roast
toe	tote	toll	told	toast
mow	moat	mole	mold	most

2. The vowel / ɔ /. Contrast columns 1 and 2, 3 and 4, and 5 and 6.

1	2	3	4	5	6
awe	awed	ball	bald	bore	bored
caw	cawed	call	called	core	cored
flaw	flawed	haul	hauled	lore	lord
paw	pawed	stall	stalled	pour	poured
saw	sawed	wall	walled	store	stored

F. Fill in the appropriate IPA symbol in the space provided. Practice reading the sentences aloud, producing / oʊ / and / ɔ / correctly.

1. T<u>o</u>ny /   / w<u>a</u>lked /   / on the b<u>oa</u>rdwalk /   / until d<u>aw</u>n /   /.

2. J<u>oe</u> /   / t<u>o</u>re /   / a sh<u>ou</u>lder /   / ligament while w<u>a</u>ter /   / skiing.

3. S<u>au</u>l /   / travels <u>o</u>ver /   / an hour to g<u>o</u> /   / to his <u>o</u>ffice /   /.

4. That <u>au</u>thor /   / <u>ough</u>t /   / to c<u>a</u>ll /   / his l<u>a</u>wyer /   /.

5. The ch<u>auffeu</u>r /   / dr<u>o</u>ve /   / c<u>au</u>tiously /   /.

6. T<u>o</u>ny's /   / car st<u>a</u>lled /   / for a l<u>o</u>ng /   / time.

7. It c<u>o</u>st /   / me f<u>ou</u>r /   / d<u>o</u>llars /   / to do an en<u>o</u>rmous /   / l<u>oa</u>d /   / of l<u>au</u>ndry /   /.

8. J<u>oe</u> /   / th<u>ough</u>t /   / he'd work <u>o</u>nly /   / for a large c<u>o</u>rporation /   /.

9. She b<u>ou</u>ght /   / a crystal b<u>ow</u>l /   / and an <u>o</u>ld /   / print at the <u>au</u>ction /   /.

10. P<u>au</u>l /   / l<u>oa</u>ned /   / me his l<u>aw</u>n /   / m<u>ow</u>er /   /.

Reading Aloud

A. This selection focuses on the production of / oʊ / and / ɔ /. Make sure you differentiate between the two vowel sounds, giving full value to the diphthong / oʊ /. Remember to link the words within the phrase and stress important words, while maintaining the conversational tone of the passage. Work for variety in pitch and clarity of articulation.

Divide the sentences into phrase units, using single and double slashes and underline the stressed words.

> **EXAMPLE:** The <u>moment</u> she <u>strode</u> on <u>board</u>, / she took <u>control</u> / and let me <u>know</u> / I wasn't going to <u>order</u> her <u>around</u>. / /

Your instructor may serve as your model for correct, fluent oral reading. Be prepared to enact this dialogue in class.

A Boat for Jackie

◆

MANNY:	Sammy, how's Jackie?
SAMMY:	At home with a cold.
MANNY :	Bet she froze when she rode the horse at her last race.
SAMMY :	Wrong. She was on a boat taking a course with the Coast Guard.
MANNY :	What for?
SAMMY:	Jackie's not a jockey anymore. She's had a couple of awful falls and decided boats were safer. So she's switched to boating.
MANNY:	You've lost me.
SAMMY:	We've gone into the boat business. I own a boat—mortgaged up to the eyeballs—and Jackie's grown very attached to it.
MANNY:	She could blow away in a storm she's so small.
SAMMY:	Small but strong. The moment she strode on board, she took control and let me know I wasn't going to order her around.
MANNY:	I never thought Jackie would choose a boat over a horse.
SAMMY:	She didn't. She chose me and the boat I bought. As long as she's the boss, she's happy. Only five feet tall but a voice like a bullhorn.
MANNY:	What kind of business are you talking about?
SAMMY:	Folks charter the boat for fishing trips up and down the coast. We stay up north until it gets too cold and then we go south. Practically an all-year-round business.
MANNY:	As long as you both like the water.
SAMMY:	Fortunately, we do. Have to go now. There are some fishing poles on order. If you ever want to go trolling, come on board.
MANNY:	Thanks, but I'll stick to betting on horses. I like to feel the ground under my feet.

*Target Sounds: / ɑ / and / ʌ /**

Distinctive Features

/ ɑ / is a low, back, unrounded vowel. / ʌ / is the lowest of the central vowels and is unrounded. Like all vowels, they are voiced.

How Are / ɑ / and / ʌ / Made?

/ ɑ / is a long vowel. The tongue is flat on the floor of the mouth, the jaw is dropped, and the mouth is open in a long oval position.

/ ʌ / is a short vowel. The center section of the tongue moves slightly toward the palate, and the mouth is in much more of a closed position than for / ɑ /. The lips are slightly apart and lax.

What Are the Problems or Patterns in Spelling?

/ ɑ / may be represented by the letters **o** or **a.**

EXAMPLE: c<u>o</u>t   f<u>a</u>ther   p<u>a</u>lm

/ ʌ / may be represented by the letters **o, u, oo,** or **ou.**

EXAMPLE: s<u>o</u>me   c<u>u</u>p   fl<u>oo</u>d   r<u>ou</u>gh

What Are the Problems in Pronunciation?

/ ɑ / may be confused with / ʌ /.

EXAMPLE: *collar* instead of *color*

may be confused with / æ /.

EXAMPLE: *hot* instead of *hat*

/ ʌ / may be confused with / ɑ /.

EXAMPLE: *duck* instead of *dock*

may be confused with / ɔ /.

EXAMPLE: *cut* instead of *caught*

may be confused with / oʊ /.

EXAMPLE: *but* instead of *boat*

---

* / ʌ / and the schwa / ə / are central vowels produced in essentially the same way. / ʌ / appears only in the stressed syllables, while / ə / appears only in the unstressed syllables.

EXAMPLE: r<u>u</u>sh / rʌʃ /   <u>a</u>lone / əloʊn /

The / ɑ / Sound

A. Variations in spelling

Repeat these words after your instructor. Observe the spelling representations for the / ɑ / sound.

are*	shot	dollar
art	gone**	psalm
far	crop	bomb
farm	hobby	foreigner**
dock	father	economics

B. Vowel length

The vowel / ɑ / is longer when it occurs before a voiced consonant.

1	2	1	2
cot	cod	lock	log
not	nod	rot	rod
cop	cob	mop	mob

C. The / ɑ / in sentence practice.

Remember to stretch or lengthen the / oʊ / sound as you read each sentence aloud.

1. Bonnie Toms was a pretty, blond college student.

2. She had an apartment in a large building in Washington, D.C.

3. She was an art major but she also studied botany and psychology.

4. Her apartment was robbed last March.

5. This bothered her father, who was a foreign correspondent in Florence.

6. Mr. Toms wanted her to get a job in Florence, where there were fewer problems.

7. But Bonnie did not want to move because her boyfriend, John, wanted her to stay in Washington.

8. When a bomb was found on her block, her father insisted that two cops guard her apartment.

9. Bob and Charles, two calm cops, watched her apartment for six months.

10. After completing her art studies, Bonnie had no problems. She married Bob, who would guard her forever.

---

* In sections of the South and East, the **r** following / ɑ / is not pronounced. The vowel / ɑ / is prolonged and is the final sound in the word.

** In some regions, the / ɑ / may be pronounced / ɔ /.

The / ʌ / Sound

A. Variations in spelling

Repeat these words after your instructor. Observe the spelling representations for the / ʌ / sound.

us	dull	flood
son	some	once
sun	rough	onion
love	uncle	stomach
oven	bubble	trouble

B. Vowel length

1. The vowel / ʌ / is longer when it occurs before a voiced consonant.

1	2	1	2
cup	cub	luck	lug
but	bud	lunch	lunge
chuck	chug	pluck	plug

2. The vowels / ʌ / and / ə / are identical except for their positions in a word. / ʌ / appears only in the stressed syllable, / ə / only in the unstressed syllable. Observe the differences in the following words.

above	/ əˈbʌv /	Russia	/ ˈrʌʃə /
tumble	/ ˈtʌmbəl /	London	/ ˈlʌndən /
button	/ ˈbʌtən /	luggage	/ ˈlʌgɪʤ /

C. The / ʌ / in sentence practice.

Pronounce the / ʌ / sound clearly in the stressed syllables as you read each sentence aloud.

1. One sunny afternoon after lunch, Mr. Mudd took a bus to New London, Connecticut.

2. When the bus broke down, Mr. Mudd was very upset.

3. He called his wife. "Honey, come up and get me. We'll be stuck in the country for a couple of hours."

4. "It's too much trouble," she said. 'I've had some problems with the oven. Besides, it's begun to rain and thunder."

5. "Well, call my brother. He's an usher at the theater until five."

6. "Your brother hurt his thumb and has enough trouble."

7. "Tell my uncle to come. We'll have supper up here."

8. "His ulcer bothered him this morning, and your mother rushed him to the doctor."

9. "This is such bad luck. They may not be done working on the bus until six o'clock," he said.

10. "There's no other way to come back. I'll get a cup of coffee and something to eat and try to ride another bus."

Listening/Speaking

A. Contrast / ɑ / and / ʌ /.

Can you *feel* the difference as you repeat after your instructor?

Can you *hear* the difference between the long / ɑ / and the short / ʌ /?

1. Your instructor will say three words from columns 1 and 2 for each pair. Indicate the pattern that you hear.

   EXAMPLE: If you hear *calm, come, calm,* the pattern is 1 2 1.

1	2	1	2	1	2
calm	come	rot	rut	shot	shut
cop	cup	bomb	bum	psalm	some
doll	dull	Don	done	stock	stuck
not	nut	cot	cut	fond	fund
dock	duck	hot	hut	collar	color
sock	suck	rob	rub	wander	wonder

2. Underline the contrastive words in these sentences. As you read aloud, remember to distinguish between the / ɑ / and / ʌ / sounds in the underlined words and produce them correctly.

   EXAMPLE: He heard a <u>shot</u> as he shut the <u>door</u>.

   a. The gun is gone.

   b. Look at the color of the collar.

   c. He's not a nut.

   d. The duck was stuck on the dock.

   e. He's got no guts.

   f. The hut was hot.

   g. He was stuck with the stock.

   h. I wonder if he'll wander away.

i. He had no luck with the lock.

j. Don is done with his work at five.

B.   Contrast / ɑ / and / æ /.

Can you *feel* the difference as you repeat after your instructor?

Can you *hear* the difference between the low back vowel / ɑ / and the low front vowel / æ /?

1. Your instructor will say three words from columns 1 and 2 for each pair. Indicate the pattern that you hear.

> **EXAMPLE:**   If you hear *rock, rack, rock,* the pattern is 1 2 1.

1	2	1	2
not	gnat	cot	cat
cop	cap	mod	mad
sod	sad	cod	cad
log	lag	adopt	adapt
lock	lack	odd	add

2. Underline the contrastive words in each sentence. As you read aloud, remember to produce the / ɑ / and / æ / sounds in the underlined words.

> **EXAMPLE:**   Our <u>cat</u> is sleeping on the <u>cot</u>.

a. The cop lost his cap.

b. It's too hot for a hat.

c. He threw his sock into a sack.

d. Don and Dan are not nuts.

e. A stack of books is in the stock room.

f. The door lacks six locks.

g. The taps and tops are in this box.

h. That gnat does not bite.

i. Those mod fashions made Mary mad.

C. Contrast / ʌ / and / æ /.

Can you *feel* the difference as you repeat after your instructor?

Can you *hear* the difference between the central vowel / ʌ / and the low front vowel / æ /?

1. Your instructor will say three words from columns 1 and 2 for each pair. Indicate the pattern that you hear.

      EXAMPLE: If you hear *luck, lack, luck,* the pattern is 1 2 1.

1	2	1	2
luck	lack	stuck	stack
bunk	bank	run	ran
rug	rag	bug	bag
mud	mad	tub	tab
cuff	calf	shrunk	shrank

2. Underline the contrastive words in these sentences. As you read aloud, remember to produce the / ʌ / and / æ / sounds in the underlined words.

      EXAMPLE: My <u>uncle</u> sprained his <u>ankle</u>.

a. Who left the rag on the rug?

b. The bug flew into the bag.

c. The mud on the rug made her mad.

d. The tab from the can fell into the tub.

e. They carried the cub into the cab.

f. The calf bit his cuff.

g. Can you run as fast as he ran?

h. The stack of papers was stuck in the drawer.

i. The tennis match took too much time.

j. The fleet of trucks left tire tracks in the mud.

Listening/Speaking

A. Listen carefully for / ɑ / and / ʌ / as your instructor pronounces each word. Write these sounds when they occur in the initial, medial, or final position using the symbols of the IPA. If / ɑ / or / ʌ / is not heard, write a dash in the space provided.

   EXAMPLE: calm /_____ɑ_____/   come /_____ʌ_____/   caught /_____—_____/

   1. much   _____   8. fond   _____   15. young   _____

   2. o'clock   _____   9. public   _____   16. industrious _____

   3. uncle   _____   10. another   _____   17. correspondent _____

   4. lock   _____   11. trouble   _____   18. money   _____

   5. supper   _____   12. problems   _____   19. bother   _____

   6. comb   _____   13. caught   _____   20. touch   _____

   7. fund   _____   14. luck   _____   21. budget   _____

B. Circle the word read aloud by your instructor.

   1. lack   lock   luck   6. cat   cot   cut

   2. stack   stock   stuck   7. lag   log   lug

   3. sack   sock   suck   8. rat   rot   rut

   4. tack   tock   tuck   9. pat   pot   putt

   5. fanned   fond   fund   10. cap   cop   cup

C. Your instructor will select one of the words in parentheses and read the entire sentence aloud. Listen carefully and circle the word you hear. Practice reading each sentence aloud using either one of the words in parentheses.

   1. Can you fix that (cot, cut)?

   2. Look for a (cop, cup).

   3. Children like to (wander, wonder) a lot.

   4. Who (shut, shot) the closet door?

   5. He lost his (luck, lock).

   6. How's your (hubby, hobby)?

7. Is he (rubbing, robbing) the desk?

8. That (dock, duck) is quite old.

9. I don't like the (collar, color).

10. She's a little (dull, doll).

D. Circle the stressed syllable as each word is read aloud. Write the number of syllables in each word. Practice aloud.

1. astronomy ____	6. sculpture ____	11. customer ____
2. foreigner ____	7. hospital ____	12. budget ____
3. subjects ____	8. job ____	13. opera ____
4. remarkable ____	9. psychology ____	14. conscience ____
5. blonde ____	10. enough ____	15. uptown ____

E. Your instructor will say three words from columns 1 and 2 for each pair. Write the pattern that you hear.

EXAMPLE: If you hear *lock, luck, lock,* write 1 2 1.

1	2	*Pattern*
1. got	gut	____ ____ ____
2. pot	putt	____ ____ ____
3. shot	shut	____ ____ ____
4. bomb	bum	____ ____ ____
5. psalm	some	____ ____ ____
6. wander	wonder	____ ____ ____
7. collar	color	____ ____ ____
8. doll	dull	____ ____ ____
9. rob	rub	____ ____ ____
10. stock	stuck	____ ____ ____

F. Listen carefully as your instructor reads each word aloud. Write / ʌ / and / ə / when they occur in the word.

      EXAMPLE: sun <u>/ ʌ /</u>   lion <u>/ ə /</u>

1. about _____

2. bunch _____

3. period _____

4. among _____

5. money _____

6. government _____

7. double _____

8. mystery _____

9. account _____

10. policeman _____

11. memory _____

12. slippery _____

13. society _____

14. cafeteria _____

15. company _____

Chapter 9 Homework Review

A. Fill in the missing sounds using the symbols of the IPA. Write the number of sounds in each word.

    EXAMPLE: grumble / grʌmbəl / ___7___

1. another   / ən___ðɚ / _____
2. uncle   / ___ŋkl / _____
3. thunder   / θ___ndɚ / _____
4. conscious   / k___nʃəs / _____
5. foreign   / f___rɪn / _____
6. not   / n___t / _____
7. onion   / _____ _____jən / _____

8. tongue   / t___ŋ / _____
9. thumb   / θ___m / _____
10. enough   / ɪn___f / _____
11. collar   / k___lɚ / _____
12. public   / p___blɪ___ / _____
13. bother   / b___ðɚ / _____
14. apartment   / ___p___rtmɪnt / _____

B. Circle the stressed syllable. Write the number of syllables in each word.

1. uptown _____
2. locked _____
3. attorney _____
4. trouble _____
5. delivery _____

6. hijacked _____
7. quality _____
8. oven _____
9. usher _____
10. another _____

11. rushed _____
12. double _____
13. young _____
14. immediately _____
15. overnight _____

C. The pronunciation of each word is given in column 2. If correct, write C. If incorrect, write I and make the corrections in column 4 using the symbols of the IPA.

    EXAMPLE: funny / fɑnɪ / ___I___ ___/ ʌ /___

1	2	3	4
Word	Pronunciation	C/I	Correction
1. bomb	/ bʌm /	_____	_____
2. public	/ pɑblɪk /	_____	_____
3. problem	/ prʌbləm /	_____	_____

1	2	3	4
Word	Pronunciation	C/I	Correction
4. closet	/ klɑzət /	_____	_____
5. lunch	/ lʌntʃ /	_____	_____
6. block	/ blɑk /	_____	_____
7. black	/ blæk /	_____	_____
8. trouble	/ trɑbəl /	_____	_____
9. not	/ noʊ /	_____	_____

D. Write the following words using the symbols of the IPA. Practice reading aloud, producing / ɑ / and / ʌ / accurately.

1. some   /   /   6. dollar   /   /

2. stocks   /   /   7. duller   /   /

3. color   /   /   8. stomach   /   /

4. collar   /   /   9. luck   /   /

5. once   /   /   10. lock   /   /

E. Fill in the appropriate IPA symbol in the space provided. Practice reading these sentences aloud, producing the / ɑ / and / ʌ / correctly.

    EXAMPLE: He was very f<u>o</u>nd / ɑ / of his <u>u</u>ncle / ʌ / D<u>o</u>n / ɑ /.

1. Enc<u>ou</u>rage /   / him to buy that rem<u>a</u>rkable /   / piece of sc<u>u</u>lpture /   /.

2. T<u>o</u>m's /   / best s<u>u</u>bjects /   / were astr<u>o</u>nomy /   / and b<u>o</u>tany /   /.

3. A d<u>o</u>llar /   / is worth n<u>o</u>thing /   / these days.

4. Ch<u>a</u>rles's /   / st<u>o</u>mach /   / pr<u>o</u>blems /   / landed him in the h<u>o</u>spital /   /.

5. That c<u>u</u>stomer /   / b<u>u</u>dgets /   / his m<u>o</u>ney /   / carefully.

6. J<u>o</u>hn's /   / c<u>o</u>nscience /   / b<u>o</u>thered /   / him.

7. The qu<u>a</u>lity /   / of the <u>o</u>pera /   / was poor.

8. The y<u>oung</u> /   / student l<u>u</u>nched /   / at the c<u>o</u>llege /   / cafeteria.

9. Those <u>o</u>nions /   / have a w<u>o</u>nderful /   / taste.

10. I w<u>o</u>nder /   / why the c<u>o</u>lor /   / of my c<u>o</u>llar /   / has faded.

Reading Aloud

A. This selection focuses on the production of / ɑ / and / ʌ /. The low back vowel / ɑ / is longer than the low central vowel / ʌ /. Be sure to drop your jaw for the / ɑ / and place your lips slightly apart for / ʌ /.

Remember to link the words within the phrase and stress important words, while maintaining the conversational tone of the passage. Work for variety in pitch and clarity of articulation.

Divide the sentences into phrase units, using single and double slashes, and underline the stressed words.

> **EXAMPLE:**   I just <u>remembered</u> / I <u>forgot</u> / to <u>lock</u> my <u>door</u>. / /

Your instructor may serve as your model for correct and fluent oral reading. Prepare to enact this dialogue in class.

The Lady on the Bus

————◆————

LADY:	Driver, is this the Number 1 uptown bus?
DRIVER:	Yes, lady.
LADY:	Are you sure? This bus seems to be another color.
DRIVER:	It's the same color as all the other buses.
LADY:	I don't want a chartered bus. Just a public one.
DRIVER:	Lady, are you getting in or not? I want to make it home for supper.
LADY:	Don't get so hot under the collar. Maybe this bus is being hijacked. Maybe you've got a gun.
DRIVER:	One of those nuts, huh?
LADY:	I'm not a nut at all. One has to be careful these days.
DRIVER:	Lady, either get on or get off!
LADY:	Young man, watch your tongue!
DRIVER:	Lady, you want me to call a cop?
LADY:	A cop? You mean a police officer? No, don't bother. A cop's not my cup of tea.
DRIVER:	You ought to be locked up.

LADY: Oh, they tried. They almost stuck me in jail overnight. But I've got too many stocks.

DRIVER: Too many stocks! In other words, you've got a lot of money.

LADY: Correct, young man. And a very good attorney as well. So it you're ever in trouble, let me know.

DRIVER: Madam, *you're* trouble. Double trouble.

LADY: Driver, stop the bus immediately. I must get off. I just remembered I forgot to lock my door.

DRIVER: What luck! Good-bye, lady. Next time, take a taxi. I don't want to be stuck with you again.

LADY: That goes for both of us. Here, my good man. I'm leaving you a dollar. Enjoy your supper.

Reviewing the Back Vowels / u ʊ oʊ ɔ ɑ /

A. Repeat after your instructor.

Can you *feel* the differences in the following words?

Can you *hear* the differences in the following words?

/ u /		/ ʊ /	/ oʊ /	/ ɔ /	/ ɑ /
pool	pull		pole	pall, Paul	pond
fool	full		fold	fall	far
cooed	could		code, coat	caught	cot
kook	cook		coke	cork	card
suit	soot		soak, sew	Salk	sock
stewed	stood		stole	stall	star
shooed	should		showed	shored	shod
wound	would, wood		woke	walk	wok
boot	bull		boat	bought	botany

B. Observe / ɑ /, / ʌ /, and / æ / contrasts.

/ ɑ /	/ ʌ /	/ æ /
cop	cup	cap
lock	luck	lack
sock	suck	sack
Don	done	Dan
cod	cud	cad
clock	cluck	clack
fond	fund	fanned
Ron	run	ran
non	none, nun	Nan

C. This dialogue focuses on the accurate production of the back vowels / u /, / ʊ /, / oʊ /, / ɔ /, and / ɑ /. Remember to link the words within the phrase and stress the important words, while maintaining the conversational tone of the dialogue. Work for variety of pitch and clarity of articulation.

Divide the sentences into phrase units, using single and double slashes, and underline the stressed words.

> **EXAMPLE:** They're <u>drooling</u> / at the <u>thought</u> of mom's <u>roast</u> <u>turkey</u> / and <u>cornbread</u> <u>stuffing</u>. / /

Your instructor may serve as your model for the correct and fluent oral reading. Prepare to enact this dialogue in class.

Home for the Holidays

◆

LUCY: Dad, is Mom home?

DAD: She's cooking. We're looking forward to seeing you tomorrow.

LUCY: Yes, well, that's why I'm calling.

DAD: What's wrong. Are you sick? Did you get the flu?

LUCY: I'm fine, but I hope you won't mind . . .

DAD: Mind what?

LUCY: I'm sort of . . . well . . . I won't be coming home alone.

DAD: Is that all! There's always room for more at the Thanksgiving table.

LUCY: What about four more?

DAD: Four more what.

LUCY: You know, four more friends. They've never been to a Thanksgiving dinner.

DAD: That's most unusual. However, we have cots we can set up in your room.

LUCY: Not exactly. These are guys—

DAD: Now, hold on, Lucy—

LUCY: Dad, don't get emotional. These are totally super human beings and all alone. Shuku's from India and makes the most marvelous cous-cous, and Han Soong is from Putien Province. He needs tutoring in spoken English, but he's a whiz at the computer. Nicki Petrovich is on the football team, quarterback position.

DAD: And who is the fourth member of this quartet?

LUCY: Walker. He owns a van. He's a real American, I mean, a native American. His folks opened a gambling resort in the North Woods.

DAD: He would have a different point of view about Thanksgiving, I should imagine.

LUCY: They're drooling at the thought of Mom's roast turkey and cornbread stuffing. I hope there's going to be warm apple pie and fruitcake. Oh, I told Nicki you played pro football until Mom made you stop.

DAD: Lucy, you're telling tales out of school and to total strangers.

LUCY: Lighten up, dad. I never would have thought college could be so rewarding.

DAD: Nothing like a liberal education, daughter.

CHAPTER TEN

Central Vowels

This diagram shows a schematic representation of the positions of the tongue in the central section of the mouth for the production of the four vowels / ɜˆ /, / ɚ /, / ə /, and / ʌ /. The central section of the tongue is elevated to its highest position, at mid-height, for the / ɜˆ / sound and descends to the lowest mid-height position for the / ʌ /. These sounds, then, may be classified as mid-central vowels.

/ ɜˆ / is the highest of the mid central vowels. The tongue tip is curled back without touching the hard palate. The tongue is tense; the lips are somewhat apart and unrounded. The / ɜˆ / is long in duration and occurs only when the vowel precedes the **r** in stressed syllables. This sound is often described as an "r-colored" vowel, which means that a slight **r** sound is added to the / ɜˆ / as the tongue is curled back.*

EXAMPLE: b<u>ir</u>d   <u>ear</u>n   p<u>er</u>son   pref<u>er</u>

/ ɚ / is also a mid central vowel but made slightly lower than the / ɜˆ /. The tongue tip is curled back without touching the hard palate, not quite as strongly as the the / ɜˆ /. The lips are slightly apart, lax, and unrounded. Th **r** quality is relatively less than in / ɜˆ /. This sound occurs only when the vowel precedes **r** in unstressed syllables.**

EXAMPLE: p<u>er</u>form   f<u>or</u>get   consid<u>er</u>   leis<u>ure</u>

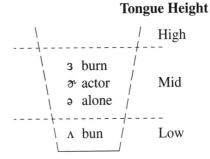

Tongue Height

FIGURE 7. Tongue positions for the central vowels.

---

* The **r** quality may not be used in sections of the South and the East.

** When the letter **r** appears between two vowels, the consonant **r** is used.

    EXAMPLE: earrings / ɪərɪŋz /   several / sɛvərəl /   tolerate / tɑləreit /

/ ə / is also a mid central vowel. It is produced with a very lax tongue; the lips are apart, lax, and unrounded. This vowel is known as the *schwa,* meaning "weak." It is very short in duration and occurs only in unstressed syllables.

EXAMPLE: all<u>o</u>wed   b<u>e</u>lieve   diffi<u>c</u>ult   dish<u>e</u>s   want<u>e</u>d   oper<u>a</u>

/ ʌ / is the lowest, central vowel. The tongue is relatively flat in the mouth, and its central section raised not quite as high as for the other central vowels. It is pronounced exactly as the / ə / with lax tongue and lips. However, it occurs only in stressed syllables.*

EXAMPLE: <u>u</u>nder   fl<u>oo</u>d   br<u>o</u>ther   s<u>u</u>n

If the back section of the tongue is raised slightly and the jaw dropped, the back vowel / ɑ / in **cot** will result in place of **cut.**

If the front section of the tongue is raised, **gist** or **jest** will result in place of **just.**

Target Sounds: / ə /, / ɚ /, and / ɝ /

Distinctive Features

/ ə /, / ɚ /, and / ɝ / are mid central vowels. Like all vowels, they are voiced.**

How Are / ə /, / ɚ /, and / ɝ / Made?

The central section of the tongue is raised to midheight in the mouth. The lips are unrounded and slightly apart in a lax position.

/ ə / is a very short vowel. It is made with the tongue lax and relatively low. The schwa occurs only in unstressed syllables.†

EXAMPLE: <u>a</u>lone   r<u>e</u>port   hist<u>o</u>ry   sof<u>a</u>

/ ɚ / is the schwa sound with an added **r** quality. The tongue tip is raised and curled without touching the hard palate. The / ɚ / appears only in unstressed syllables.

EXAMPLE: p<u>er</u>suade   f<u>ir</u>e   fact<u>or</u>   pleas<u>ure</u>

---

* / ʌ / is often confused with / ɑ /, the low back vowel. See pages 000–000 for detailed practice.

Note: The vowel / ʌ / does not appear in most languages, thereby providing a problem for many non-native speakers.

** These sounds are produced with "r color" in GAD. However, the **r** quality may be omitted in sections of the South and the East.

† The / ʌ /, a counterpart of the / ə /, appears only in stressed syllables. See pages 000–000 for further discussion and practice.

/ ɜˆ / is long in duration with a strong **r** quality. The tongue tip is tense as it is raised and curled back without touching the hard palate.

EXAMPLE: h<u>er</u>b   occ<u>u</u>rred   t<u>er</u>minal   det<u>er</u>

What Are the Problems or Patterns in Spelling?

/ ə / may be represented by the letters **a, i, o,** and **e.**

EXAMPLE: <u>a</u>bil<u>i</u>ty   pr<u>o</u>vide   pr<u>e</u>pare   fact<u>o</u>ry   d<u>e</u>partm<u>e</u>nt

/ ɚ / may be represented by the letters **er, or, re,** and **ure.**

EXAMPLE: p<u>er</u>spire   f<u>or</u>got   requi<u>re</u>   runn<u>er</u>   capt<u>ure</u>

/ ɜˆ / may be represented by the letters **ea, er,** and **or.**

EXAMPLE: <u>ea</u>rnest   det<u>er</u>mine   pref<u>er</u>   w<u>or</u>d

What Are the Problems in Pronunciation?

/ ə / may be diphtongized and pronounced / eɪ / in the article <u>a</u>.

EXAMPLE: *a book* / eɪ bʊk / instead of / ə bʊk /

may be pronounced / oʊ / when emphasis is given to the unstressed syllable.

EXAMPLE: *o'clock* / oʊklɑk / instead of / əklɑk /

/ ɚ / may be pronounced / ɔ / when emphasis is given to the unstressed syllable.

EXAMPLE: *act<u>or</u>* / æktɔr / instead of / æktɚ /

/ ɜˆ / may be pronounced / ʌ /.

EXAMPLE: *th<u>u</u>d* instead of *th<u>ir</u>d*

may be pronounced / ɑr /.

EXAMPLE: *f<u>ar</u>m* instead of *f<u>ir</u>m*

may be pronounced / ɔr /.

EXAMPLE: *f<u>or</u>m* instead of *f<u>ir</u>m*

Note: Most non-native speakers and some native speakers may need to work on distinguishing and producing the / ɜˆ / sound.

The / ə / Sound

A. Variations in spelling

Repeat these words after your instructor. Observe the different spellings for the / ə / sound.

away	capable	zebra
predict	nation	camera
appear	delicious	banana
occur	rented	idea
o'clock	psychology	operator
oppose	recall	general

B. The / ə / in sentence practice.

Remember to produce the / ə / with the tongue and lips in neutral position as you read aloud.

1. Maria had a poor memory.

2. She didn't recall her last two positions.

3. She couldn't obtain any recommendations.

4. When she applied for a job as a secretary, she had no references.

5. An interviewer asked her about her ability to write reports.

6. "I know how to operate several data processing machines," answered Maria confidently.

7. "I can use a word processor very well. I've also prepared many reports."

8. "I'm also familiar with statistics, and I can even design some research programs for you."

9. "I believe you may be overqualified for a position in this office."

10. "I'd advise you to try elsewhere," responded the interviewer sympathetically.

The / ɚ / Sound

A. Variations in spelling

When **r** follows a vowel in an unstressed syllable, the vowel / ɚ / may be produced.*

---

* In parts of the East and the South, the **r** quality may be omitted.

1. Observe the use of the / ɚ / when it appears in a prefix.

forget	pursue
persuade	percent
correct	surprised
perform	perspire

2. Observe the use of the / ɚ / when it appears in a suffix.

better	modern
scholar	tutor
lecture	actor

3. Observe the use of the / ɚ / when it appears in other unstressed syllables.

fire	exercise
inquire	information
hired	requirement

B. The / ɚ / in sentence practice.

As you read each sentence aloud, be sure to raise the tongue tip and curl it back slightly for the / ɚ / sound.

1. Henrietta inquired about a tutor for history, her worst subject.

2. She couldn't tolerate the two-hour history lectures.

3. Her professor forgot his subject and gave little information.

4. Her tutor, Henry, was southern and a better lecturer than her teacher.

5. Henry wanted to be an actor but was persuaded to tutor in order to earn some money.

6. He persisted in helping Henrietta to picture historical events.

7. Henrietta never liked her Western Civilization course, but she did pass.

8. Henry was hired for another semester.

9. He tutored other students successfully and helped to correct their papers.

10. Instead of becoming an actor, he became a history teacher.

The / ɜ˞ / Sound

A. Variations in spelling: stressed syllables

When **r** follows a vowel in a stressed syllable, the vowel / ɜ˞ / may be produced.

Repeat these words after your instructor. Observe the different spellings for the / ɜ˞ / sound.

fur	hurt	kernel
word	urge	worthy
shirt	heard	terminal
stir	thirst	colonel

B. Vowel length

1. The vowel / ɜ˞ / occurs in stressed syllables.

thirsty	determine	thirteen
reserved	purchase	personal
murder	occurs	university

2. The vowel / ɜ˞ / is longer when it occurs before a voiced consonant.

hurt	heard	surf	serve
Bert	bird	shirt	shirred
curt	curd	purse	purrs

C. The / ɜ˞ / in sentence practice.

As you read each sentence aloud, be sure to raise and tense the tongue tip and curl it back strongly without touching the palate.

1. Have you heard how Herman and Myrna met?

2. They were returning from Germany and happened to be seated next to each other.

3. Herman observed that Myrna seemed on the verge of tears.

4. He asked if she was nervous, or if this was her first flight.

5. She told him her room had been burglarized. Her fur coat, worth thirty-three hundred dollars, had been stolen, as well as pearl earrings and a sterling silver bracelet.

6. "No wonder you're disturbed," Herman said.

7. Myrna burst out fiercely, "I could have murdered those burglars!"

8. Herman was determined to pursue the relationship, and Myrna was not averse at all.

9. In no time they were married.

10. Herman's wedding present to Myrna was a fur coat to replace the one that had been stolen.

Listening/Speaking

A. Contrast / ɜˆ / and / ʌ /.

Can you *feel* the difference as you repeat after your instructor?

Can you *hear* the difference between / ɜˆ / and / ʌ /?

1. Your instructor will say three words from columns 1 and 2 for each pair. Indicate the pattern that you hear.

   EXAMPLE: If you hear *bird, bud, bird,* the pattern is 1 2 1.

1	2	1	2
bird	bud	third	thud
burn	bun	turn	ton
circle	suckle	pert	putt
hurt	hut	shirt	shut
stern	stun	search	such
girl	gull	Bert	but
fern	fun	curd	cub

2. Underline the contrastive words in each sentence. As you read aloud, remember to produce the / ɜˆ / and / ʌ / sounds in the underlined words.

   EXAMPLE: <u>Fern</u> thought it was <u>fun</u> to dance at the disco.

   a. Did you hear the thud on the third floor?

   b. Don't burn the bun.

   c. But Bert can't come.

   d. The girl fed the gull on the beach.

   e. His shirt was caught as the door slammed shut behind him.

   f. The bird settled on a rosebud.

   g. A circle of bees surrounded the honeysuckle flowers.

   h. Kurt placed the hurt actor in the hut.

   i. The search for a cancer cure began such a long time ago.

   j. We can't turn the piano because it weights a ton.

B. Contrast / ɜˆ / and / ɑr /.

1. Your instructor will say three words from columns 1 and 2 for each pair. Indicate the pattern that you hear.

Can you *feel* the difference as you repeat after your instructor?

Can you *hear* the difference between / ɜˆ / and / ɑr /?

> **EXAMPLE:**   If you hear *fur, far, fur,* the pattern is 1 2 1.

1	2	1	2
fur	far	firm	farm
bird	bard	curve	carve
dirt	dart	stir	star
curt	cart	hurt	heart
heard	hard	burn	barn

2. Underline the contrastive words in each sentence. As you read aloud, remember to produce the / ɜˆ / and / ɑr / sounds in the underlined words.

> **EXAMPLE:**   Mr. <u>Stars</u> always <u>stirs</u> his coffee before he drinks it.

a. The firm refused to sell the old farm to the actor.

b. Carve a sign near the dangerous curve.

c. Although he was hurt, his heart was not affected.

d. In the far north, a fur coat is necessary.

e. I heard how hard that exam was.

f. Luckily the barn did not burn.

g. That cat always lurks near the lark's nest.

h. Don't dart into that dirt road.

i. The man with the cart was curt.

j. Don't stir until you see a star.

C. Contrast / ɜˆ / and / ɔr /.

Can you *feel* and *hear* the differences between / ɜˆ / and / ɔr /?

1. Your instructor will say three words from columns 1 and 2 for each pair. Indicate the pattern that you hear.

> **EXAMPLE:**   If you hear *word, ward, word,* the pattern is 1 2 1.

1	2	1	2
were	wore	firm	form
word	ward	worm	warm
fur	four	shirt	short
burn	born	turn	torn
were	war	first	forced

2. Underline the contrastive words in these sentences. As you read aloud, remember to produce the / ɝ / and / ɔr / sounds in the underlined words.

a. A short man in a blue shirt appeared.

b. We heard that the senator did hoard gasoline.

c. He was the first person who was forced to leave.

d. The doctors never mentioned the word "cancer" on the ward.

e. I did not turn in the torn coat I had found.

f. Fill out the application form for the firm.

g. The actress bought four fur coats.

h. The owner confirmed that he had conformed to the law.

i. When we were there, he wore a top hat.

j. The first worm appeared on a warm day.

Listening/Writing

A. Listen carefully for / ɝ / and / ɚ / as your instructor pronounces each word. Write these sounds when they occur in the initial, medial, or final position using the symbols of the IPA. If / ɝ / or / ɚ / is not heard, write a dash in the space provided.

EXAMPLE: burn /____ɝ____/ other /____ɚ____/ born /____—____/

1. Germany	_____	7. morning	_____	13. personally	_____
2. information	_____	8. reserved	_____	14. protect	_____
3. world	_____	9. hijackers	_____	15. surprised	_____
4. mother	_____	10. journey	_____	16. nerve	_____
5. birthday	_____	11. nurse	_____	17. passengers	_____
6. Thursday	_____	12. concerned	_____	18. burglarized	_____

B. Circle the word read aloud by the instructor.

1. firm	form	farm		6. burn	born	bar
2. bird	bored	bard		7. turn	torn	tarn
3. heard	hoard	hard		8. stir	store	star
4. word	ward	wad		9. shirt	short	shot
5. fur	four	far		10. curt	court	cart

C. Your instructor will select one of the words in parentheses and read the entire sentence aloud. Listen carefully and circle the word you hear. Practice reading each sentence aloud using either one of the words in parentheses.

1. The laundry lost my (shirts, shorts).

2. Was your poem about the (bards, birds) ever published?

3. Did you get a (burn, barn)?

4. I heard all about those (words, wards).

5. His (firm, farm) is located in New York State.

6. We didn't get that (fur, far).

7. Those are lovely (birds, buds).

8. Where's his old (firm, form)?

9. That is an unusual looking (girl, gull).

10. His (firm, farm) went bankrupt.

D. Circle the stressed syllables as each word is read aloud. Write the number of syllables in each word. Practice aloud.

1. curfew ____		6. personally ____		11. hypodermic ____
2. determine ____		7. available ____		12. whipped ____
3. generally ____		8. burglarized ____		13. pursued ____
4. disturbed ____		9. jewelry ____		14. entire ____
5. journey ____		10. surprised ____		15. disguise ____

E. Your instructor will say three words from columns 1 and 2 for each pair. Write the pattern that you hear.

    EXAMPLE: If you hear *third, thud third*, write 1 2 1.

	1	2	Pattern
1.	third	thud	_____ _____ _____
2.	turn	ton	_____ _____ _____
3.	search	shut	_____ _____ _____
4.	hurt	hut	_____ _____ _____
5.	firm	farm	_____ _____ _____
6.	heard	hard	_____ _____ _____
7.	hurt	heart	_____ _____ _____
8.	curve	carve	_____ _____ _____
9.	word	ward	_____ _____ _____
10.	firm	form	_____ _____ _____
11.	shirt	short	_____ _____ _____
12.	turn	torn	_____ _____ _____

Chapter 10 Homework Review

A. Fill in the missing sounds using the symbols of the IPA. Write the number of sounds in each word.

    EXAMPLE: world / w _ɜ^_ ld /   _4_

1. purchased / p___ tʃ___ ___ ___ / _____   7. heard   / h___ d /   _____

2. computer / k___ ___ pju___ ___ / _____   8. beeper   / ___ ___ p___ /   _____

3. turned   / t___ n___ /   _____   9. cursor   / k___ s___ /   _____

4. bother   / ___ ɑ___ ___ /   _____   10. absurd   / əp___ ___ d /   _____

5. illiterate / ɪ___ ___ tə___ ___ t / _____   11. respect / r___ ___ p___ kt / _____

6. Internet / ___ nt___ nɛ___ / _____   12. surprised / s___ p___ ___ zd / _____

B. Circle the stressed syllable. Write the number of syllables in each word.

1. discovered _____   6. personally _____   11. protect   _____

2. problem _____   7. disturbed _____   12. information _____

3. available _____   8. surprised _____   13. international _____

4. purchase _____   9. identity _____   14. reserved _____

5. pursued _____   10. expert _____   15. disappeared _____

C. Write the following words using the symbols of the IPA. Practice reading aloud, producing / ɜ^ /, / ɚ /, and / ə / accurately.

1. nerve   /   /   6. disturbed /   /

2. confirm /   /   7. birthday /   /

3. hard   /   /   8. predict /   /

4. hurt   /   /   9. early   /   /

5. heard   /   /   10. pursued /   /

D. Fill in the appropriate IPA symbol in the space provided. Practice reading the sentences aloud, producing / ɜˆ /, / ɚ /, and / ə / accurately.

1. Colonel /   / Korn /   / left early /   / in the morning /   /.

2. Circle /   / the correct /   / word /   / on that form /   /.

3. Your income tax return /   / is due by Thursday /   /.

4. The farmer /   / was firm /   / when he said, "No."

5. Did you earn /   / any money /   / to buy more shirts /   / and shorts /   /?

6. His circle /   / of friends made frequent journeys /   / to Russia /   /.

7. Bert /   / reserved /   / thirteen /   / plane seats for his birthday /   / party /   /.

8. The burglars /   / cursed /   / when they were caught /   /.

9. Thirty /   / passengers at the airport /   / terminal /   / received third- /   / degree burns /   /.

10. The hearse /   / carried the governor /   / to the burial /   / grounds near the church /   /.

E. The pronunciation of each word is given in column 2. If correct, write C. If incorrect, write I and make the corrections in column 4 using the symbols of the IPA.

EXAMPLE: firm / fɚm /   I   / fɜˆm /

1	2	3	4
Word	Pronunciation	C/I	Correction
1. world	/ wɔrld /	_____	_____
2. search	/ sɜˆtʃ /	_____	_____
3. murder	/ murdɚ /	_____	_____
4. word	/ wɔrd /	_____	_____
5. ward	/ wɔrd /	_____	_____
6. hurt	/ hʌt /	_____	_____
7. hut	/ hʌt /	_____	_____
8. turn	/ tɔrn /	_____	_____
9. nurse	/ nurs /	_____	_____
10. journal	/ ʤɜˆnəl /	_____	_____

Reading Aloud

A. This dialogue focuses on the accurate pronunciation of the central vowels: / ɜˆ /, / ɚ /, and / ə /. Be sure to use the / ɜˆ / in stressed syllables and the / ɚ / and / ə / in unstressed syllables. Remember to link the words within the phrase and stress important words, while maintaining the conversational tone of the dialogue. Work for variety in pitch and clarity of articulation.

Divide the sentences into phrase units, using single and double slashes and underline the stressed words.

EXAMPLE: I <u>represent</u> an <u>international</u> <u>firm,</u> / and my <u>own</u> <u>mother</u> / doesn't <u>respect</u> my <u>work</u>. / /

Computer Mom

◆

HERBERT: Mother, I purchased a computer for your birthday, but it's untouched.

MOTHER: That's not true. I turned it on. And then I turned it off. Too much bother.

HERBERT: My mother—computer illiterate in this modern world!

MOTHER: Herbert, how dare you call me illiterate?

HERBERT: Don't call me Herbert. My name is Bert. How do you manage without e-mail and the Internet with those wonderful Web sites.

MOTHER: I have a phone. And I've heard of cell phones, and beeper, and caller ID, and call waiting.

HERBERT: At least learn the word processor. You don't know a mouse from a monitor, a cursor from a printer. This is very disturbing to me.

MOTHER: You're absurd to take it personally.

HERBERT: But I'm an expert. I represent an international firm, and my own mother doesn't respect my work.

MOTHER: Now, Herbert—

HERBERT: It's Bert! You're giving me an acute case of nervous indigestion.

MOTHER: You sound just like your father.

HERBERT: There must be some way to persuade you. Wait! I have an idea. You play solitaire, right?

MOTHER: Calms my nerves. Better than liquor.

HERBERT: I can teach you solitaire on the computer. Watch. There are the cards, on the monitor.

MOTHER: Herbert—I mean Bert—what a surprise!

HERBERT: Now, just observe me as I drag the mouse from here to there.

MOTHER: You forgot to put the heart three on the club four. Permit me to take over. Uh-oh, I've discovered a problem. The computer won't let you cheat!

HERBERT: In time, I'm certain you'll find an answer to that.

Reviewing the Central Vowels / ɜˆ ɚ ə ʌ /

A. Review Practice

1. The / ɜˆ / and / ʌ / sounds

   Practice producing the following words.

/ ɜˆ /	/ ʌ /
burn	bun
turn	ton
search	such
girl	gull
hurt	hut
stern	stun

   Can you *feel* the difference as you repeat after your instructor?

   Can you *hear* the difference as you produce each of the central vowels?

2. The / ə / sound

   Practice producing the schwa without **r** coloring in the unstressed syllables.

umbrella	prevent	correct
banana	avoid	tolerate
profession	oppose	statistics
machine	reduce	successfully

3. The / ɚ / sound

   Practice producing the schwa with **r** coloring in the unstressed syllables.

information	culture	surprised
require	personality	discovered
registered	unpopular	pursued
hijackers	forever	her

B. Vocabulary

Vocabulary words from the two reading selections in Exercise C are listed below. After you have completed the vocabulary exercise for the first selection, prepare to read the passage aloud in class. Do the same with the second reading passage.

1. Divide the following words from Passage 1 into syllables. Circle the stressed syllable, and write the number of syllables in each word.

Passage 1: Memories

a. chaos _____

b. uncertainty _____

c. scurried _____

g. particular _____

h. easier _____

d. inconvenient _____

e. frustrating _____

f. atmosphere _____

i. fulfill _____

j. differences _____

Select five words from the previous list and compose a sentence for each. Underline each selected word in the sentence, and practice reading aloud using the correct pronunciation.

a. _____

b. _____

c. _____

d. _____

e. _____

2. Divide the following words from Passage 2 into syllables. Circle the stressed syllable, and write the number of syllables in each word.

Passage 2: Space Shuttle

a. shuttle _____

b. rocket _____

c. constructed _____

d. technicians _____

e. philosophical _____

f. undertaking _____

g. destruction _____

h. mechanical _____

i. understandably _____

j. spectacular _____

k. Columbia _____

l. tedious _____

Select five words from the list above and compose a sentence for each. Underline each selected word in the sentence, and practice reading aloud using the correct pronunciation.

a. _____

b. _____

c. _____

d. _____

e. _____

C. *Reading Passages*

These selections focus on the accurate pronunciation of the central vowels: / ɜˆ /, / ʌ /, / ɚ /, and / ə /. Be sure to use the / ɜˆ / and / ʌ / in stressed syllables and the / ɚ / and / ə / in unstressed syllables.

Remember to link the words within phrases and stress important words, while maintaining the conversational tone of the passage. Work for variety in pitch and clarity of articulation.

Divide the sentences into phrase units, using single and double slashes and underline the stressed words.

EXAMPLE: <u>Aboard</u> the <u>space</u> <u>shuttle</u> *Columbia,* / <u>all</u> <u>systems</u> were <u>set</u> to <u>go</u> / <u>when</u> a <u>bug</u> was <u>discovered</u> / in <u>one</u> of the <u>engines</u>. / /

A tape or your instructor may serve as your model for correct and fluent oral reading. Prepare to read aloud in class.

Memories

———◆———

I'm finally a senior in college. Last September, I registered for the last time. The chaos, the uncertainty about courses, and the terrible course schedules will be out of my life forever.

I shall always remember the hectic and disorganized atmosphere during the registration period. Each semester, the lines seemed to get longer and the confusion seemed to increase as students scurried about to get their courses. Hundreds of students milling around a registration room or a department office made me nervous. I always wondered if there would be any courses left for me to take.

At times, it was very difficult to determine which courses would be interesting and would still fulfill the requirements for graduation. I would often inquire about who was teaching a particular course. After I became aware of the differences among teachers and their teaching styles, I was sometimes able to avoid an unpopular professor.

It was especially frustrating when major courses were offered at inconvenient hours. A course in accounting, for example, was given only at three o'clock. That was an impossible hour for me. I was either working or helping my family.

It's all over now. I'll be graduating in June. Do you think my life will be easier when I'm finished with school?

Exercise

Select the / ɚ / and / ə / words in this passage and write them in the appropriate columns.

/ ɚ /	/ ə /	/ ɚ /	/ ə /
_____	_____	_____	_____
_____	_____	_____	_____
_____	_____	_____	_____
_____	_____	_____	_____
_____	_____	_____	_____

Space Shuttle

◆

Aboard the space shuttle *Columbia,* all systems were set to go when a bug was discovered in one of the engines. While government officials wondered what had occurred, technicians began the tedious job of locating the problem. For a moment, it was touch and go. But it was decided to stop the countdown. It would be some time before the trouble was discovered. Members of the crew were understandably upset at the cancellation of the flight, but they were philosophical.

Their lives were on the line, and they were lucky nothing was left undone. A rocket constructed of hundreds of parts was subject to human and mechanical error. The public loved to watch the spectacular thrust of power as the rocket shot into the atmosphere. The men and women involved in the undertaking just hoped that nothing would go wrong. Better to wait another month, and not risk the destruction of the rocket and the lives of those who flew it.

Exercise

Select the / ʌ / and / ɑ / words in this passage and write them in the appropriate columns.

/ ʌ /	/ ɑ /	/ ʌ /	/ ɑ /
_____	_____	_____	_____
_____	_____	_____	_____
_____	_____	_____	_____
_____	_____	_____	_____

syllable

consonants

Diphthongs

vowels

lateral and glides

diphthongs

Quotations from China

———◆———

Heavenly King was intelligent,

Spat a lot of spittle into his hand,

Clapped his hand with a noise,

Produced Heaven and Earth,

Tall grass made insects,

Stones made men and demons

Made male and made female,

How is it you don't know?

All

All is fate

All is cloud

All is beginning without an end.

All language is repetitious

All contact a first encounter

All love is in the heart.

The following diphthongs appear in General American Dialect.

/ aɪ /	in *aisle*	/ eɪ /	in *fame**
/ ɔɪ /	in *oil*	/ oʊ /	in *foam**
/ aʊ /	in *owl*		

/ ɪr ~ ɪɚ /	in *peer*	/ ɛr ~ ɛɚ /	in *pair*
/ ɔr ~ ɔɚ /	in *pour*	/ ʊr ~ ʊɚ /	in *poor*

A diphthong is a combination of two adjacent vowel sounds that form a single vowel sound. The unique feature of diphthongs is the glide or shift from one vowel to another as the tongue moves from one articulatory position to another. The first element in the diphthong is notably strong and long; the second is weak and short.

A diphthong functions as a vowel. A syllable contains only one vowel sound; similarly, it can contain only one diphthong. Like a vowel, a diphthong is voiced and produced orally. It can be sung, and it forms the core or nucleus of a syllable.

EXAMPLE: ice   why   right

A diphthong can stand alone as a word.

EXAMPLE: I / aɪ /   eye / aɪ /

A diphthong can also stand alone as a syllable.

EXAMPLE: idea / aɪ dɪə /   identity / aɪ dɛn tɪ tɪ /

While a diphthong is longer in duration than a vowel, it too is longer before a voiced consonant.

EXAMPLE: sight side   clout cloud   race raise   ice eyes

When a diphthong appears in a word at the end of a phrase or sentence, it tends to be longer in duration.

EXAMPLE: *Why* did he ask?   I don't know *why.*

The expression of feeling and emotion may be conveyed through variations in pitch, volume, and duration of diphthongs, as well as vowels.

Diphthongs may be classified according to the position of the final element in the glide. *Front diphthongs* end in the front vowel / ɪ /. *Back diphthongs* end in the back vowel / ʊ /. There are four diphthongs that close with the central vowel, or schwa / ə /, and these are know as *central diphthongs.***

---

* These sounds are pronounced as diphthongs in American English. They are considered variants of the vowels / e / and / o / and are discussed fully in Part 4.

** The technical terms for these diphthongs are *fronting, retracting,* and *centering.* For pragmatic purposes we have simplified these terms.

Variants of the *front* diphthong / aɪ / or / ɑɪ / as in **time** and / ɔɪ / in **toil** are regional and social markers.* In the production of / aɪ /, the tongue glides from the low front vowel / a / to the high front / ɪ /. In the production of / ɔɪ / the tongue shifts from the mid back vowel / ɔ / to the high front / ɪ /.

The *back* diphthong / aʊ / or / ɑʊ / as in **town** also has sociolinguistic variations.** In the production of / aʊ /, the tongue glides from the low front vowel / a / to the high back vowel / u /.†

The *central* diphthongs are / ɪɚ / as in **beer,** / ɛɚ / as in **bear,** / ɔɚ / as in **bore,** and / ʊɚ / as in **boor.** In the production of these diphthongs, the tongue glides from the vowel positions of / ɪ /, / ɛ /, / ɔ /, and / ʊ / to the midcentral vowel / ɚ /.

Dialectal variations are most apparent in the production of the diphthongs, particularly the central diphthongs. In regions of the South and the East, the final **r** following a vowel is often omitted. In sections where General American Dialect is spoken, the **r** following a vowel is pronounced, although it is not as strong as in the initial of medial position. The **r** following a vowel functions as a vowel, not as a consonant, in these spelling configurations.

The nonphonemic variants of the central diphthongs do not signal differences in meaning. However, they may affect a listener's attitude toward the speaker based on region or social class.

	ch<u>eer</u>	ch<u>air</u>	c<u>ar</u>	c<u>ore</u>	c<u>ure</u>
East, South	/ ɪə /	/ ɛə /	/ ɑː /	/ ɔə /	/ ʊə /
GAD	/ ɪɚ /	/ ɛɚ /	/ ɑɚ /	/ ɔɚ /	/ ʊɚ /
GAD (**r**-colored)††	/ ɪr /	/ ɛr /	/ ɑr /	/ ɔr /	/ ʊr /

---

* Nonstandard pronunciations for / aɪ / are / ɔɪ / as in / tɔɪm / and / a / as in / tam /.

** Nonstandard pronunciations for / aʊ / are the nasalized / æ̃ʊ / as in / tæ̃un / or / ɛʊ / as in / tɛun /.

† The / aɪ /, / ɔɪ /, and / aʊ / diphthongs are phonemic. When words with a diphthong are compared with words containing the first vowel element in the diphthong, differences in meaning may be noted.

EXAMPLE: type—top   oil—all   bound—bond

†† Some instructors may prefer the last series of pronunciations.

CHAPTER ELEVEN

Front Diphthongs

Target Sounds: / aɪ / and / ɔɪ /

Distinctive Features

/ aɪ / begins with a low back vowel / a /.*
/ ɔɪ / begins with a mid-back vowel / ɔ /.

Both diphthongs end with the high front vowel / ɪ /. They are voiced.

How Are / aɪ / and / ɔɪ / Made?

/ aɪ / consists of two sounds that are produced as a single unit. The first is longer and made with the tongue flat in the mouth, which is opened wide. The second is short and made with the tongue shifting to a higher position. The lips are spread slightly. The tongue tip remains behind the lower front teeth.

EXAMPLE: aisle   style   cry

/ ɔɪ / is made with the back of the tongue raised to midheight and gliding into the high front position for the / ɪ /. The lips are somewhat rounded for the first element and slightly spread for the second.

EXAMPLE: oyster   loiter   annoy

---

* The vowel / a / is not included in the IPA chart in this text because it is not used in GAD. However, its use in the diphthong is common. An alternate pronunciation is the diphthong / ɑɪ /, which begins with the low back vowel / ɑ /. The mouth is less wide open, and the tongue is relatively low.

What Are the Problems or Patterns in Spelling?

/ aɪ / may be represented by the letters **y, uy, eigh, igh,** and **ie.**

EXAMPLE: m<u>y</u>   b<u>uy</u>   h<u>eigh</u>t   s<u>igh</u>t   d<u>ie</u>   qu<u>ie</u>t

/ ɔɪ / may be represented by the letters **oy** and **oi.**

EXAMPLE: enj<u>oy</u>   ch<u>oi</u>ce   <u>j</u><u>oi</u>n

What Are the Problems in Pronunciation?

/ aɪ / may be shortened and pronounced / a / or / ɑ /.

EXAMPLE: *lot* instead of *light*

may be shortened and pronounced / ʌ /.

EXAMPLE: *cut* instead of *kite*

may be pronounced / ɔɪ / and nasalized.

EXAMPLE: *oil* instead of *aisle*

/ ɔɪ / may be shortened and pronounced / ɔ /.

EXAMPLE: *tall* instead of *toil*

may be pronounced / ɝ /.

EXAMPLE: *verse* instead of *voice*

may be pronounced / aɪ /.

EXAMPLE: *pint* instead of *point*

Note: Speakers from the New York area, the Caribbean, and the South may need to work on distinguishing and to producing / ɑɪ /, or / aɪ /, and / ɔɪ /.

The / aɪ / Sound

A. Variations in spelling

Repeat these words after your instructor. Observe the different spellings for the / aɪ / sound.

I	iron	guide
eye	pride	type
ice	high	sign
my	height	lied
buy	rhyme	hire
why	quiet	choir

B. Vowel length

1. The diphthong / aɪ / is longer before a voiced consonant.

1	2	1	2
height	hide	light	lied
bite	bide	sight	sighed
life	live	tight	tied

2. The diphthong / aɪ / is longer when it is the last sound in the word.

1	2	1	2
buy	bide	rye	ride
sigh	side	try	tried
tie	tide	cry	cried

C. Divide each sentence into phrase units and link the words within each phrase. Stress the important words as you read aloud using a wide-open mouth for the / a /, the first element in the diphthong.

1. Mike was a pilot and he loved to fly.

2. One night, Mike's wife asked him to give up flying.

3. "Why should we give up this high income?" Mike asked quietly.

4. "This five-room apartment on Riverside Drive is quite nice."

5. "What good is a high-rise apartment when you're away so much of the time?" Eileen cried.

6. "I'm much too busy flying," sighed Mike.

7. "I'm tired of a life without you," replied Eileen.

8. "Why don't you fly with me again?" said Eileen. "You've been retired far too long."

9. "Oh, Eileen, I'd love to fly again. You won't mind?"

10. Eileen laughed, "Mind? Now I can fly with the finest flight attendant on the airline."

Listening/Writing

A. Listen carefully for / aɪ / as your instructor pronounces each word. Write these sounds when they occur in the initial, medial, or final position using the symbols of the IPA. If / aɪ / is not heard, write a dash in the space provided.

EXAMPLE: type   /_____aɪ_____/   lived   /_____—_____/

1. typical	_____	6. trial	_____	11. quit	_____
2. typewriter	_____	7. child	_____	12. quite	_____
3. sight	_____	8. chilled	_____	13. quiet	_____
4. site	_____	9. choir	_____	14. sign	_____
5. sit	_____	10. rhyme	_____	15. lock	_____

B. Circle the stressed syllable as each word is read aloud. Write the number of syllables in each word. Practice aloud.

1. hire	_____	5. quiet	_____
2. requirements	_____	6. rehired	_____
3. trial	_____	7. provides	_____
4. retired	_____	8. frightened	_____

Chapter 11 Homework Review

A. Write the following words using the symbols of the IPA. Note the number of sounds in each word.

1. five /   / _____
5. smiled /   / _____

2. twice /   / _____
6. typed /   / _____

3. signed /   / _____
7. sighed /   / _____

4. height /   / _____
8. tried /   / _____

B. Fill in the appropriate IPA symbol in the space provided. Practice reading the sentences aloud, producing / aɪ / accurately.

> **EXAMPLE:** I tri̱ed / aɪ / to phone you twi̱ce / aɪ /.

1. Cly̱de /   / was not hi̱red /   / because he li̱ed /   / about his ty̱ping /   /.

2. The si̱ght /   / of the si̱ck /   / chi̱ld /   / fri̱ghtened /   / the pi̱lot /   /.

3. Ei̱leen /   / did not try̱ /   / to sing in the cho̱ir /   /.

4. The qui̱et /   / gui̱de /   / in the Empi̱re /   / State Building cri̱ed /   /.

5. Isaac's /   / last fli̱ght /   / to I̱reland /   / was fi̱ve /   / years ago.

The / ɔɪ / Sound

A. Variations in spelling

Repeat these words after your instructor. Observe the different spellings for the / ɔɪ / sound.

boy	voiced	joint
oil	annoy	broil
coins	avoid	appoint
choice	royalty	ointment

B. The / ɔɪ / in sentence practice.

Divide each sentence into phrase units and link the words within the phrase. Stress the important words as you read aloud.

1. As a young boy, Roy Floyd was a joy to his parents.

2. He enjoyed his toys, collected coins, and, in time, became a lawyer.

3. He had, however, a foible about food.

4. He would eat only oysters broiled in oil and soy sauce.

5. Stomach pains began to annoy him, so he made an appointment with his physician, Dr. Freud.

6. "You are poisoning your system," the doctor said. "No more oysters."

7. Roy recoiled in horror. "Oh, no, a life devoid of oysters!"

8. Dr. Freud said, "Broiled steak, hard-boiled eggs, and loin lamb chops."

9. He added, "Make an appointment in three months. Until then—"

10. "No more oysters," Roy Floyd whispered. "I know I have no choice."

Listening/Writing

A. Listen carefully for the / ɔɪ / as your instructor pronounces each word. Write these sounds when they occur in the initial, medial, or final position using the symbols of the IPA. If / ɔɪ / is not heard, write a dash in the space provided.

EXAMPLE: c<u>oi</u>l /_____ɔɪ_____/   call /_____—_____/

1. coins _____	4. verse _____	7. joint _____
2. early _____	5. voice _____	8. broil _____
3. oily _____	6. avoid _____	9. soil _____

10. ball _____   12. brawl _____   14. tall _____

11. boil _____   13. toil _____   15. ointment _____

B. Circle the stressed syllable as each word is read aloud. Write the number of syllables in each word. Practice aloud.

1. poisoned _____   5. boisterous _____   9. voices _____

2. ointment _____   6. boiled _____   10. avoided _____

3. choices _____   7. appointment _____   11. enjoy _____

4. annoyed _____   8. royalty _____   12. employ _____

NAME: _____ DATE: _____

Chapter 11 Homework Review

A. Write the following words using the symbols of the IPA. Note the number of sounds in each word.

1. toy   /   / _____   4. voiced   /   / _____

2. boys   /   / _____   5. joined   /   / _____

3. oil   /   / _____   6. sirloin   /   / _____

B. Fill in the appropriate IPA symbol in the space provided. Practice reading the sentences aloud, producing / ɔɪ / accurately.

    EXAMPLE: Don't av<u>oi</u>d / ɔɪ / using a strong v<u>oi</u>ce / ɔɪ /.

1. R<u>oy</u>'s /   / v<u>oi</u>ce /   / ann<u>oy</u>ed /   / everyone.

2. Fl<u>oy</u>d /   / found the ancient c<u>oi</u>ns /   / buried in the s<u>oi</u>l /   /.

3. R<u>oy</u> /   / made an app<u>oi</u>ntment /   / with the empl<u>oy</u>ment /   / agency.

4. The b<u>oy</u>s /   / felt the br<u>oi</u>ling /   / sun as they t<u>oi</u>led in the <u>oi</u>l /   / fields.

5. It's too <u>ea</u>rly /   / to br<u>oi</u>l /   / those sirl<u>oi</u>n /   / steaks.

Back Diphthongs

Target Sounds: / aʊ / ~ / ɑʊ /

Distinctive Features

The / aʊ / ~ / ɑʊ / diphthong begins with / a /* or / ɑ / and ends with a high back vowel / ʊ /. The diphthong is voiced.

How Is / aʊ / Made?

The tongue starts flat in a low front position with the mouth opened wide; the lips are unrounded. It shifts to a high back position with considerable rounding of the lips. The first element in the diphthong is longer than the second. The tongue tip remains behind the lower front teeth.

EXAMPLE: out   aloud   now

What Are the Problems or Patterns in Spelling?

/ aʊ / may be represented by the letters **ou** and **ow**.

EXAMPLE: d<u>ou</u>bt   c<u>ow</u>ard

---

* The vowel / a / is not included in the IPA in this text because it is not used in GAD. However, its use in the diphthong is common. An alternate pronunciation is the diphthong / ɑʊ /, which begins with the low back vowel / ɑ /. The mouth is less wide open, and the tongue lies flat in the mouth.

What Are the Problems in Pronunciation?

/ aʊ / may be shortened and pronounced / ɑ /.

EXAMPLE: *bond* instead of *bound*

   clod instead of *cloud*

   may be pronounced / ɛəʊ / or / æʊ / or / ãʊ /.*

EXAMPLE: *down* / dɛəʊn / instead of / daʊn / ~ / dɑʊn /

   round / ræʊnd / instead of / raʊnd / ~ / rɑʊnd /

The / aʊ / ~/ ɑʊ /Sound

A. Variations in spelling

Repeat these words after your instructor. Observe the different spellings for the / aʊ / or / ɑʊ / sound.

now	our	flowers
how	doubt	shouting
crowd	brown	pronounce
ground	south	accountant

B. Vowel length

1. The diphthong / aʊ / ~ / ɑʊ / is longer before a voiced consonant.

1	2	1	2
bout	bowed	house (n)	house (v)
clout	cloud	lout	loud

2. The diphthong / aʊ / ~ / ɑʊ / is longer when it is the last sound in the word.

how	plow	bow
now	row	cow

---

* This nasalized diphthong may be heard in New York City.

Note: Many non-native and some native speakers from the New York area may need to work on distinguishing and producing / aʊ / or / ɑʊ /.

C. The / aʊ / ~ / ɑʊ / in sentence practice.

Divide each sentence into phrase units and link the words within each phrase. Stress the important words as you read aloud.

1. Howard was a circus clown who dreamed about becoming a radio announcer.

2. But clowns never make any sounds. Howard's mouth was always closed.

3. So he always bowed without making a sound.

4. How could Howard become a radio announcer if he never made a sound?

5. "It's now or never," said Howard aloud. He moved to a small town, where he avoided crowds and practiced pronouncing words aloud.

6. He found he liked the sound of his voice.

7. "I'll never be a clown again," he vowed, "now that I've found my voice."

8. Howard returned to his hometown in the South and found a letter addressed to him.

9. He was astounded that he had been offered a job as a radio announcer for a program called "Uptown-Downtown."

10. In time, Howard became so rich that he bought a house and found a spouse. Today he is very proud of his success as a radio announcer.

Listening/Writing

A. Listen carefully for / aʊ / ~ / ɑʊ / as your instructor pronounces each word. Write these sounds when they occur in the initial, medial, or final position using the symbols of the IPA. If / aʊ / or / ɑʊ / is not heard, write a dash in the space provided.

EXAMPLE: bound /___aʊ___/   bond /___—___/

1. hour _____	6. clod _____	11. pronounce _____
2. how _____	7. cloud _____	12. account _____
3. ounce _____	8. clawed _____	13. vowed _____
4. flaws _____	9. crowd _____	14. brown _____
5. flowers _____	10. know _____	15. pronunciation _____

B. Circle the stressed syllable as each word is read aloud. Write the number of syllables in each word. Practice aloud.

1. announcer _____

2. astounded _____

3. bowed _____

4. accountant _____

5. scowled _____

6. doubtfully _____

7. counter _____

8. our _____

9. chowder _____

10. pound _____

11. counselor _____

12. pronounced _____

Chapter 12 Homework Review

A. Write the following words using the symbols of the IPA. Note the number of sounds in each word.

1. brown   /   / _____   4. frowned   /   / _____

2. found   /   / _____   5. now   /   / _____

3. crowd   /   / _____   6. loudly   /   / _____

B. Fill in the appropriate IPA symbol in the space provided. Practice reading the sentences aloud, producing / aʊ / accurately.

   EXAMPLE: The man at the c<u>ou</u>nter / aʊ / spoke l<u>ou</u>dly / aʊ /.

1. H<u>ow</u> /   / did you like the play, "<u>Ou</u>r /   / T<u>ow</u>n /   /?"

2. H<u>ow</u>ard /   / spilled his ch<u>ow</u>der /   / on the lunch c<u>ou</u>nter /   /.

3. Her acc<u>ou</u>ntant /   / was d<u>ou</u>btful /   / ab<u>ou</u>t /   / eating tr<u>ou</u>t /   /.

4. The ann<u>ou</u>ncer /   / b<u>ow</u>ed /   / after the cr<u>ow</u>d /   / sh<u>ou</u>ted /   / for him.

5. Mary was ast<u>ou</u>nded /   / that she had lost two p<u>ou</u>nds /   / and three <u>ou</u>nces /   /.

CHAPTER THIRTEEN

Central Diphthongs

Target Sounds: /ɪr ~ ɪɚ/, /ɛr ~ ɛɚ/, /ɔr ~ ɔɚ/, and /ʊr ~ ʊɚ/

Distinctive Features

The high and mid-front vowels / ɪ / and / ɛ / and the high and mid back vowels / ʊ / and / ɔ / combine with the central vowel / ɚ / to form the diphthongs / ɪɚ /, / ɛɚ /, / ɔɚ /, and / ʊɚ /. They are voiced.

How Are These Diphthongs Made?

These diphthongs combine two adjacent vowel sounds to form a single unit. The first element in each diphthong starts with a different sound which is stronger and longer than the second. The tongue glides from the originating position into the schwa / ɚ /.*

/ ɪr ~ ɪɚ / begins with the front section of the tongue placed high in the mouth. The lips are lax and slightly spread. The tongue glides down and centrally for the schwa / ɚ /.

EXAMPLE: e<u>ar</u>   st<u>eer</u>   m<u>erely</u>

/ ɛr ~ ɛɚ / begins with a front vowel / ɛ /. The tongue is raised to midheight in the mouth; the lips are lax and somewhat apart. The tongue moves down to the midcentral schwa / ɚ /, completing the diphthong.

EXAMPLE: <u>air</u>   f<u>are</u>   <u>pear</u>

---

* The second element of these diphthongs is **r**-colored, or made with a slightly curled up tongue. This pronunciation is commonly used in GAD. Sections of the East and South omit the **r,** producing the schwa without the **r**-colored / ə /, as in **fare** / fɛə /. These are known as "colorless-**r** words."

/ ɔr ~ ɔɚ / begins with the mid back vowel / ɔ /. The back section of the tongue is raised to midheight; the lips are somewhat rounded. The tongue glides down to the schwa / ɚ /, completing the diphthong.

EXAMPLE: pour   more   or   hoarse

/ ur ~ uɚ / begins with the high vowel / u /. The back section of the tongue is raised high in the mouth; the lips are very rounded and tense. The tongue shifts downward to the schwa / ɚ /, completing the diphthong.

EXAMPLE: poor   sure   tour

What Are the Problems or Patterns in Spelling?

These diphthongs are used in configurations where **r** follows a vowel in stressed syllables.

/ ɪr ~ ɪɚ / may be represented by **ear, eer, e,** and **ere.**

EXAMPLE: <u>ear</u>   car<u>eer</u>   <u>e</u>ra*   m<u>ere</u>ly

/ ɛr ~ ɛɚ / may be represented by **air, ear, eir, ere,** and **are.**

EXAMPLE: <u>air</u>   w<u>ear</u>   th<u>eir</u>   w<u>a</u>ry   wh<u>ere</u>   decl<u>are</u>

/ ɔr ~ ɔɚ / may be represented by **oar, oor, our, or, ar,** and **ou.**

EXAMPLE: <u>oar</u>   d<u>oor</u>   c<u>our</u>se   sh<u>or</u>t   w<u>ar</u>d   f<u>or</u>ge   <u>ore</u>   y<u>our</u>

/ ur ~ uɚ / may be represented by **our, oor, ure, ur, ure,** and **ou.**

EXAMPLE: t<u>our</u>   sp<u>oor</u>   s<u>ure</u>ly   d<u>ur</u>ing*   p<u>ure</u>   y<u>ou</u>'re

What Are the Problems in Pronunciation?

/ ɪr / and / ɛɚ / may be confused.

EXAMPLE: *fear* instead of *fare*

beer instead of *bear*

/ ɔr / and / uɚ / may be confused.

EXAMPLE: *tore* instead of *tour*

pour instead of *poor*

---

* When **r** appears between two vowels, it functions as a consonant.

    EXAMPLE: era / ɪrə /   during / durɪŋ /

Note: Some native and non-native speakers and those from the Caribbean may need to work on distinguishing and producing these diphthongs.

The / ɪɚ /Sound

A. Variations in spelling

Repeat these words after your instructor. Observe the different spellings for the / ɪɚ / sound.

hear	fear
steer	cheer
here	ear

B. The / ɪɚ / in sentence practice.

Divide each sentence into phrase units and link the words within the phrase. Stress the important words as you read aloud.

1. Ian Greer found he was developing queer symptoms.

2. First his eyes would tear, and then his ears would ring.

3. When he walked, he would veer from side to side.

4. Then one day, he couldn't hear, he couldn't steer his car and jammed his gears.

5. Sick with fear, he went to his doctor, who ran a series of tests.

6. "Have no fear," the doctor said cheerfully. "Tell me, do you drink beer?"

7. "Nearly a six-pack every day," Ian said.

8. "You have an allergy to beer," his doctor said.

9. Ian went home, poured all his beer down the drain, and in one year, he could see, hear and steer his car.

10. He never drank soda again.

The / ɛɚ /Sound

A. Variations in spelling

Repeat these words after your instructor. Observe the different spellings for the / ɛɚ / sound.

bear	stair	where
fair	their	wear
stare	there	wares

B. The / ɛɚ / in sentence practice.

Divide each sentence into phrase units and link the words within each phrase. Stress the important words as you read aloud.

1. Claire and Blair wanted to share an apartment in the New York area.

2. They found an airy apartment in a converted warehouse where Claire's father once worked.

3. "There's no elevator and I can't bear all those stairs," Claire sighed.

4. "Have no fear, We'll put a chair at the top of the stairs," declared Blair.

5. "We have plenty of air and space," Claire said, staring around the bare room.

6. "The price is fair," Blair pointed out. "We don't dare let it go."

7. Claire agreed, "A rare find!" And we'll have a couple of rare steaks to celebrate."

8. "Fair enough," her friend said, and they raced down the stairs, prepared to sign a lease.

Listening/Speaking

A. Contrast / ɪɚ / and / ɛɚ /.

1	2	1	2	1	2
hear	hare	here	hare	cheer	chair
fear	fare	steer	stare	rear	rare
mere	mare	peer	pair	sheer	share
dear	dare				

Can you *feel* the difference as you repeat after your instructor?

Can you *hear* the difference between / ɪɚ / and / ɛɚ /?

B. Underline the contrastive words in each sentence. As you read aloud, remember to produce the / ɪɚ / and / ɛɚ / sounds in the underlined words.

> **EXAMPLE:**   I can't <u>bear</u> to have more <u>beer</u>.

1. I hear you have a pet hare.

2. Mary fears that train fares will be rising again.

3. Harry did not dare to kill the deer.

4. Cheers for the person who brings more chairs to our party.

5. It is rare to own two rear view mirrors.

6. Why are you staring at the steering wheel?

7. I won't shed a tear if you tear up those pictures.

8. Don't throw those beer bottles at the bear.

9. We're going to wear hats at the funeral.

10. Each of my peers bought several pairs of gloves at the factory.

Listening/Writing

A. Listen carefully for / ɪɚ / and / ɛɚ / as your instructor pronounces each word. Write these sounds when they occur in the initial, medial, or final position using the symbols of the IPA. If / ɪɚ / or / ɛɚ / is not heard, write a dash in the space provided.

EXAMPLE: queer /____ɪɚ____/ quiet /____—____/ care /____ɛɚ____/

1. clear	_____	6. nearly	_____
2. Clare	_____	7. hear	_____
3. ear	_____	8. beer	_____
4. air	_____	9. hair	_____
5. merely	_____	10. chair	_____

11. share _____
12. sheer _____
13. peer _____
14. pair _____
15. pear _____

B. Circle the stressed syllable as each word is read aloud. Write the number of syllables in each word. Practice aloud.

1. series	_____	6. feared	_____
2. warehouse	_____	7. staring	_____
3. celebrate	_____	8. Mary	_____
4. prepared	_____	9. area	_____
5. cheerfully	_____	10. airy	_____

Chapter 13 Homework Review

A. Write the following words using the symbols of the IPA. Note the number of sounds in each word.

1. dear   /   / _____   6. bear   /   / _____

2. deer   /   / _____   7. pair   /   / _____

3. dare   /   / _____   8. pear   /   / _____

4. beer   /   / _____   9. pare   /   / _____

5. bare   /   / _____   10. hear   /   / _____

B. Fill in the appropriate IPA symbol in the space provided. Practice reading the sentences aloud, producing / ɪɚ / and / ɛɚ / accurately.

    EXAMPLE: Did you p<u>eer</u> / ɪɚ / at those p<u>ears</u> / ɛɚ /?

1. Cl<u>ai</u>re /   / always sh<u>a</u>res /   / her ch<u>ai</u>rs /   / with n<u>ea</u>rby /   / neighbors.

2. No one c<u>a</u>red /   / about the f<u>ea</u>rful /   / d<u>ee</u>r /   /.

3. Wh<u>ere</u> /   / are the r<u>ea</u>r /   / st<u>ai</u>rs /   /?

4. Are you aw<u>a</u>re /   / that th<u>ei</u>r /   / candidate was ch<u>ee</u>red /   / by the entire audience?

5. The d<u>a</u>ring /   / p<u>ai</u>r /   / who voted for increased f<u>a</u>res /   / are my p<u>ee</u>rs /   /.

The / ʊɚ / and / ɔɚ / Sounds

A. Variations in spelling

Repeat these words after your instructor. Observe the different spellings for the / ʊɚ / sound.

poor	boor
sure	cure
tour	lure

B. The / ʊɚ / in sentence practice.

Remember to round the lips for the first sound of the diphthong as you read each sentence aloud.

1. Mary has toured the moors of England.

2. She was sure she wanted to live there forever more.

3. She was lured there by the solitude and stillness.

4. The air on the moor was quite poor, and life was very dour.

5. People were poor and for that there was no cure.

6. Her only friend was a boor.

7. She was assured that a health cure could be found on the moor.

8. Even though the rural life was poor, Mary was still sure she wanted to live on the moor.

The / ɔɚ / Sound

A. Variations in spelling

Repeat these words after your instructor. Observe the different spellings for the / ɔɚ / sound.

pour	store
tore	four
more	chore

B. The / ɔɚ / in sentence practice.

Divide each sentence into phrase units and link the words within the phrase. Stress the important words as you read aloud.

1. Cora was bored with school.

2. She tore up her notebooks and said, "No more."

3. She went to live at the seashore, where it always poured.

4. Life at the seashore was not a bore.

5. She loved the roar of the ocean.

6. She explored the native flora and fauna and became interested in the local folklore.

7. To support herself, she worked in a store selling imported coffee.

8. She bought a house that she planned to restore.

9. Life at the seashore was definitely not a bore.

Listening/Speaking

A. Contrast / ʊɚ / and / ɔɚ /.

1	2	1	2
moor	more	tour	tore
dour	door	sure	shore
poor	pour	boor	bore

B. Underline the contrastive words in each sentence. As you read aloud, remember to produce the / ʊɚ / and / ɔɚ / in the underlined words.

> **EXAMPLE:**   Tom <u>tore</u> / ɔɚ / up the booklet about his <u>tour</u> / ʊɚ /.

1. More stories about your life on the moor would be interesting.

2. Folklore may lure me to New England.

3. Please pour some water for those poor thirsty children.

4. I tore up that expensive tour booklet.

5. We were sure it wouldn't rain at the shore.

6. That boor I met at your party was a bore.

7. More people are leaving the moor.

8. The door was opened by a lady with a dour expression.

9. Sure, let's go to the shore.

Listening/Writing

A. Listen carefully for / ʊɚ / and / ɔɚ / as your instructor pronounces each word. Write these sounds when they occur in the initial, medial, or final position using the symbols of the IPA. If / ʊɚ / or / ɔɚ / is not heard, write a dash in the space provided.

EXAMPLE: cure /____ʊɚ____/   door /____ɔɚ____/   mood /____—____/

1. store _____	5. bore _____	9. lure _____
2. boor _____	6. boar _____	10. poor _____
3. moor _____	7. boor _____	11. pore _____
4. more _____	8. tour _____	12. pour _____

B. Circle the stressed syllable as your instructor reads each word aloud. Write the number of syllables in each word.

1. door _____	5. touring _____	9. rural _____
2. doing _____	6. doubtfully _____	10. explored _____
3. shouted _____	7. chores _____	11. employed _____
4. tousled _____	8. cured _____	12. restore _____

Chapter 13 Homework Review

A. Write the following words using the symbols of the IPA. Note the number of sounds in each word.

1. more   /   /   _____   4. shore   /   /   _____

2. tours   /   /   _____   5. pure   /   /   _____

3. sure   /   /   _____   6. poor   /   /   _____

B. Fill in the appropriate IPA symbol in the space provided. Practice reading the sentences aloud, producing / ʊɚ / and / ɔɚ / accurately.

      EXAMPLE: He was lured / ʊɚ / to the area because of the folklore / ɔɚ /?

1. The father was assured /   / that his child would be cured /   /.

2. When he was poor /   / he lived in a rural /   / area /   /, not in the suburbs.

3. I'm not sure /   / I could live at the seashore /   /.

4. She insured /   / the store /   / she had restored /   /.

5. Four /   / birds soared /   / over the moors /   /.

Reviewing the Diphthongs / ɪɚ ɛɚ ɔɚ ʊɚ /

A. Practice pronouncing the following words.

Can you *feel* the difference as you repeat after your instructor?

Can you *hear* the difference as you pronounce each of the diphthongs?

1. Compare the front diphthongs.

/ aɪ /	/ ɔɪ /
vice	voice
tie	toy
buy	boy
I'll	oil
kind	coined
sigh	soy

2. Compare the back diphthong with the front diphthong.

/ aʊ /	/ aɪ /
how	high
bound	bond
found	find
mound	mind
loud	lied
crowd	cried

3. Compare the central diphthongs.

/ ɪr ~ ɪɚ /	/ ɛr ~ ɛɚ /	/ ʊr ~ ʊɚ /	/ ɔr ~ ɔɚ /
sheer	share	sure	shore
tear	tear	tour	tore
beer	bear	boor	bore
leer	lair	lure	lore
mere	mare	moor	more
peer	pare	poor	pour

4. Compare front diphthongs and vowels.

/ aɪ /	/ ɑ /	/ ɔɪ /	/ ɔ /
light	lot	coil	call
psych	sock	oil	all
write	rot	toil	tall
like	lock	joy	jaw
fire	far	boil	ball
tire	tar		

5. Compare the back diphthongs and vowels.

/ aʊ /	/ ɑ /
bound	bond
found	fond
cloud	clod
our	are
shout	shot
doubt	dot

B. Review Passage

This passage focuses on the accurate production of all the diphthongs: / aɪ /, / ɔɪ /, / aʊ /, / ɪɚ /, / ɛɚ /, / ɔɚ /, and / ʊɚ /. Be sure to produce these accurately.

Remember to link the words within the phrase and stress the important words, while maintaining the conversational tone of the dialogue. Work for variety in pitch and clarity of articulation.

Divide the sentences into phrase units, using single and double slashes, and underline the stressed words.

EXAMPLE: I'll <u>try</u> to <u>keep</u> an <u>open</u> <u>mind</u>, / <u>provided</u> / you <u>keep</u> the <u>sound</u> <u>level</u> / <u>down</u>. / /

Your instructor may serve as your model for correct and fluent oral reading. Prepare to read aloud in class.

Flatfoot Floogie with a Floy Doy

◆

GRANDMA: Turn down that sound. You're about to destroy what's left of my hearing.

SPIKE: Grandma, what are you shouting about?

GRANDMA: I can't stand all that noise.

SPIKE: Noise! I'm listening to the Backstreet Boys.

GRANDMA: Then listen somewhere else. My poor old ears can't take it.

SPIKE: Fair enough. How about the Wiseguys or Snoopy Doggy Dog. You've got your choice of techno or rap.

GRANDMA: Give me the good old times—the Andrews Sisters and the Dorsey Brothers.

SPIKE: Never heard of them.

GRANDMA: I'm sure you've heard of the Rolling Stones.

SPIKE: They should have retired years ago. They had their fair share of fame. They can't give up the limelight.

GRANDMA: I'm reminded of some awfully funny songs, like "Flatfoot Floogie with a Floy Doy."

SPIKE: Talk about weird!

GRANDMA: No more weird than what I'm hearing on your CDs. How many years do you give their careers?

SPIKE: I don't care. Right now, I just go with the flow. So, what is your desire? You have your choice—techno or rap.

GRANDMA: Who is this Eminem I keep hearing about?

SPIKE: Grandma, trust me, he's not your style!

GRANDMA: The tone of your voice tells me to rely on your judgment. Well, now, I'll try to listen with an open mind, provided you keep the sound level down. Agreed?

SPIKE: Agreed. The Wiseguys followed by a singer you'll like, Celine Dion.

GRANDMA: You're sure?

SPIKE: I'm sure.

APPENDIX A

Pronunciation of the Letter x

The letter **x** may be pronounced / ks / or / gz /.

1. When **x** is followed by a voiceless consonant, it is pronounced / ks /.*

    EXAMPLE: expense / ɪkspɛns /   extra / ɛkstrə /

2. When **x** occurs in a stressed syllable, it is pronounced / ks /.

    EXAMPLE: excellent / ɛksələnt /   taxi / tæksɪ /

3. When **x** is followed by a vowel in a stressed syllable, it is pronounced / gz /.

    EXAMPLE: exam / ɪgzæm /   exact / ɪgzækt /

Exercise

Practice these words aloud. Select five words from each group and compose a sentence for each. Prepare to read your sentences aloud in class.

/ ks /		/ gz /	
expel	extension	exit**	exert
express	excited	exile**	exorbitant
taxes	excess	exist	exonerate
exhale	axis	examine	exhibit
exercise	execute	example	exhausted
extreme	extraordinary	exaggerate	executive
external	exodus		

---

* / ks / also occurs when **x** is the last letter of the word.

    EXAMPLE: six   fix   mix   sex

** Exceptions to the rules.

443

/ ks /

1. _____

2. _____

3. _____

4. _____

5. _____

/ gz /

1. _____

2. _____

3. _____

4. _____

5. _____

* Exception to rule number 2.

Consonant Clusters

Initial

bl ____	fl ____	gl ____	kl ____*	pl ____	sl ____
bland	flue	glue	clip	plead	slogan
blaze	flunk	globe	clarify	pledge	slacks
bleach	flash	glass	clergy	plant	slurred
blanket	flight	glacier	client	playbill	slavery
blister	flavor	glorious	clarinet	plaintiff	slapped
blunder	fluoride	gloomily	classical	plagiarize	slippery

br ____	fr ____	gr ____	kr ____*	pr ____	tr ____
brief	fraud	grave	crave	prompt	trace
brand	frail	graft	craft	primary	trachea
brain	frantic	grumble	crisis	profound	traitor
bruise	fractions	graduate	cream	precaution	tragic
bridge	fragments	gradual	crumble	predominant	traditions
broker	fragrance	grateful	credentials	preliminary	transcript

str ____	skr ____	spr ____	shr ____	dr ____	thr ____
strive	scrap	sprawl	shrub	drugs	thruway
stroke	scrape	spruce	shrill	draft	threaten
struck	scribble	spring	shrimp	drift	throttle
strong	scratch	spread	shrunk	drenched	thriftily
strength	screen	sprouts	shriek	dramatic	thriller
struggle	scramble	sprained	shrewd	draftsman	threshold

_____

* Refers to IPA symbols.

Final

_____ ft	_____ kt*	_____ lt	_____ nt	_____ pt	_____ st
rift	tact	fault	dent	adopt	past
raft	elect	built	faint	swept	twist
left	impact	dealt	lint	script	waste
gift	contact	tilt	meant	accept	passed
coughed	restrict	belt	count	except	disgust
laughed	balked	melt	frequent	stamped	glanced

_____ ld	_____ nd	_____ mp	_____ sp	_____ sk*	_____ nth
weld	wind (v)	lump	gasp	ask	tenth
mold	mend	damp	lisp	task	ninth
build	kind	chimp	clasp	desk	month
child	wound (v)	dump	cusp	disc	seventh
ruled	chained	stump	rasp	brisk	eleventh
trailed	blend	champ	grasp	mask	

_____ ns*	_____ lth	_____ ts	_____ dz*
once	health	bets	beds
license	wealth	rates	raids
balance	stealth	bites	bides
bounce	filth	seats	seeds
defense		mates	maids
inheritance		goats	goads

---

* Refers to IPA symbols.

APPENDIX C

Evaluations

Oral and written performances are evaluated at the end of a unit or at the end of a series of lessons. The purpose of frequent testing is (1) to observe and reduce students' problems in understanding basic speech concepts and in using accurate speech patterns, (2) to provide immediate teacher and class feedback and assistance, and (3) to reinforce learning in the classroom.

Students are given a diagnostic reading passage at the beginning and at the end of the semester in order to gauge progress. The dialogues serve as experiences in structured conversation; they also function as oral test performances before the class. See the Speech Evaluation Form on page 000 for grade determination.

Written quizzes are given often to evaluate understanding and application of the phonological principles taught in class. These are short (fifteen to twenty minutes). They review the vocabulary from the dialogues and reading passages, and they assess the following skills: distinguishing voiced and voiceless sounds and final consonants; segmenting phonemes, syllables, and sentences appropriately; using the IPA as a meaningful tool, discriminating sounds, and distinguishing stressed and unstressed syllables in words.

Sample questions from the written quizzes fall into two categories—one group involves teacher participation, the other group only written materials. In the first category of tasks, the student indicates on paper the speech patterns heard as the teacher reads aloud. In the second, students rely on their perceptions of their own speech patterns in response to written words. In our regular class quizzes, each test item is longer than in the shortened version below.

Sample Test Items: Written

I. Listen carefully as your instructor reads the following:

    A. In the spaces provided, indicate the pattern that you hear. If you hear *sue, zoo, sue,* write 1 2 1.

1	2			
race	raise	____	____	____
ship	chip	____	____	____

B. Circle the stressed syllable in each word.

ex   pen   sive   pro   mised   per   mit (v)

C. Listen to the pronunciation of the underlined word in the sentence. If it is correct, write C; if incorrect, write I in the space provided.

1. Would you like a <u>cup</u> / kʌ___ / of coffee?   C/I _____

2. That's a nice <u>suit</u> / su___ / you're wearing.   C/I _____

D. If you hear the voiced **th,** write / ð /. If you hear the voiceless **th,** write / θ /.

thought / ___ /   brother / ___ /   truthful / ___ /

II. Read the following questions carefully.

A. Circle the word that doesn't belong.

was   does   yes   his

B. Write the sounds of the underlined letters using the symbols of the IPA.

bac<u>ked</u> /   /   wan<u>ted</u> /   /   lug<u>ged</u> /   /

C. Circle the stressed syllable in each word. Indicate the number of syllables.

apologized _____   appreciate _____   jumped _____

D. Fill in the missing sounds using the symbols of the IPA. Write the number of sounds in each word.

thought / ___ ɔ ___ / _____   stays / s ___ eɪ ___ / _____

E. Is the pronunciation of the following words correct (C) or incorrect (I)?

planed / plænt / _____   looked / lʊkt / _____

F. What is the final sound in each word? Indicate if the sound is voiced (V) or voiceless (VL).

cape /   / _____   ache /   / _____   mix /   / _____

G. Read the following sentence aloud to yourself.

She decided not to answer the phone, although she knew it was her brother, who had just arrived from Florida.

1. Divide the previous sentence into meaningful phrase units.

2. List five stressed words from this sentence.

3. List five unstressed words from this sentence.

H. Write the following words using the symbols of the IPA.

know /   /   called /   /

I. Transcribe the following words.

/ tɔkt / _____   / lʌntʃɪz / _____

J. Write the number of voiceless consonants in each of the following words.

kick _____   attack _____   stopped _____

NAME: _____ **DATE:** _____

Speech Evaluation Form

Oral Performance _____
(Name/Type of activity)

SOUNDS

    Target Sounds* /   /

    Articulation

PHRASING

    Pausing

    Linking

STRESSING (Pi, Vo, Du)**

    Syllable

    Word

OVERALL

    Volume

    Rate

    Eye Contact

    Pronunciation

    Intelligibility

COMMENTS   **Grade** _____

Grade Score

A	B	C	D	F
1	2	3	4	5

_____

* Refer to the target sounds studied in the current lesson(s).

** Evaluate the use of pitch, volume, and duration.

Index